THE CONSTITUTIONAL STRUCTURE OF EUROPE'S AREA OF 'FREEDOM, SECURITY AND JUSTICE' AND THE RIGHT TO JUSTIFICATION

This book explores the implications of freedom as a non-domination-oriented view for understanding EU security regulation and its constitutional implications. At a time when the European borders are under pressure and with the refugee and migration crisis, which escalated in 2015, the idea of exploring a constitutional theory for the 'Area of Freedom, Security and Justice' (AFSJ) might seem to be a utopian project. This appears especially true in the light of the increased threat of terrorism in Europe (and on a global scale) and where the expanding EU security agenda is often advanced through the administrative law path, in contrast to the constitutional trajectory. Add to this the prolonged financial crisis, which continues to cast a long shadow on the future development of EU integration, and which suggests that Europe needs to 're-invent itself' beyond the sphere of economics. Therefore, it is precisely because of the current uncertainties regarding the progress of the EU and the constitutional law project that a constitutional take on the AFSJ is of particular importance. The book investigates the meaning of non-domination and the idea of justice and justification in the area of EU security regulation. In doing so, it focuses on the development of an AFSJ, what it means, and why it represents a fascinating example of contemporary constitutional law with interacting layers of security regulation, human rights law and transnational legal theory at its core.

Volume 5 in Hart Studies in Security and Justice

Hart Studies in Security and Justice

Series editor: Liora Lazarus

The interplay between security and justice has always featured prominently in legal scholarship, but it has taken on a particular urgency since the new Millennium. The new scholarly questions that arise are theoretical, doctrinal and empirical, cutting across a range of traditional sub-disciplines within the legal academy. They address some of the most pressing legal issues of our time, such as the legal status of the 'the war on terror', the nature of states of exception, targeted killing, preventive pre-trial detention, mass surveillance and the numerous other threats that security poses to human rights, the rule of law and liberal democracy.

The purpose of this series is to engage with security and justice scholarship broadly conceived, and to promote a sophisticated and complex understanding of the important challenges it faces. The series is inclusive, promoting new and established scholars from a range of disciplines. It covers doctrinal, empirical, historical and theoretical work, as well as studies which focus on domestic, comparative and international dimensions of emerging security and justice fields. The series also strives to promote the most inclusive range of politics and methodologies, scrutinizing received wisdom and established paradigmatic approaches, and promoting an intellectual dialogue between its authors and the wider field of law as a whole.

Recent titles in this series:

Surveillance, Privacy and Trans-Atlantic Relations
Edited by David Cole, Federico Fabbrini and Stephen Schulhofer

Parliament's Secret War
Veronika Fikfak and Hayley J Hooper

Permanent States of Emergency and the Rule of Law
Alan Greene

The Constitutional Structure of Europe's Area of 'Freedom, Security and Justice' and the Right to Justification

Ester Herlin-Karnell

•HART•
OXFORD • LONDON • NEW YORK • NEW DELHI • SYDNEY

HART PUBLISHING

Bloomsbury Publishing Plc

Kemp House, Chawley Park, Cumnor Hill, Oxford, OX2 9PH, UK

HART PUBLISHING, the Hart/Stag logo, BLOOMSBURY and the Diana logo are trademarks of Bloomsbury Publishing Plc

First published in Great Britain 2019

A catalogue record for this book is available from the British Library.

Library of Congress Cataloging-in-Publication data

Names: Herlin-Karnell, Ester, author.

Title: The constitutional structure of Europe's area of 'freedom, security and justice' and the right to justification / Ester Herlin-Karnell.

Description: Oxford, UK ; Portland, Oregon : Hart Publishing, 2019. | Series: Hart studies in security and justice | Includes bibliographical references and index.

Identifiers: LCCN 2018053609 (print) | LCCN 2018055179 (ebook) | ISBN 9781509912506 (EPub) | ISBN 9781509912490 (hardback)

Subjects: LCSH: Internal security—Law and legislation—European Union countries. | National security—Law and legislation—European Union countries. | Criminal justice, Administration of—European Union countries. | BISAC: LAW / International.

Classification: LCC KJE5977 (ebook) | LCC KJE5977 .H47 2019 (print) | DDC 342.24/0418—dc23

LC record available at https://lccn.loc.gov/2018053609

ISBN: HB: 978-1-50991-249-0
ePDF: 978-1-50991-251-3
ePub: 978-1-50991-250-6

Typeset by Compuscript Ltd, Shannon
Printed and bound in Great Britain by TJ International Ltd, Padstow, Cornwall

To find out more about our authors and books visit www.hartpublishing.co.uk. Here you will find extracts, author information, details of forthcoming events and the option to sign up for our newsletters.

Acknowledgements

THIS BOOK BEGAN life half a decade ago; not in Europe, but in New York City. In 2013 I spent a semester at New York University School of Law, where I had the privilege of serving as an Emile Noël fellow at the Jean Monnet Center for International and Regional Economic Law & Justice. I was also fortunate to spend a couple of months as a visiting fellow at the University of Michigan Law School, Ann Arbor. The early thoughts of structuring this book developed in those outstanding academic environments, coinciding with the beginning of the migration crisis on the other side of the Atlantic back in Europe. I was also extremely fortunate that Rainer Forst was a fellow the same year at NYU, as we began a series of discussions and exchanges around his essential notion of a right to justification that has informed my thinking ever since. The ideas developed in the present book were further progressed during a fellowship at the Centre for Global Constitutionalism of the WZB, the Berlin Social Science Center during 2014 and 2015. I am extremely grateful to Joseph Weiler, Gráinne de Búrca, Daniel Halberstam and Mattias Kumm, respectively, for making these fruitful research visits possible. I am also extremely grateful to the Dutch Research Council (NWO Veni grant) for a very generous research grant that sponsored the work during those visits. The VU Amsterdam University Research Chair funding scheme and Access Europe Amsterdam sponsored a number of conferences where I was able to present and further discuss my work on the arguments developed in this book.

The benefits of being an academic are, of course, multiple. I had the privilege of visiting the Global Trust Centre at Tel Aviv University in the autumn of 2015, which was extremely helpful for my thinking of constitutional justice. It was at a time when Europe was again experiencing a number of terror attacks, starting with the Paris attacks of November 2015, and I will never forget the experience of watching the news from outside Europe. A few weeks later, I had the opportunity of meeting with former Chief Justice of Israel, Aharon Barak, for a long, very interesting discussion about proportionality and due process rights, building on the experience of that country's recent legal challenges. This followed with a 2017 visit at the Minerva Centre for the Rule of Law under Extreme Conditions at the University of Haifa. I would like to thank Eyal Benvenisti at Tel Aviv University and Amnon Reichman and Michal Gal at the Minerva Centre and their respective research groups for hosting me for fruitful intellectual exchanges. Thanks also to Toronto Law School for inviting me to continue my work as a visiting fellow in 2017, and to Malcolm Thorburn for helpful discussion of the ideas developed in this book. I am likewise grateful to the EU Law discussion group at Oxford University Faculty of Law, the Global

Law research group at Queen Mary University School of Law London, Bar-Ilan Faculty of Law, the EU Law Cluster at Leicester University School of Law and the EU law Center at Gothenburg Law School for inviting me to present ideas from this book in various forums.

Several people were generous with time and input and had a significant impact on the ideas presented in this in book through different stages of its progress. In addition to those thanked above, I am especially indebted to Ori Aronson, Estella Baker, Ulad Belavusau, Iris Canor, Sionaidh Douglas-Scott, Myriam Feinberg, Alon Harel, Aravind Ganesh, Oxana Golynker, Poul F Kjaer, Matthias Klatt, Kai Möller, Sivan Shlomo-Agon, Arthur Ripstein, Enzo Rossi, Valentina Vadi, Jonathan Yovel, Bertjan Wolthuis and Katja Ziegler. Needless to say all mistakes are my own.

I am also very grateful to Chris Engert and Vicki Hillyard for their excellent help with revision and copy-editing and to Hart Publishing for believing in this project and providing excellent support. Finally, on a personal level, thanks to my family for their love, encouragement and great inspiration!

Table of Contents

List of Abbreviations

AFSJ	Area of Freedom, Security and Justice
CIA	Central Intelligence Agency
CJEU	Court of Justice of the European Union
EAW	European Arrest Warrant
ECHR	European Convention on Human Rights
ECtHR	European Court of Human Rights
EPPO	European Public Prosecutor's Office
ESMA	European Securities and Market Authority
EU	European Union
IT	Information Technology
NATO	North Atlantic Treaty Organization
TEU	Treaty on European Union
TFEU	Treaty on the Functioning of the European Union (Treaty of Lisbon)
TFTP	Terrorist Finance Tracking Program
PNR	Passenger Name Record
UK	United Kingdom
UN	United Nations
US	United States of America

Table of Cases

EU Law Cases

ECHR Case Law

National Case Law

Table of Legislation

EU Directives

EU Regulations

Former EU Third Pillar Instruments

Other Sources

Part I

1

Introduction

I. THE IDEA OF THE BOOK

THIS BOOK[1] EXPLORES the implications of freedom as a non-domination-oriented view for understanding EU security regulation and its constitutional implications. When I began writing this book, the European Schengen system was under extreme pressure, from recent terrorist attacks across Europe to the refugee and migration 'crisis' which escalated in 2015 and has developed into an extreme challenge both to tackle and to resolve. It seemed as if the idea of exploring a constitutional theory for the Area of Freedom, Security and Justice (AFSJ), would be something of a utopian project. Yet the expanding EU security agenda is at present often advanced through the path of administrative law, in contrast to the constitutional trajectory. Add to this the prolonged financial crisis that began in 2007/08, which continues to cast a long shadow on the future development of EU integration, and which suggests that Europe needs to 're-invent itself' beyond the sphere of economics. Therefore, it is precisely because of the current uncertainties regarding the progress of the EU and the constitutional law project that a constitutional take on the AFSJ is of particular importance. This book zooms in on the concepts of non-domination and justice theory in the context of the trajectory of the AFSJ. The book discusses what the AFSJ means, and why it represents a fascinating example of contemporary constitutional law with interacting layers of security regulation, human rights law and transnational legal theory at its core.

Specifically, the book takes as its starting point the claim that the European AFSJ is currently being constructed through the notion of security, while simultaneously being mainstreamed with the EU legal constitutional framework.

[1] Some of the early thoughts of what is now this book have appeared in Ester Herlin-Karnell, 'The Concepts of Non-Domination and Justification in EU security-related context' in Ester Herlin-Karnell and Matthias Klatt (eds), *Constitutionalism Justified* (Oxford, Oxford University Press, 2019), forthcoming; Ester Herlin-Karnell, 'The Domination of Security and the Promise of Justice: On Justification and Proportionality in Europe's "Area of Freedom, Security and Justice"' (2017) *Transnational Legal Theory* 79, Ester Herlin-Karnell, 'Two Conceptions of Justice in EU Constitutionalism. The shaping of security law in Europe' (Amsterdam, VU University of Amsterdam, 2014; and Ester Herlin-Karnell, 'Europe's Area of Freedom, Security and Justice Through the Prism of Constitutionalism: Why the EU Needs a Grammar of Justice to Improve Its Legitimacy WZB', discussion paper, SP IV 2014–801, Berlin (2014).

This poses challenges as to what kind of security the EU specifically sets out to establish, and how it can be reconciled with the notions of freedom and justice. The book serves the purpose of critically examining and exploring the impact of a justice-oriented approach in the AFSJ sphere by linking the long-standing debate on justice to what specific justification the EU owes to both the citizens and the Member States when enacting new security-dominated legislation. But first I should explain what I mean by an AFSJ. In legal terms, the EU sets out to establish an AFSJ (Article 3 TEU and Article 67 TFEU) and this domain concerns security issues, border control, anti-terrorism law and crime, and hence embodies a new and sensitive field in the EU, one which is currently being transformed from largely being an isolated justice and home affairs space, to that of a European security regulation hub. The work assesses the AFSJ through the lens of constitutionalism, by firstly constructing the building-blocks for understanding security regulation in Europe and, secondly, by looking at the practical legal examples of security regulation, counter-terrorism and criminal law, and migration law, as representing salient examples of policy areas that need to be tackled through the prism of justice. The book sets out to argue that the balance between freedom, security and justice, and how this balance is being struck, is a question that is best approached through the framework of constitutionalism.[2] I will try to tell the story of the development of the AFSJ, and why a theoretical and legal theory understanding of it is lacking, and go on to address the issue of how it could be improved and/or achieved.

The book suggests, borrowing from Alon Harel and others, that the republican vision of freedom as non-domination is in line with the global constitutionalism project individuals do not live 'at the mercy' of national constitutions.[3] In Harel's view, freedom does not merely require that rights be not violated; it also demands that these rights be publicly recognised, in which the global norm contributes to freedom from static constitutions. This book sets out to use a similar template of the value of constitutionalism as its starting point. It does this by adopting the benchmark of freedom as non-domination in order to view justice as 'non-domination' in the AFSJ context, and how it could be achieved through attention to a right to justification in the AFSJ setting. The right to justification, then, and in line with Rainer Forst's theory, is intimately connected to justice-centred reasoning, and allows individuals equality and the right to justification for any decisions that concern them.[4] The book builds on this and goes on to argue that there is a connection between the notions of justice and justification, and explains why their full comprehension enhances the legitimacy of the EU's AFSJ project. It argues that the notion of justice, despite its contested nature, offers a helpful lens for viewing the AFSJ as part of

[2] Alon Harel, *Why Law Matters* (Oxford, Oxford University Press, 2014).

[3] ibid.

[4] Rainer Forst, *Justification and Critique: Towards a Critical Theory of Politics* (Cambridge-Malden MA, Polity Press, 2014).

the EU constitutional landscape. In addition, it contends that we need to analyse the notion of justice in the AFSJ by starting from the position of security as domination.

But what does it mean to refer to the concept of justice in this context? For John Rawls, justice is a condition that requires that everyone be allocated a fair share of the benefits in society if people are to be bound by an obligation of a fair share (the 'Duty of Fair Play').[5] According to this view, the beneficiary has an obligation to provide a fair return.[6] However, Rawls argued that only when the system is just can obligations of fair play apply. For him, we can never be bound to support or comply with unjust arrangements.[7] Thus, while justice is a highly contested concept, this book argues that it is nonetheless still a useful one. After all, how could the EU construct an AFSJ space without a shared sense of justice and solidarity? Why should justice be debated at EU level at all, rather than in the different spheres of justice of the Member States themselves, one may legitimately ask? It is true that Rawls, when constructing his basic structure of society, did not explicitly discuss justice in the global, or even in the international, arena. As Forst argues, though, there is good reason to believe that Rawls' theory of justice could be extended beyond the nation state, provided that we have the right constitutional toolkit to do so.[8] Central to this tool kit is the link not only between justice and justification, but also with that of legitimacy. Hence, the question of legitimacy will run like a thread throughout the book and it will be suggested that the constitutional structure – properly understood – could be anchored in a holistic reading of the AFSJ in which it is seen as part of the EU constitutional venture and with several global elements. Moreover, by looking at the meaning of 'non-domination' as a realisation of justice, as I argue throughout this book, this will help us to link the rather abstract right to justification to the more 'concrete' proportionality test, and will confirm the need for both ex ante and ex post checks of the EU legislative domain.

II. THE STRUCTURE OF THE BOOK

In this section, I will set out the structure and underlying idea of the book in more detail. The book seeks to construct a normative framework for understanding

[5] John Rawls, *A Theory of Justice* (Cambridge MA, Harvard University Press, 1971) discussed in John Simmons, *Justification and Legitimacy: Essays on Rights and Obligations* (Cambridge, Cambridge University Press, 2001) 5–8.

[6] Simmons (ibid), and see, also, Andrea Sangiovanni, 'On the Relation Between Justice and Legitimacy: A Framework for the EU', paper presented at the workshop Towards a Grammar of Justice in EU Law, 6–7 November 2014, at the VU Centre for European Legal Studies and Access Europe Workshop.

[7] Simmons, *Justification and Legitimacy* (2001) 5–6.

[8] Rainer Forst, 'Transnational Justice and Democracy: Overcoming Three Dogmas of Political Theory' in Eva Erman and Sofia Näsström (eds), *Political Equality in Transnational Democracy* (Basingstoke, Palgrave Macmillan, 2013) 41–59.

the parameters of the AFSJ. As already mentioned, in so doing, the book aims to use the notion of non-domination as the normative grounding by which to understand the emerging AFSJ space by linking it to the function of justification in the EU security context. Hence, the book charts the broader contexts of justifications beyond the nation state, and asks what conclusions we can draw from them in the setting of the AFSJ. In doing so, the book critically examines and explores the impact of a justice-oriented approach to the AFSJ.

A constitutional structure, as Aharon Barak explains, creates the required nexus between constitutional language and the implications inferred from it.[9] The constitutional structure is then based upon a constitution's architecture. At its heart, the EU has its constitutional construction in its commitment to human rights, democracy and the rule of law. As Mattias Kumm has argued, the constitutional character of EU law should be understood as a debate about how to understand the conditions of constitutional legitimacy and European authority.[10] Moreover, a constitutional thinking of justice goes to the heart of the question of how to address the current EU crisis and the increasing demands for an improved democratic yardstick and 'better regulation'. But most importantly for this project, it explores the constitutional structure of the AFSJ and what justice means in a security-related context.

A. Part I

Part I of the book explains the constitutional make-up of the EU and places the AFSJ project within the wider EU constitutional context. It does so by briefly outlining how much of the EU venture is crisis-driven, and how the many layers of EU integration are interrelated and overlapping. It situates the book within both the context of the broader European political landscape and the many constitutional challenges that the EU is currently facing. This part of the book is theory-oriented in that it uses the EU security discourse to demonstrate that, when measuring freedom against the benchmark of non-domination, the EU's security measures are presently close to what could be characterised as 'domination'. This is necessary in order to supply the normative base upon which the AFSJ components follow. After all, much of the EU's action is grounded in a preventive approach through the use of a security vocabulary.[11]

[9] Aharon Barak, *Human Dignity: The Constitutional Value and the Constitutional Right* (Cambridge, Cambridge University Press, 2015).

[10] See Mattias Kumm, 'Constitutionalism and the Cosmopolitan State, An Integrated Conception of Public Law' (2013) 20 *Indiana Journal of Global Legal Studies* 605–28.

[11] See, for example, Kaarlo Tuori, 'A European Security Constitution?' in David Jenkins, Amanda Jacobsen and Anders Henriksen (eds), *The Long Decade: How 9/11 Changed the Law* (Oxford, Oxford University Press, 2014); Christian Kaunert, Sarah Léonard and Patryk Pawlak (eds), *European Homeland Security: A European Strategy in the Making?* (Abingdon, Routledge, 2012); Massimo Fichera and Jens Kramer (eds), *Law and Security in Europe: Reconsidering the Security Constitution* (Cambridge, Intersentia, 2013), Cian C Murphy, *EU Counter-Terrorism: Pre-Emption and the Rule of Law* (Oxford, Hart Publishing, 2012).

This is achieved by setting out the key concepts in, predominantly, republican theory as being particularly relevant in the security context.[12] This introductory part then discusses what this means in both the concrete AFSJ context and in the EU setting more broadly by discussing the question of non-domination in the specific setting of legitimacy, and addresses how the two questions are related. The introduction sets out the legal and political set-up of the AFSJ and the broader questions that it asks. The second chapter looks at the theoretical parameters for understanding non-domination in political theory, and how it could be translated to the EU-AFSJ context by turning to security regulation. These chapters lay the groundwork for the Part II, which looks at why the question of justice is tied to the right to justification and the legitimacy process.

B. Part II

Part II scrutinises what it means to speak of an AFSJ area that both respects and fosters a common sense of justice. It explains why justice, both in the AFSJ context and beyond, should be seen as a constitutional question and not merely as an administrative concept of the right to access to justice in concrete court cases.[13] In other words, the chapter argues that justice, as an overall ambition, should be reflected in the overall architecture of the AFSJ project. In doing so, the chapter looks at the contested concept of justice and discusses the question as to how justice could become more than simply an administrative notion. In addition, the chapter investigate the idea of a constitutional concept of justice, and explores it in the context of rights-based judicial review and explains why constitutionalism matters for the construction of an AFSJ. Moreover, this part of the book examines the connection between justice and justification, and explains why their full comprehension enhances the legitimacy of the AFSJ project. This part is, admittedly, fairly abstract, in that it scans the main theoretical issues and scholarship[14] for understanding justice and justification (details in chapter three), but the questions outlined in this part of the book will be applied to the practical examples supplied in Part III. Chapter four looks more concretely at the link between justice and justification, and how these could be translated in the idea of proportionality. In particular, this part sets out to argue that the theoretical grounding of the right to justification, and its clear link to

[12] See, for example, Philip Pettit, *On the People's Terms: A Republican Theory and Model of Democracy* (Cambridge: Cambridge University Press, 2012).

[13] On critical justice in legal context, see Sionaidh Douglas-Scott, *Law after Modernity* (Oxford, Hart Publishing, 2013) and Andrew Williams, *The Ethos of Europe: Values, Law and Justice in the EU* (Cambridge, Cambridge University Press, 2010); see, also, Rainer Forst, *The Right to Justification: Elements of a Constructivist Theory of Justice* (Chichester-New York, Columbia University Press, 2012).

[14] See, for example, John Rawls, *A Theory of Justice*, rev edn (Cambridge MA, Harvard University Press, 1999), and see below for further literature review in ch 3.

justice reasoning in the AFSJ context, could and should be linked to the practical use of the principle of proportionality in EU law (which is practice-dependent). In addition, it argues that proportionality – in broader constitutional terms – is best seen as an overarching principle for understanding the constitutional conundrums facing the AFSJ. The AFSJ security focus is assessed against the yardstick of reasonable disagreement and the question of which justifications are 'good enough' by turning to the principle of proportionality. Hence, the book looks at proportionality both as a mechanism and as a method, and, as such, one which is closely associated with the rule of law – in order to understand good governance and the underlying architectural balance. In advancing this argument, I set out to demonstrate the actual implications and need for an increased use of proportionality in AFSJ cases, which unites the desire for justice as an expression of the general right of justification with the EU regulatory endeavour to ensure good governance in a broad sense.

C. Part III

Part III looks explicitly at how the EU principle of proportionality might serve as a principle for balancing freedom, security and justice, by examining the recent important cases that add to the understanding of the AFSJ and its constitutional significance.

Specifically, this part uses proportionality as a method for testing the robustness of the reasons given in decision-making, in terms of both legislation and adjudication. Chapter five explores these questions through a mixed normative and empirical approach. It uses a case study (or hands-on approach). In doing so and thereby testing the propositions outlined in this project, the book turns to two areas as useful testing grounds for the implications of constitutional justice in the AFSJ. It examines two areas, admittedly moving targets, of particular importance: the EU's response to the refugee/migration crisis, and the ongoing EU fight against terrorism and crime. The practical cases are supplied as illuminating examples of the delicate question of justice and justification, and the quest for legitimacy.

Both examples seriously challenge the EU's legitimacy claim. The chapter also tentatively discusses the extent to which the Charter of Fundamental Rights successfully provides the groundwork for a right to justification in EU decision-making, particularly with regard to how the proportionality principle is applied.

Chapter six addresses the difficult question of how the constitutional framework outlined in this book works when applied in the multi-speed context, in which not all the Member States are on board the EU ship of integration. This means that AFSJ co-operation operates in an archipelago-like landscape. For example, the UK and the Republic of Ireland have an option to opt into the AFSJ legislation, but have, as their default choice, an exemption from AFSJ legislation (although the UK is leaving the whole EU project, it has signalled its interest in remaining in security co-operation).[15] Denmark has opted out from the whole AFSJ acquis. How can this fragmented landscape be kept (and hang) together and contribute to the establishing of an AFSJ area within a constituent framework of constitutional rights? There are two concerns here: legitimacy; and constitutional rights. Does constitutionalism pre-suppose a global or European environment? Expressed differently, the chapter briefly assesses the distinctive character of proportionality in this regard as a balancing mechanism. It discusses it in the broader framework of differentiated integration looking at it in order to place the AFSJ in context.

Chapter seven sums up the argument.

III. WHY CONSTITUTIONALISM MATTERS FOR CONSTRUCTING THE AFSJ SPHERE

Before exploring the questions as outlined above, perhaps it is warranted to discuss briefly why constitutionalism is important here. This section sets out the development of the AFSJ by exploring it from the perspective of constitutional law and the need for a clarification of what kind of AFSJ space could adequately ensure justice. The hope is to demonstrate that a turn to justice as a theoretical concept could help the EU in framing the questions that it ought to be asking and, as such, are needed for the development of the AFSJ domain. A constitutional reading of justice would then be one that integrates Treaty-based values, such as a high level of human rights, with a critical reading of the rule of law.[16] This could usefully be referred to as a constitutionalised vision of justice for the AFSJ. At its core, the question relates to the connection between a theoretical understanding of justice and the practical implications that it has as a governance device for AFSJ matters, via, for example, the operation of the mutual recognition and the assumption of EU mutual values and trust which carries the AFSJ forward in the integration process. However, perhaps it should be mentioned that some scholars, such as Martti Koskenniemi, largely reject the terminology of values and argue that, instead of assuming that values exist, such values must be reached through public political discourse.[17] The risk of a kind of *jus cogens*-related (that certain legal rules cannot be contracted out)

[15] The United Kingdom's exit and the new partnership with the European Union available at: https://assets.publishing.service.gov.uk/government/uploads/system/uploads/attachment_data/file/589191/The_United_Kingdoms_exit_from_and_partnership_with_the_EU_Web.pdf.

[16] Douglas-Scott, *Law after Modernity* (2012) and on the history of the AFSJ, e.g. Massimo. Fichera, "Sketches of a Theory of Europe as an Area of Freedom, Security and Justice", in M. Fletcher, E. Herlin-Karnell and C. Matera (eds), *The EU as an Area of Freedom, Security and Justice*, (Abingdon: Routledge, 2016), Chapter 3, pp. 34–56.

[17] Itamar Mann, *Humanity at Sea: Maritime Migration and the Foundations of International Law* (Cambridge, Cambridge University Press 2016); Martti Koskenniemi, 'Constitutionalism as Mindset: Reflections on Kantian Themes about International Law and Globalization' (2007) 8 *Theoretical Inquiries in Law*, 9, 35–36.

vocabulary of human rights, as Itamar Mann observes, is that dominant actors could use such a framework to impose their own values. Mann still argues that the very existence of human rights imposes on members of humanity the duty to enforce human rights. But when responsibility falls on everyone's shoulders, as he points out, no one ends up accepting individual responsibility.[18] Ironically, and despite the solidarity principle in EU law, in the European context, only some Member States have shown a political willingness to solve the migration crises at EU level, and thus solidarity in an EU context remains extremely vague.

What, then, is the point of constitutionalism in a security-dominated AFSJ? Should we not focus more on accountability as inherent in the administrative law project of the EU, which is undoubtedly an extremely important task for the EU? Perhaps this would fit the current model of EU security regulation better than that of a constitutionalist world view of the EU?[19]

Before addressing the meta level, however, we need to know what constitutionalism is proper. It is often said that national constitutionalism is justified for at least two reasons.[20] First, it is based upon consent and hence the decision to become a citizen of a particular state means that one accepts the constitutional essentials of that state. Secondly, the idea of constitutionalism is based upon fairness, democratic values, the rule of law and protection of human rights.[21] A constitution in this context means a set of fundamental principles and institutions according to which a state is organised. In the EU context, which is a supranational organisation, constitutional essentials are coupled to the constitutional structure of the EU.[22] Moreover, the idea of justice forms an integral part of the constitutional structure of the AFSJ. Specifically, the idea of justice within the AFSJ is coupled with the notion of justice seen as non-domination, as will be explored in more detail in chapter two below.

Justice, then, is, from this perspective, the new key to understanding the very survival of the EU venture. But, while justice, according to Rawls, is the first virtue of the basic structure of society,[23] Hegel famously said that the clash of justice with justice defined tragedy.[24] While the EU is facing an ongoing drama

[18] Mann (ibid) 223–25.

[19] Peter L Lindseth, *Power and Legitimacy, Reconciling Europe and the Nation-State* (Oxford: Oxford University Press, 2010).

[20] Liav Orgad, *The Cultural Defense of Nations: A Liberal Theory of Majority Rights* (Oxford, Oxford University Press, 2015) 212–13.

[21] John Rawls, *Justice as Fairness: A Restatement* (Cambridge MA, Harvard University Press, 2001). And see Alon Harel, *Why Law Matters* (2014).

[22] Arthur Ripstein would describe this as the obligations of individuals who go to another state to recognise that state as a de facto rightful condition in Kantian terms: Arthur Ripstein, *Force and Freedom: Kant's Legal and Political Philosophy* (Cambridge MA, Harvard University Press, 2009) 298; see also John Simmons, 'Human Rights World Citizenship', in Simmons (n 5) 195–96, also discussed in Ripstein.

[23] Rawls, *Justice as Fairness* (2001); see, also, Rainer Forst, *Justification and Critique: Towards a Critical Theory of Politics* (Cambridge-Malden MA, Polity Press, 2014) 3.

[24] Yirmiyahu Yovel, *Spinoza and Other Heretics: The Marrano of Reason*, Vol 1 (Princeton NJ, Princeton University Press, 1989) 13.

in terms of various constitutional crises, Europe has had to tackle serious injustices throughout its history.[25] The phenomenon of EU justice would, by and large, seem to be an evolving process.

IV. INTRODUCTION TO THE CONTESTED CONCEPT OF JUSTICE AND THE EU SECURITY STATUS QUO

The importance of a secure society is undeniable but, if there is too much security, can there still be justice? For about a decade now, the EU's internal security mission, in line with global trends, has dominated the policies of the AFSJ as an expression of the fight against terrorism. The significance of achieving security has spilled over to the more general ambition of a market-based approach to the EU's fight against crime and the financing of terrorism, which, in turn, has led to a preventive approach, a coupling of the market-based approach within the internal market with that of the AFSJ and the achieving of security through penal measures.[26] These are only brief examples, but at their core there is an innate need for the EU to work out a strategy for the AFSJ. It is true that the EU's multi-annual AFSJ programmes and the plans set out in these ambitious agendas reflect a wish among EU institutions to be firm about the future application of the rule of law.[27] However, there is a striking absence in the political discussion on how to shape this area and what justice can add to the debate.

As indicated above, Forst argues that there is good reason to believe that Rawls' theory of justice could be extended beyond the nation state, provided that we have the right constitutional toolkit to do so.[28] While it might seem politically naïve, in the current European climate, to claim a cosmopolitan-based justice,[29] and while some 'old' Member States still have problems with 'new' Member States, the conception of justice could still inform the European Treaty-based interpretation of what it means to refer to solidarity. It is precisely here that a justice deficit exists, and it is here that the question of what kind of justification the EU owes to those on its territory becomes a burning issue. The impact of a constitutional meaning of justice and the extent to which it could function as a visualising tool for remedying some of the problems facing the EU in the current wave of populism and disintegrative tendencies in the

[25] On the role of statehood and the formation of EU and global regime, see Poul F Kjaer, *Constitutionalism in the Global Realm: A Sociological Approach* (Abingdon, Routledge, 2014).

[26] See for example, Directive 2018/843 on the prevention of the use of the financial system for the purposes of money laundering or terrorist financing, *OJ L 156, 19.6.2018, p. 43–74.*

[27] COM(2015) 185 final, The European Agenda on Security, and COM(2014) 158 final, Communication from the Commission, A new EU framework to strengthen the Rule of Law.

[28] Forst, 'Transnational Justice and Democracy' (2013).

[29] See, however, Mathias Risse, 'Taking up Space on Earth: Theorizing Territorial Rights, the Justification of States and Immigration from a Global Standpoint' (2015) 4 *Global Constitutionalism* 81–113.

Member States remains a considerable challenge and dilemma for the construction of the AFSJ.[30] Justice, in this sense, is critical, in that it insists on more than an empty assertion of justice and involves more than mere procedure.[31] In legal terms, these values may be deduced from the Charter and the preamble of the EU Treaty.

Recently, a debate has taken shape with regard to the application of 'justice' as a possible substitute for the lack of democratic credentials in the EU space. Jürgen Neyer has argued, more specifically, that the EU, as a transnational feature, cannot live up to its democratic credentials, and that the main democratic deficit lies with the Member States, not with the EU. In trying to cure this seemingly terminate EU illness, Neyer sets out to 'borrow' concepts from Forst's theory of the right to justification and justice philosophy as a better template for non-state law than that of democracy.[32] In Neyer's view, the EU would be better off by not focusing so much on the basic demand for democracy, which is something it cannot live up to anyway, and, instead, leaving it to the Member States to 'tick that box'. He argues that the EU does not have a monopoly on power and has no political equality, which makes it fundamentally flawed as a state entity and hence able to 'escape' or avoid state measurements.[33] Yet even an 'amended' version of the EU project, ergonomically designed for post-national law, still has to comply with basic democratic principles.

In the light of the EU's promise to establish an AFSJ, too strong a focus on security appears to be highly problematical. Nevertheless, the EU's security mission equally follows from the ambitions set out in the Treaty, since the EU promises to ensure a high level of security even where there is no clear division between internal and external security (Article 3 TEU and Article 67 TFEU). The focus on security, has to a great extent overshadowed the need to ensure due process rights within the EU. And, although the EU is currently improving the situation for suspects by adopting legal safeguards, and the Court of Justice has from time to time handed down rulings in favour of the individual, this is currently not enough for the AFSJ, which places equal value on all of its components of freedom, security and justice. Security has largely functioned as an identity-building power, which has largely shaped Europe with regard to security governance. As Karlo Tuorli puts it: war and crime, external and internal security, are hard to keep separate in combating terrorism, which leads to the emergence of a security constitution.[34] Similarly, I have previously pointed to

[30] TRS Allan, *Constitutional Justice: A Liberal Theory of The Rule of Law* (Oxford, Oxford University Press, 2003). See, also, Aharon Barak, 'On Constitutional Implications and Constitutional Structure' in David Dyzenhaus and Malcolm Thorburn (eds), *Philosophical Foundations of Constitutional Law* (Oxford, Oxford University Press, 2015) ch 3.

[31] For example, Douglas-Scott (n 13) above.

[32] Jürgen Neyer, *The Justification of Europe: A Political Theory of Supranational Integration* (Oxford, Oxford University Press, 2012).

[33] ibid.

[34] Kaarlo Tuori, 'Ultima Ratio as a Constitutional Principle' (2013) 3 *Oñati Socio-legal Series* 6–20.

the emergence of a preventive regime, increasingly mainstreamed with EU law on general market construction.[35] Indeed, much of the EU's involvement has been centred on the need to secure a high level of security, which is reflected in the basic market rationale in the EU in which the achievement of security is part of the market focus. It is a confirmation of the many different layers that underlie the AFSJ; how the external and internal security features interact – making the application of mainstream constitutional principles in the AFSJ a particularly difficult task for the EU legislator. The latter concern is shared by many political scientists, who have described the EU state of play as one of a European homeland security in the making.[36]

So security seems currently to dominate the AFSJ project.[37] Indeed, famously, for Hobbes, the whole point of the political enterprise is security. It is for security against each other and security against outsiders that we set up the sovereign.[38]

V. JUSTICE, EU LEGAL DEBATE AND THE EXTERNAL ASPECT

The idea of justice brings its own problems, as it casts light on some burning, albeit difficult, governance questions in the EU. More specifically, the notion of justice highlights the difficulty of reconciling the issue of how to solve the democratic deficit with the EU's greater aspiration of becoming a just, modern and effective actor on the international scene. Furthermore, the AFSJ is, in itself, as mentioned above, a very broadly defined field of law which deals with a wide EU policy area that ranges from security and criminal law to border control and civil law co-operation. Therefore, although the AFSJ is identified as one policy area, it is quite obvious that the task of identifying the underlying values in this divergent area, and how these values drive the development of the AFSJ, is of paramount importance, and it is precisely here that the concept of justice ought to guide the EU as a constitutional compass.

Moreover, while it is sometimes suggested that the EU has lost its grand narrative, when trying to navigate back to the European trajectory, it is arguably not particularly helpful to view the Member States as on a road to serfdom,[39]

[35] Ester Herlin-Karnell, 'The Development of EU Precautionary Criminalization' (2011) 2 *European Criminal Law Review* 149.

[36] Eg Christian Kaunert, Sarah Léonard and Patryk Pawlak (eds), *European Homeland Security* (2012); Fichera and Kramer (eds), *Law and Security in Europe* (2013); Marieke de Goede, 'The SWIFT Affair and the Global Politics of European Security' (2012) 50 *Journal of Common Market Studies* 214–30.

[37] On the concept of security in international law, see, for example, Liora Lazarus, 'The Right to Security' in Rowan Cruft, Matthew Liao and Massimo Renzo (eds), *The Philosophical Foundations of Human Rights* (Oxford, Oxford University Press, 2015), ch 23. On emergency laws, see, for example, David Dyzenhaus, *The Constitution of Law: Legality in a Time of Emergency* (Cambridge, Cambridge University Press, 2006).

[38] On Hobbes and security see eg, Jeremy Waldron, 'Safety and Security' (2006) 85 *Nebraska Law Review* 454–507.

[39] Friedrich A von Hayek, *The Road to Serfdom* (Chicago IL, Chicago University Press, 1944).

dominated by the superpower of the EU. Rather, there is a need to conceptualise the notion of justice in the European space so as to foster mutual resonance from within. In creating such a EU polity, the question of how best to tackle the various crises in the EU today and the associated constitutional crisis[40] is increasingly being placed at the top of the European agenda. Nevertheless, the political nature of the EU enterprise – in the contemporary discussion of European integration – often points in the direction of Carl Schmitt's theory of the political and its impact on the legal architecture.[41] The key to understanding the concept of 'political' in Schmittian thought is often said to lie in the fact that the state is not a static entity.[42] Whereas the evolving character of European law is a well-known feature of the Union as a non-static entity, the integrationist vision has always been the driving force for the EU and we now clearly seem to have arrived at the constitutional movement where the question of legitimacy has to be placed on the EU legal table. It has been argued that, independently of what we can learn from constitutional theorists in the previous century, the societal framework is still as important as ever.[43] This (arguably) means we cannot simply transpose old theories onto the contemporary debate; instead, we need to think harder – and more innovatively – about how to contextualise them into timeless concepts. The key point that scholars such as Gunther Teubner make is that the origins of the constitutional question can be found in processes of societal differentiation.[44] The norms of EU law processes are relevant to the broader and constantly changing societal settings in which they operate. In this complex structure of the EU, in upholding its constitutional standards, the rule of law and the principle of legality are a *sine qua non* for any discussions of legitimacy, given the public law nature of much of the EU's activities in the controlling of coercive power and respecting human rights. This raises questions. For one thing, the notion of legitimacy and the aspiration to achieve justice are not necessarily the same thing. After all, law may be just without having been legitimately enacted, and legitimate while failing to be just.[45] The rule of law pre-supposes, therefore, that both of these criteria are fulfilled. And it is here, as will be

[40] Jürgen Habermas, *The Crisis of the European Union: A Response* (Cambridge, Polity Press, 2013); Marc Amstutz, 'Eroding Boundaries: On Financial Crisis and an Evolutionary Concept of Regulatory Reform' in Poul F. Kjaer, Gunther Teubner and Alberto Febbrajo (eds), *The Financial Crisis in Constitutional Perspective: The Dark Side of Functional Differentiation* (Oxford, Hart Publishing, 2011) 223–68; Gunther Teubner, *Constitutional Fragments: Societal Constitutionalism and Globalization* (Oxford, Oxford University Press, 2012).

[41] Alexander Somek, 'What is a Political Union' (2013) 14 *German Law Journal* 561.

[42] Martin Loughlin, 'The Concept of Constituent Power' (2013) 13 *European Journal of Political Theory* 218–37; Carl Schmitt, *The Concept of the Political* (Chicago, Chicago University Press, 2007, G Schwab trans) 26 and 38.

[43] Teubner, *Constitutional Fragments* (2012). Poul F Kjaer, 'Between Integration and Compatibility' in Paulius Jurčys, Poul F Kjaer and Ren Yatsunami (eds), *Regulatory Hybridization in the Transnational Sphere* (Leiden, Nijhoff, 2013).

[44] ibid.

[45] Charles Larmore, 'What is Political Philosophy?' (2013) 10 *Journal of Moral Philosophy* 276–306.

elaborated below, that critical justice enters the picture. Sionaidh Douglas-Scott, for example, has argued that the rule of law could be reflected in the EU justice paradigm beyond its Treaty-based assertion.[46] The key to understanding justice is to take a holistic view of it; this makes it more than an empty notion, and substantiates the democratic values that it embodies. If interpreted as a critical legal concept, justice must form a core part of the rule of law.

This political dimension of the EU's view of justice is crucial for understanding the EU's communication with the international sphere and the role of law in this dialogue.[47] In a broader EU and transnational context, the question of the conferral of powers, for example, is so much more than the mere consideration of whether a law was enacted legitimately.[48] This is because the whole existence of EU law builds and relies on the willingness of the Member States to accept the supranational structure of the 'EU beast'. The EU project and its legal framework have therefore developed upon a slightly schizophrenic basis: the EU has always had to balance its own powers with those of the Member States, while at the same time seeking to advance the European project and its ideas.

In the context of the normative foundation for human rights, Allen Buchanan has asked what it would take to produce reliable factual information of the sort that is likely to be relevant for specifying and justifying claims about human rights.[49] Could we translate this statement into the constitutional AFSJ context? Justice, then, in the AFSJ, seems central to the ambition of realising freedom and thereby ensuring rights. Accordingly, it could be argued that the EU legal system encompasses a broader notion of justice than the basic constitutional principle upon which other EU principles are based (the rule of law[50]). For all these reasons, therefore, there has to be a connection between the aspiration for justice and that of the overall legal architecture or, to put it differently, the governance ambition of securing legitimacy in the European system. This would seem particularly important in an AFSJ context, considering that it is a sensitive area.

VI. CONCLUSION

As will be explored below, while Rawls anchored justice in the basic structure of society as a response to the question of how government action could be

[46] Sionaidh Douglas-Scott, 'The Problem of Justice in the European Union: Values, Pluralism, and Critical Legal Justice' in Julie Dickson and Pavlos Eleftheriadis (eds), *Philosophical Foundations of EU Law* (Oxford, Oxford University Press, 2012) 412–48.

[47] On the difficulties with global justice, see Thomas Nagel, 'The Problem of Global Justice' (2005) 33 *Philosophy and Public Affairs* 113–47. On justice in legal theory discourse, see Rawls, *A Theory of Justice* (1999) 171.

[48] Joel Colón-Rios, *Weak Constitutionalism: Democratic Legitimacy, and the Question of Constituent Power* (Abingdon, Routledge, 2012) 102–25.

[49] Allen Buchanan, 'Human Rights and the Legitimacy of the International Order' (2008) 14 *Legal Theory* 39–70.

[50] On the rule of law fundamentals, see, for example, Lon L Fuller, *The Morality of Law* (New Haven CT, Yale University Press, 1969).

justified and designed,[51] a broader discourse on what public reasoning means in the context of the relationship between the individual and the state has emerged at the transnational level and with great relevance for the EU. As such, it is intimately connected to what kind of justification citizens are entitled to as the EU project expands. Because of the rapid development of the AFSJ in recent years and its crisis-driven agenda a serious awareness and critical reflection as to how the EU could construct a just order of security regulation is warranted.

The book will try to show why we need more than a conception of justice in the EU that is simply centred on the administration in concrete court cases, but one that operates as part of the EU's constitutional governance endeavour, which is part of the constitutional structure of the EU, not a rival theory. The book does this by demonstrating the uniqueness of the constitutional structure of the AFSJ and why it is a particularly useful testing-field of 'justifications' as one of the most urgent and dynamic domains at present, and where the idea of justice as non-domination will add to a grammar of justice and thereby help improve the EU's credibility.

While security concerns have dictated the AFSJ discourse as an EU crisis-management tool for tackling terrorism since 9/11, the general security mission within the AFSJ has now had to deal with the increasing migration and refugee crisis (which started in 2015), which has had the effect of jeopardising the legitimacy of the EU as an AFSJ space. Regardless of whether one is a consequentialist focusing on outcome, or whether one cares about the law as such,[52] justice seen as non-domination has important implications for how we think about the AFSJ. This is why a serious reflection on what 'freedom, security and justice' really means for Europe and the rest of the world is so important. This book embarks on an exercise in tracing the reasons as to why this is the case.

[51] Rawls (n 14). See, also, Andrea Sangiovanni, 'Justice and the Priority of Politics to Morality' (2008) 16 *Journal of Political Philosophy* 137–64.

[52] Harel (n 2) ch 2.

2

The Concept of Non-domination in the EU Security-related Context

I. INTRODUCTION

IN THIS CHAPTER, I investigate the implications of a non-domination-oriented view for understanding EU security regulation. I will ask how the non-domination template fits the constitutional legal model, and what it adds to the understanding of the establishment of an AFSJ in the specific case of the EU. Moreover, I will tentatively look at the relationship between the question of coercion and domination, as well as the question regarding non-arbitrariness in the constitutional context. Specifically, the chapter links the question of security regulation to the longstanding debate in political theory on the connection between freedom and non-domination, and to the constitutional debate on the formation of security regulation in Europe. As noted in chapter one, a turn to global constitutionalism is in line with the republican vision of freedom as non-domination, as it rests on the idea that individuals do not live at the mercy of national constitutions and that global norm-setting contributes to freedom from static constitutions.[1] In line with this, for James Bohman, for instance, the most robust version of a model of global governance is a theory of republican constitutionalism understood as an obligation to form a political community beyond the nation state.[2] Thus, this chapter sets out to use a similar template of the value of constitutionalism. It does this by adopting the benchmark of freedom as non-domination in order to view justice as non-domination in the AFSJ context, and how it could be achieved through attention to a right to justification.

The chapter takes as its starting point the claim that the AFSJ is currently being constructed through the notion of security. As noted in the introduction, this poses challenges as to exactly what kind of security the EU sets out to establish, and how it can be reconciled with the notions of freedom and justice. The concept of non-domination is commonly seen as one of the most

[1] Alon Harel, *Why Law Matters* (Oxford, Oxford University Press, 2014) ch 2.

[2] James Bohman, 'A Response to my Critics: Democracy across Borders' (2010) 3 *Ethics & Global Politics* 71–84.

central concepts in republican theory,[3] and this chapter argues that it is through security seen as domination that we will understand the EU's strategy in AFSJ matters. The chapter will try to cast a clarifying light on the debate, and thereby provide both a platform and a theoretical foundation for understanding the concept of non-domination in political theory, before addressing its forms and shapes in the EU security context.

Certainly, the classic benchmark for testing the level of freedom in a given society is commonly the republican yardstick of non-domination.[4] Thus, in the republican tradition, non-domination is a personal and common good, one which everyone desires.[5] As Niko Kolodny notes, 'if the only thing that holds them [the others for invading] back is their "arbitrary" or "unilateral" will, then, according to the Domination Interpretation, you are objectionably under their power. You are dominated by them. You stand to them as the slave stands to a benevolent master.'[6]

While the master–slave example is the most obvious instance of domination, it is far from the only one.[7] There are more recent examples, and the difficulty is to translate the 'domination' criterion, as a device for measuring freedom, to the meta level. It could be argued that the sweeping generality in which the concept of security is being used echoes domination, thereby seriously hampering both freedom and justice.

For this reason, the EU security regulation regime will serve as a good test case. Thus, it seems easy to conclude that the security discourse requires a more elaborate vocabulary and a more nuanced approach to what is actually at stake when invoking its blanket term. And how the balance should be struck between security needs and the need to ensure adequately high human-rights standards is a question that is best asked and answered through the framework of constitutionalism.[8]

The chapter is structured as follows. Part II looks at the notion of freedom as non-domination, and also addresses some of the main critiques against this, predominantly, republican benchmark. Part III looks at the relevance of coercion for understanding the concept of domination, and tentatively explores the relationship with the question of power as such. Part IV investigates the

[3] Philip Pettit, *Just Freedom: A Moral compass for a Complex World* (New York, Norton, 2014).

[4] See, for example, Adam Tomkins, *Our Republican Constitution* (Oxford, Hart Publishing, 2005) 46–52.

[5] Philip Pettit, *On the People's Terms: A Republican Theory and Model of Democracy* (Cambridge, Cambridge University Press, 2012), and Fabian Schuppert, 'Non-domination, Non-alienation and Social Equality: Towards a Republican Understanding of Equality' (2015) 18 *Critical Review of International Social and Political Philosophy* 440–45.

[6] Niko Kolodny, 'Being Under the Power of Others', available at http://sophos.berkeley.edu/kolodny/BeingUnderThePowerOfOthers2.pdf.

[7] Tomkins, *Our Republican Constitution* (2005) 46–52.

[8] On constitutionalism see e.g. Mattias Kumm, "Constituent Power, Cosmopolitan Constitutionalism, and Post-positivist Law", (2016) 14 *I-CON*, pp. 697–711, and Alon Harel, *Why Law Matters* (Oxford, Oxford University Press, 2014).

question of legitimacy and justification as a closely associated question to that of non-domination. Thereafter, the chapter briefly assesses the impact of non-domination and legitimacy in the EU constitutional landscape, before addressing it in the specific context of security seen as domination and the implications for the AFSJ.

II. THE CONCEPT OF 'FREEDOM AS NON-DOMINATION' AS A CONSTITUTIONAL SET-UP: CHARTING THE MAIN DEBATE

This section will seek to clarify the meaning of non-domination before moving on to argue that the idea of non-domination is central to understanding the EU's commitment to justice.

As indicated, the idea of non-domination as the basis for freedom is an essential feature of a republican world view. In short, the notion of domination is a vertically constructed concept and means that some form of inequality, in terms of unfairness or the like, occurs, which is generally considered as domination.[9] The ideal of non-domination is therefore structurally egalitarian in that non-domination can only be achieved if all are equal in some fundamental sense, such as equality before the law, for example. Furthermore, freedom as non-domination is not only a social good, which means that there are legal and social arrangements in place which ensure non-domination, it is also a common good in so far as it aims at reducing the vulnerability of everybody (and of every social group).[10] Indeed, Isaiah Berlin famously distinguished between 'two conceptions of liberty', namely, a positive and a negative notion of freedom.[11] With the negative conception of freedom, people are free simply to the extent that their choices are not interfered with. This is in line with the liberalism expressed by John Stuart Mill, for example, and has been the dominant view of freedom.[12] The positive conception is trickier: it is freedom in the sense that groups or individuals exercise self-control or self-mastery. Berlin associated the positive conception of freedom to the 'enlightened rationalism' of thinkers such as Spinoza and Hegel.[13] Yet, according to the republican understanding of freedom, in order to be free, it is not sufficient that the person is not coerced

[9] Eoin Daly, 'Freedom as Non-domination in the Jurisprudence of Constitutional Rights' (2015) 28 *Canadian Journal of Law and Jurisprudence* 289–316.

[10] Pettit, *Just Freedom* (2014); Philip Pettit, *Republicanism: A Theory of Freedom and Government* (Oxford, Oxford University Press, 1997) 122–23.

[11] Isaiah Berlin, 'Two Concepts of Liberty' in *Four Essays of Liberty* (Oxford, Oxford University Press, 1958).

[12] John Stuart Mill, *On Liberty* (London, Longman, Roberts & Green, 1869), which has formed much of modern criminal law based upon the harm principle (according to the harm principle, the only purpose for which power can rightfully be exercised over any other member of a civilised community against his or her will is to prevent harm being done to others). For an overview, see, for example, AP Simester and Andreas von Hirsch, *Crimes, Harms and Wrongs: On the Principles of Criminalisation* (Oxford, Hart Publishing, 2011) ch 2.

[13] ibid, and discussion in Daly, 'Freedom as Non-domination' (2015).

or is unlikely to be coerced: in order to be free, it is also necessary that the potential victim does not live at the mercy of the inclinations of his or her potential violators.

As Arthur Ripstein argues, though, a problem here is the way in which different exercises of negative liberty interact with each other, which depends on the particular purposes that the people in question are pursuing, or what Immanuel Kant would call the matter of their choice. If our private purposes come into conflict, so too must our negative freedom. As Ripstein explains, Kant conceives of freedom differently.[14]

For Kant, a system of equal freedom is one in which each person is free to use his/her own powers, individually or co-operatively, in order to set his/her own purposes, and he/she is the one who decides what ends he/she will use his/her means in order to pursue those ends.[15] Kant's conception of the right to independence is a right within a system of reciprocal limits on freedom.[16] Freedom is an individualisation of the universal principle of right in one's own person, and demands that each person exercise his/her choice in ways that are consistent with the freedom of all.[17] Thus, to satisfy the Kantian principle of non-instrumentalisation, the state must secure persons against domination.

The exact contours of domination and its relation to freedom and equality are, however, still debatable. Despite its contested nature, the conception of domination, according to, for example, Fabian Schuppert, is commonly marked by three important features:[18] 1) domination is seen as a problem in specific social relationships; 2) domination is understood as being structure-based, meaning that it is not a particular outcome of domination which matters (eg, that I dare not speak my mind), but the structure of the social relationship itself; and 3) domination is identified as the use of arbitrary interference or alien control. The notion of domination is complex and appears to have something in common with other cognate concepts such as injustice, inequality and exclusion, and this is why this concept is particularly interesting for constitutional lawyers.[19]

In Pettit's terms, however, domination means something along the lines of, 'living under any agent who possesses the capacity to interfere with choices in an arbitrary manner'.[20] To be free, therefore, requires one consciously to have the personal, natural and social resources to be able to satisfy one's will. With arbitrary power, Pettit does not mean a decision that is based upon the subjective judgement or preference of the agent as such, but rather one based solely upon

[14] Arthur Ripstein, *Force and Freedom: Kant's Legal and Political Philosophy* (Cambridge MA, Harvard University Press, 2009) 32–33.

[15] ibid, 33.

[16] ibid.

[17] ibid, 35–36.

[18] Schuppert, 'Non-domination (2015).

[19] Mira Bachvarova, 'Non-domination's Role in Theorizing Global Justice' (2013) 9 *Journal of Global Ethics*, 173–85; Daly (n 9).

[20] Pettit, *On the People's Terms* (2012).

the agent's pleasure.[21] This approach has recently been criticised by Michael Thompson, who suggested that the classic focus on arbitrariness as the central element of domination is mistaken, and what is needed is a Weberian view of domination as being informed by societal strictures. In addition, he argues that domination in the modern world is often not arbitrary, but it is very strategic and routinised.[22] According to this view, domination cannot be reduced merely to an agent, but must be seen as being generated by the logic of the social structure. Others have argued that the concept of non-domination also has to entail an element of equality.[23] For Christian Rostbøll, 'The reason why freedom as independence involves equality is that the issue is not the empirical likelihood of being secure against interference, but, rather, the normative or categorical one of not being dependent on some particular or private will for the ability to pursue one's ends'.[24] Thus, freedom in the republican sense does not consist of an absence of interference as such, but, rather, of an absence of domination.[25] Indeed, Jean-Jacques Rousseau can also be seen in this tradion, in that the political and legal order does not preserve freedom, but instead constitutes it.[26]

According to Rainer Forst, a discourse-theoretical notion of (non-) domination, unlike a neo-republican version, does not focus on the robustness of the protection of the secured spheres of individual freedom of choice. Instead, it focuses on the normative standing of persons as justificatory equals and normative authorities within a political and social order as an order of justification. For Forst, political domination has two important dimensions: the rule by unjustifiable norms, and the lack of appropriate discursive arenas and institutional structures of justification to contest given justifications and to construct discursively generally and reciprocally acceptable justifications that lead to authoritative norms.

In any case, while many scholars have criticised the republican take on freedom, that is, democracy as grounded in freedom as non-domination, rather than equality, more recently, the question of non-domination has reached the limelight anew as a more general stricture for understanding power structures.[27] The freedom argument for democracy has been criticised for relying either on the idea that political activity (Aristotelian) is the highest good, or on an untenable equation of the people in their collective capacity.[28] As pointed out by

[21] ibid.

[22] Michael J Thompson, 'Reconstructing Republican Freedom. A Critique of the Neo-republication Concept of Freedom as Non-domination' (2013) 39 *Philosophy and Social Criticism*, 277–98.

[23] Rainer Forst (informal statement, discussion with the author) who adopts a non-consequentialist position.

[24] Christian F Rostbøll, 'Kant, Freedom as Independence, and Democracy' (2016) 78 *The Journal of Politics* 792–805.

[25] Eoin Daly, *Rousseau's Constitutionalism, Austerity and Republican Freedom* (Oxford, Hart Publishing, 2017) 17.

[26] ibid.

[27] Daly (n 9) above.

[28] Christian F Rostbøll, 'Non-domination and Democratic Legitimacy' (2015) 18 *Critical Review of International Social and Political Philosophy* 424–39.

Christian Rostbøll, this has led some contemporary political thinkers to ground democracy in equality, rather than freedom, and to suggest that the value of democracy is instrumental.[29] Pettit, of course, suggests an 'eye-ball test' as a criterion for social non-domination, ie, depending on our social context, we can look people in the eyes without the need for ingratiation or deterrence.[30] He is criticised for not taking into consideration the complex reality of choice and thereby fails to consider sufficiently how choice itself may, in some cases, be an important aspect of dominating structures.[31]

Others, like David Estlund, object to this view on the relation between non-domination and freedom, and consider the appeal of democracy to be associated with the importance of fair procedures.[32] Viewed from the lens of law, this debate seems to be related to the discussion on the value of constitutionalism as such.[33] More trivially, it also seems to be connected to the debate on harmonisation (full harmonisation or minimum) of national law within the supranational framework of the EU.

A. Coercion and Domination in Power Structures

The question of power is, as Forst notes, the first question of justice and the right to justification,[34] and lies at the very heart of a non-domination-oriented conception of law and justice.[35] Therefore, we need to place the question of justice in the AFSJ in the context of what (non-)domination means proper. In the EU context, the question of non-domination is usually framed as a question of equality among Member States.[36] Indeed, Max Weber famously defined the nation state as one of a legitimate monopoly of force and power.[37] In addition, non-domination is, of course, the republican benchmark or key for understanding justice, and is considered by some to be incentive-compatible, rather than ideal.[38] Yet, while the idea of non-domination for measuring freedom is

[29] ibid.

[30] Daly, *Rousseau's Constitutionalism* (2017) 127–28.

[31] ibid, 129.

[32] David Estlund, *Democratic Authority: A Philosophical Framework* (Princeton, NJ, Princeton University Press, 2008); Rostbøll, 'Non-domination' (2015).

[33] Harel, *Why Law Matters* (2014) ch 2.

[34] Forst (n 4).

[35] Philip Pettit, 'A Republican Law of Peoples' (2010) 9 *European Journal of Political Theory* 70–94, and Ian Shapiro, 'On Non-Domination' (2012) 62 *University of Toronto Law Journal* 293–336, 311.

[36] See, for example, Jürgen Neyer, *The Justification of Europe: A Political Theory of Supranational Integration* (Oxford, Oxford University Press, 2012).

[37] Max Weber, *Economy and Society*, Vol 1 (Berkeley-Los Angeles CA, University of California Press, 2013); see also Rainer Forst, 'Noumenal Power' (2015) 23 *The Journal of Political Philosophy* 111–27.

[38] Pettit (n 6).

a well-known concept in political theory,[39] in a legal context, it seems more common to refer to coercion, rather than to the notion of domination as such. For example, for Ronald Dworkin, any conception of law must explain why law is the legitimate authority for coercion.[40] A state is said to coerce its citizens because it issues commands (laws) backed by the threat of sanctions.[41] And for John Rawls, political power is always coercive power.[42] Moreover, any coercive political community must respect the dignity of those over whom it exercises dominion by showing equal concern and respect for all.[43] In addition, it has been proposed that the ideal of non-domination can be interpreted as a normative argument for cosmopolitan democracy.[44]

Indeed, any textbook on criminal law starts with the question of coercion, and explains how it is an obstacle to freedom as well as a means to it.[45] As Mattias Kumm has recently pointed out, individual actors might not always be motivated to do what is required by justice. The institutionalisation of a constitutional system seeks to add non-moral incentives – the threat of institutionalised sanctions of some kind – to support and stabilise justice-respecting behaviour and to counter domination.[46] But coercion, just like domination, is an essentially contested concept.[47] According to Ripstein, any questions about coercion are to be answered by considering the potential costs of granting a certain type of power to the state.[48] Ripstein adopts the Kantian approach in which, without a state, all uses of force are arbitrary. The coercive power of the state, he concedes, may well be needed both to deter malefactors and to assure citizens of one another's compliance with the law. The point that he makes is that the ways in which the state may legitimately exercise its coercive power cannot de-limit what justice itself is. As indicated, for Rawls, political power is always coercive power and always backed by the government's use of sanctions.[49] Perhaps, this is in line with the Dworkinian course of reasoning

[39] But see Andrea Sangiovanni, 'The Irrelevance of Coercion, Imposition, and Framing to Distributive Justice' (2012) 40 *Philosophy and Public Affairs* 79–110.

[40] Ronald Dworkin, *Law's Empire* (Oxford, Hart Publishing, 1999) 190.

[41] See, for example, HLA Hart, *The Concept of Law*, 3rd edn (Oxford, Clarendon Press, 2012) ch 3; see, also, discussion in a global context, for example, Laura Valentini, *Justice in a Globalized World: A Normative Framework* (Oxford, Oxford University Press, 2011).

[42] John Rawls, *Political Liberalism* (New York, Columbia University Press, 1993).

[43] Ronald Dworkin, 'A New Philosophy for International Law' (2013) 41 *Philosophy & Public Affairs* 2–30.

[44] James Bohman, 'Nondomination and Transnational Democracy' in Cécile Laborde and John Maynor (eds), *Republicanism and Political Theory* (Oxford, Blackwell, 2008) 190–218.

[45] See, for example, Lindsay Farmer, *Making the Modern Criminal Law: Criminalization and Civil Order* (Oxford, Oxford University Press, 2016).

[46] Mattias Kumm, 'Constituent Power, Cosmopolitan Constitutionalism, and Post-positivist Law' (2016) I-CON, 697.

[47] Ian Shapiro, 'On Non-Domination' (2012) 62 *University of Toronto Law Journal*, 293–336.

[48] Arthur Ripstein, 'Authority and Coercion' (2004) 32 *Philosophy & Public Affairs*, 2–35.

[49] John Rawls, *Political Liberalism* (New York, Columbia University Press, 1993) ch 1.

that fundamental values of equal concern and respect are interpreted in the light of their role in a coercive order.[50] After all, it was Dworkin who stated that: 'It [consistency in law] requires that the various standards governing the state's use of coercion against its citizens be consistent in the sense that they express a single and comprehensive vision of justice.'[51]

For him, coercive political organisations undermine the dignity of their members unless each accepts a reciprocal responsibility to the others to respect collective decisions, provided that these decisions meet the appropriate conditions. Moreover, Dworkin famously linked the general justification for the exercise of the coercive power of the state with that of the moral obligation of citizens to obey the law.[52] Thus, every conception, in Dworkin's terms, faces the same dilemma, as it asks the question of whether anything can justify coercion in ordinary politics? In contrast, Rawls' notion of justification is rather a justification of coercion coupled to the question of the extent to which coercion is a necessary price to pay for people living in a state together.[53]

What does this tell us about the EU system and the question of coercion and domination? In the EU context, this involves the use of arbitrary powers and can be traced back, for example, to poorly drafted legislation and deficient legal reasoning in the Court of Justice of the European Union (CJEU). As a result, domination was not wiped off the agenda by the creation of the EU and its genesis as a peace project; instead, a different form of domination developed: that of the extraordinary powers of the CJEU and the European Commission, the two strongest EU institutions. Thinly reasoned judgments by the CJEU or badly drafted legislation are perhaps also candidates for what could conceivably be viewed as domination in an EU setting, in which such arbitrariness can be seen in a lack of proportionate reasoning by EU agents, overriding the concerns of the Member States. The EU is not a state, even though it increasingly comprises state-like features, and the very lack of coercive power is often highlighted as one of the criteria that distinguishes the EU from a nation state.[54] Despite the EU's lack of traditional coercive powers, the entry into force of the Treaty of Lisbon in 2009, and thereby the increased role of the Union legislator, means that the EU has gained increased sanctioning powers because of being entrusted with some monopoly of force. Yet, perhaps it is worth asking whether the theory of coercion as the benchmark for assessing legitimacy of the nation state[55] really matters to the EU? From the start,

[50] Dworkin, *Law's Empire* (1999) 190–91; see, also, John Simmons, 'Justification and Legitimacy' (1999) 109 *Ethics* 739–71; see, also, Ronald Dworkin, *Justice for Hedgehogs* (Cambridge MA, Harvard University Press, 2011).

[51] Dworkin (n 40) 134.

[52] ibid, 190–91; see, also, Simmons, 'Justification and Legitimacy' (1999) 739.

[53] Sangiovanni, 'Framing to Distributive Justice' (2012).

[54] Neyer, *The Justification of Europe* (2012).

[55] Andreas Føllesdal and Simon Hix, 'Why there is a Democratic deficit in the EU: A Response to Majone and Moravcsik' (2006) 44 *Journal of Common Market Studies*, 533–62.

the EU has been built on a decentralised system, in which the Member States act as the gatekeepers and enforcers of EU law on the national stage. Not only do the Member States run the risk of infringement procedures being initiated by the EU Commission, but their national courts have been turned into 'infiltrators' by the CJEU and are required to enforce EU law in the domestic setting. However, as the EU is taking on more state-like features, it inevitably has to address some of the core 'old nation state' questions: the need to justify any and all use of coercive powers and to tackle the issue of what it means to refer to justice within a Union of 28 Member States (although the UK is about to leave through its Brexit negotiations in 2018). Thus, as the EU pushes forward with deterrent measures to ensure a high level of security, the status quo in AFSJ law has become one of a 'too preventive' regime, in which the safeguards of the individual are lost, despite the high values of the treaties. Perhaps, it could even be argued that the rights in the EU Charter of Fundamental Rights (Charter) and the European Convention on Human Rights (ECHR) at present appear to be somewhat empty assertions, in so far that not enough is being done at political level to ensure a European culture of due process where the nation state no longer supplies adequate legal safeguards.

III. NON-DOMINATION, JUSTICE AND EU SECURITY REGULATION

This section will aim to advance the argument that it is through security seen as domination that we will understand the EU's strategy in AFSJ matters. While the EU's heavy reliance on security as a justificatory tool for the EU's presence both on the internal and the external scene has been criticised by academics in the last decade, it still plays an important role as the main driving force for the furthering of the EU security agenda.[56] Consequently, the large majority of the measures adopted in the EU's suppression of terrorism have been characterised by a strong preventive focus closely related to that of market creation. It confirms a precautionary approach to the fight against crime. From the perspective of justice, such an approach has been problematical since the basic due-process fundamentals were not given significant weight in the supranational state of security.[57] It could be asked what domination, more specifically, comprises in an EU security context?

When discussing justice in the AFSJ setting, we need to recognise justice as a concept which is closely related to the governance structure of the AFSJ as such. Central to this argument, as noted above, is the importance of viewing justice

[56] See for example, EU Security Agenda 2015–2020, COM (2015) 185 final and the EU Security Union, available at http://europa.eu/rapid/press-release_IP-17-5202_en.htm (last accessed November 2018). See also Sionaidh Douglas-Scott, 'The Problem of Justice in the European Union' in Julie Dickson and Pavlos Eleftheriadis (eds), *Philosophical Foundations of EU Law* (Oxford, Oxford University Press, 2012) 412–48.

[57] For example, Massimo Fichera and Jens Kramer (eds), *Law and Security in Europe: Reconsidering the Security Constitution* (Cambridge, Intersentia, 2013).

as a process, not as a static phenomenon. Yet, here we have what amounts to the first challenge to the argument. After all, the process-based lens, as seen in security theory, is generally considered to be highly problematical.[58] The claim is that security is often deployed and manipulated through strategies of power, which are easily corrupted. The problem with the interlinked relationship of security and the political is that there is an obvious lack of a guarantee that the discursive framework of security will be used for good purposes.[59] The classic problem with the EU's governance endeavour with regard to the AFSJ is that it is tilted towards an overly strong security dogma. Security theorists, beyond the EU sphere – and in keeping with Michael Foucault, for example – have asked what it is that is positive about the state of exception in international law.[60] But, while security is discursive and too much of it is problematical from a human rights perspective, justice is also useful, not as an 'all or nothing' concept, but as an umbrella concept for measuring fairness. Thus, there is a well-known dichotomy between the different components of the AFSJ. The argument, as presented here though, is that the merit of viewing something as a process, rather than as a static enterprise, is different when it comes to justice, as compared to the slippery concept of security.[61] And the reason for this is the linkage of justice and legitimacy in the EU context; it is an evolving – both normatively and functionally – but necessary process. The notion of non-domination could then be formulated as a constitutional right to freedom and justice, in that nobody is to be subject to arbitrary power.[62]

Against this backdrop, and given the strong emphasis on security for the construction of the AFSJ, we need to pause and reflect upon the level of justice (we can call it a culture of fairness) that could be achieved. The question of power, as Forst points out, is the first question of justice and the right to justification,[63] and lies at the very heart of a non-domination-oriented conception of law and justice.[64] One question that automatically arises when discussing the EU's security mission is how it is related to the identity of the AFSJ, and the extent to which this identity mission is more broadly tied to the EU's symbolic function. This is because, just like 'security', terms such as 'symbolic' run the risk of being used in an overly broad way. Added to this is the tendency

[58] Andrew W Neal, 'Foucault in Guantánamo: Towards an Archaeology of the Exception' (2006) 37 *Security Dialogue* 31–46.

[59] ibid.

[60] Michael Foucault, see e.g. Security, Territory, Population: Lectures at the Collège de France, 1977–1978, discussed in Andrew W Neal (n 58).

[61] Carl Schmitt, *Political Theology: Four Chapters on the Concept of Sovereignty*, (transl, Cambridge, The MIT Press, 1985).

[62] Rainer Forst, *The Right to Justification: Elements of a Constructivist Theory of Justice* (Chicester-New York, Columbia University Press, 2012); Daly (n 9).

[63] Rainer Forst, *Normativity and Power: Analysing Social Orders of Justification* (Oxford, Oxford University Press, 2017) 38.

[64] Philip Pettit, 'A Republican Law of Peoples' (2010) 9 *European Journal of Political Theory* 70–94, and Shapiro, 'On Non-Domination' (2012) 293–336, at 311.

towards ill-defined legislation, and concealment[65] in the legislative process, which arguably constitutes domination at the expense of adequate high human rights protection (discussed further in Chapter 5 below). A critical notion of justice within the AFSJ is therefore linked to the basic right of justification as a counter-measure to domination. Yet, it still does not tell us much of the concrete meaning of non-domination for understanding AFSJ law. Admittedly, the idea is simple. It could be argued that, at macro level, 'domination' may be identified in the way in which the EU uses security to extend its objectives to new areas. At micro level, conversely, 'domination' may be identified in the way in which the security dogma deprives individuals of some of their basic due process rights, which were traditionally guaranteed by the nation state, as the current system is so oriented towards a preventive regime.

As Forst argues, 'there is at least one fundamental moral demand that no culture or society may reject: the unconditional claim to be respected as someone who deserves to be given justifying reasons for the actions, rules, or structures to which he or she is subject'.[66] Under Forst's theory, these justifications are to be structured by considerations of reciprocity and generality. The justification must have two features: it must exhibit reciprocity and generality.[67] Forst understands reciprocity as follows: participants act reciprocally when they do not seek simply to advance their own interests, but rather afford a similar status to the interests of others. Participants motivated by a sense of reciprocity accord to others the same benefits and opportunities that they call for themselves. The second feature of the right of justification is generality: participants honour this constraint when they include all and do not arbitrarily exclude anyone.[68] Moreover, according to Evan Fox-Decent, given the entrenched nature of the domination that pervades contemporary border regimes, borders are a 'moral context' to which the duty of justification applies, and so it applies to all who are affected, including outsiders.[69] Significantly, the duty is borne by the state, since the state produces the moral context of domination typical of border regimes.[70]

[65] Deirdre Curtin, 'Overseeing Secrets in the EU: A Democratic Perspective' (2014) 52 *Journal of Common Market Studies* 684–700.

[66] Forst, *The Right to Justification* (2012).

[67] Simon Caney, *Justice beyond Borders: A Global Political Theory* (Oxford, Oxford University Press, 2005).

[68] Arthur Ripstein, 'The Innate Right of Humanity and the Right to Justification' in Ester Herlin-Karnell and Matthias Klatt (eds), *Constitutionalism Justified* (Oxford, Oxford University Press, forthcoming).

[69] Evan Fox-Decent, 'Constitutional Legitimacy Unbound' in David Dyzenhaus and Malcolm Thorburn (eds), *Philosophical Foundations of Constitutional Law: Legality in a Time of Emergency* (Oxford, Oxford University Press, 2016) 119–40; Evan Criddle and Evan Fox-Decent, *Fiduciaries of Humanity: How International Law Constitutes Authority* (Oxford, Oxford University Press, 2016).

[70] This appears similar to the debate in legal discourse on proportionality: that there can be no simple formula, but that what is required is a multifaceted understanding. The picture is more complex and requires a political understanding of the specific context in which it operates.

The AFSJ sets out to secure justice and freedom through a high level of security. The notion of freedom, as stipulated in the AFSJ paradigm, does not really promise any philosophical statement, but is rather a re-affirming of the right to free movement, ie, the fundamental freedoms and the safeguarding of the rule of law. Yet, the idea of freedom, if the aspiration is for the AFSJ to become a justice space, must be tied to the quest for non-domination, as discussed above. This is where the link between justice and freedom becomes visible. The idea of the EU constructing an area of freedom and justice, while at the same time ensuring security, might, at first sight, signify a striking imbalance between the different parameters of freedom, security and justice. Yet, the construction of a true AFSJ space pre-supposes a balance, but how this balance is to be achieved is a messy task for the EU. Therefore, as indicated above, it could be argued that it is not justice in any administrative sense that is being balanced, but a broader conception of justice as a European notion of fairness as proclaimed in the values of the Treaty of Lisbon. Lawyers may propose that the imaginative creation of citizenship, as developed in CJEU case law, has to some extent resolved the democratic problem or deficit in the EU and that it ensures a European concept of freedom.[71] The point for lawyers, accordingly, is that the law can be used in a strategic way that, in combination with participation rights and citizen initiatives (Article 20 TFEU), puts some flesh on the bare bone of the European skeleton. But this seems to place the burden of justification for attaining freedom on the citizens, and not on the EU or the Member States when they are limiting freedom within AFSJ policies such as security regulation. This apparent, revised burden of justification is highly problematical in a security-related context. After all, it could be argued that the notion of justification is deeply associated with the question of how to create a European legal culture in AFSJ matters, one that genuinely cares for the individual. In the following, I propose that the core of AFSJ law be properly framed as a question of how the EU justifies its endeavours. It is contended that the freedom component, when viewed against the current domination of security, is a reasonable expectation for ensuring justice. Legitimacy in turn is central for understanding what counts as a sound justification.

IV. LEGITIMACY AND JUSTIFICATION

For Rawls, a contractualist conception of justice is based upon a notion of public justification.[72] According to this view, the use of political power is fully proper only when 'it is exercised in accordance with a constitution the essentials of which all citizens as free and equal may reasonably be expected to endorse

[71] Case C-85/96, ECR 1998, I-02691.

[72] Rawls, *Political Liberalism* (1993) discussed in Wilfried Hinsch, 'Justice, Legitimacy, and Constitutional Rights' (2010) 39 *Critical Review of International Social and Political Philosophy* 39–54; and see Wojciech Sadurski, 'Reason of State and Public Reason' (2014) 27 *Ratio Juris* 21–46.

in light of the principles and ideals acceptable to their common human reason'. In this view, a well-ordered society is a fair system of social and political co-operation which is effectively regulated by a public conception of justice. But, as argued by Wilfried Hinsch, the requirement of public justification means that the basic norms of a well-ordered society must secure the consent of citizens whose moral, philosophical and religious views are, at least partially, incompatible. It is, therefore, not inconceivable that no publicly justified political principles can be found.[73]

It seems as if the question of legitimacy is also contingent on the right to justification.[74] Indeed, Bernard Williams has famously argued that a state 'has to be able to offer a justification of its power to each subject'.[75] And, for Hannah Arendt, the question of justification is inherently connected to that of legitimacy, where the former depends on how the purported government has acquired its powers and the quality of the justification given.[76] Yet it is often said that the notion of legitimacy speaks to the moral quality of power relations between specific agents (independently of the 'justness' of allocating goods, rights and duties between those agents).[77] The point is to establish the rule of law by setting boundaries to the social power of the various actors so that social affairs are governed by principle and not by force. In a democracy, there will always be those who voted against the current regime. For Dworkin, for example, this is the classic problem of legitimacy, as it rides on the back of another problem, that of political obligation, and is linked to the question of the justification of state action. This is in contrast with John Simmons, who seems to argue that there is a difference between legitimacy and the question of justification, and who associates the question of legitimacy with how states are created.[78] In line with this, Joel Colón-Ríos has argued that it is an issue of the constitutional pedigree of the nation state.[79]

The question of coercion, just like that of non-domination, then seems to be tied to the question of legitimacy. It is also about the legitimacy of the

[73] Hinsch, 'Justice' (ibid).

[74] Simmons (n 50), also discussed in Joel Colón-Ríos, *The Legitimacy of the Juridical: Weak Constitutionalism, Democracy, and Constituent Power* (Abingdon, Routledge, 2012) ch 6. See, also, Jean L Cohen, *Globalization and Sovereignty: Rethinking Legality, Legitimacy, and Constitutionalism* (Cambridge, Cambridge University Press, 2012).

[75] See Bernard Williams, 'Realism and Moralism' in *In the Beginning was the Deed: Realism and Moralism in Political Argument* (Princeton NJ, Princeton University Press, 2005) 1–17, also discussed in: David Dyzenhaus, 'Process and Substance as Aspects of the Public Law Form', (2015) 74 *Cambridge Law Journal*, 284–306; see, also, Jan Pieter Beetz and Enzo Rossi, 'EU Legitimacy in a Realist Key', WZB Centre for Global Constitutionalism Discussion Paper (2015) SP IV 2015-802.

[76] See generally Hannah Arendt, On Violence (Orlando FL, Harcourt Brace & Company, 1970).

[77] See, for example, Colón-Ríos, *The Legitimacy of the Juridical* (2012).

[78] Simmons (n 50) discussed in: Colón-Ríos (n 74). See, also, Cohen, *Globalization and Sovereignty* (2012).

[79] Colón-Ríos (n 74). Moreover, for example, Pettit argues that there can be no effective system of justice without the state. For him, the question of justice is – deep down – one of legitimacy as non-interference. The distinction non-interference/non-domination appears somewhat vague.

general structure of authority, in which the idea of public reason is intimately connected. As Mira Bachvarova points out, the concept of non-domination in a global context can usefully be turned into a question of legitimacy while still retaining the republican idea of freedom.[80]

Moreover, in Rawlsian terms, and according to his 'liberal principle of legitimacy', the use of political power is fully proper only when 'it is exercised in accordance with a constitution the essentials of which all citizens as free and equal may reasonably be expected to endorse in light of the principles and ideals acceptable to their common human reason'.[81] It has been suggested that legitimacy is the logical correlate of the individual obligation to comply with the lawfully imposed duties that flow from the legitimate institutional processes. The question of legitimacy is of great relevance to our understanding of coercion and domination, as closely associated questions. As indicated, Max Weber approached legitimacy as a subcategory of domination, by which he meant the probability that certain specific commands would be obeyed by a given group of persons. Furthermore, every genuine form of domination implies a minimum of voluntary compliance, that is, an interest in obedience. Hence, Weber used the word 'legitimate' in order to characterise one type of domination: the type in which obedience is based in part upon the belief that the command in question is binding. In this sense, society has legitimacy when its members are willing to assume the disciplines and burdens which membership entails.[82] Does that then mean that an unjust society, which is still valued by some of its members, is legitimate? This is where the questions of justice and justification usually enters the debate, and in which human rights and the rule of law requires a quality check.[83]

Modern constitutionalism seems to make two fundamental departures from Philip Pettit's constitutional vision.[84] The first concerns the justification of judicial review. Pettit conceives of judicial review as an instrument, among others, for bringing about contestation. For him, the question of which instruments a particular legal system should adopt is an empirical question about how best to promote contestability.[85] According to some scholars, in Joseph Raz's theory of legitimate authority, legitimacy is ultimately derived from the citizens' interest in following the directives of the given authorities, rather than from any facts about the authorities themselves.[86] For Jürgen Habermas, laws are legitimate

[80] Bachvarova, 'Theorizing Global Justice' (2013).

[81] Rawls (n 49).

[82] Discussed in Simmons (n 50) citing Tom R Tyler, *Why People Obey the Law* (Princeton NJ, Princeton University Press, 2006).

[83] Forst, *Justification* (2012).

[84] Jacob Weinrib, Dimensions of Dignity: The Theory and Practice of Modern Constitutional Law (Cambridge, Cambridge University Press, 2016).

[85] Discussed further in Jacob Weinrib, *Dimensions of Dignity* (2016).

[86] Discussed in Sadurski, 'Reason of State' (2014).

if they can be conceived as both self-imposed and binding.[87] He is well known for grounding his account of democratic politics, with its guiding normative idea of legitimacy in what people would agree to in the absence of coercion.[88] Yet, it has been suggested that Habermas does not specify specific institutions, but instead argues that people would be persuaded to adopt/accept the best arrangement through uncoerced deliberations.[89] Moreover, Habermas has been criticised for ignoring the importance of the question of power, in contrast to Michel Foucault's view on domination, which is rooted in the recognition of power as one of the characteristics of politics.[90] Nonetheless, as pointed out by the same commentator, Foucault does not distinguish between different uses of power and is therefore vulnerable to the accusation that he disregards other aspects of human behaviour than just power.[91] As Ian Shapiro points out, regardless of whether political theorists see freedom as a feature of justice or an alternative to it, they treat it as the coin of the realm in judging the legitimacy of political institutions. For Shapiro (citing James Madison), democratic competition offers the best hope for mitigating domination, and working to protect and expand the democratic dimension is, in his view, the best path forward for those who regard non-domination as the bedrock of justice. For Allen Buchanan, too, legitimacy is an ecological notion which makes sense when one thinks of how it fits into the system.[92] This seems a very suitable picture for Europe. Surely the EU could learn from the political theory debate?

What then is the concept of legitimacy? For Forst, legitimacy is, in the first instance, descriptive, as it owes its overlaying, more salient function of normative criticism or defence to other resources.[93] As one commentator points out, though, legitimacy, it has been argued, is normally based upon what is considered to be successful practice in procedural and factual terms.[94]

Again, this seems to take us from legitimacy to the eternal question about the meaning of 'justice'. After all, the debate on justice in EU law arguably concerns how to justify the EU project, and is, therefore, also a question about quality. Applying a Rawlsian account to the theory of justice would, in any case, imply

[87] Jürgen Habermas, *Between Facts and Norms: Contributions and Discourse Theory Law and Democracy* (Cambridge, Polity Press, 1996), also in Michel Rosenfield, 'Constitutional versus Administrative Ordering in an era of Globalization and Privatization, Reflections on Sources of Legitimation in the Post Westphalian Polity' (2011) 32 *Cardozo Law Review* 2339–68.

[88] Shapiro (n 47) 311.

[89] ibid.

[90] ibid, and Michel Foucault, *The Archeology of Knowledge and the Discourse on Language* (New York, Vintage Books, 1972).

[91] Shapiro (n 47) 293–336, at 311.

[92] Allen Buchanan, *The Heart of Human Rights* (Oxford, Oxford University Press, 2013) 198.

[93] Rainer Forst, 'Legitimacy, Democracy and Justice', paper presented at VU Amsterdam, 6–7 November 2014, 'Towards a Grammar of Justice in EU Law'.

[94] Sebastiano Maffettone, 'Global Legitimation and Reasonableness' in Giovanni Sartor, Giorgio Bongiovanni and Chiara Valentini (eds), *Reasonableness and Law* (Dordrecht-Heidelberg-London-New York, Springer, 2009) 147–62.

using reasonableness as an adequate standard for measuring legitimacy at EU level and for linking it to the broader debate on justice.

In brief, it could be argued that the EU legal system encompasses a broader notion of justice than the basic constitutional principle upon which other EU principles are based. However, in order to be legitimate, and as already touched upon above, a regime must not only aim to be just, but also to demonstrate a level of justice that defines the conditions under which the state may rightly justify its coercive power.[95]

V. JUDICIAL REVIEW AND NON-DOMINATION

What, then, of the function of courts in the justice process? For Rawls, judicial review should be understood simply as a practice of some degree of reliance on an independent judiciary for the effectuation of the constitutional essentials.[96]

The idea of judicial review is commonly seen as the hallmark of the constitutionalist way of thinking about law. Central to the idea of freedom as non-domination, according to neo-republican thinkers like Pettit, is a strong form of judicial review as a vital check on arbitrary powers.[97] The reason for this is that what constitutes non-arbitrary intervention is best preformed through a non-political procedure. Perhaps, this appears in contrast to other republican thinkers, such as Richard Bellamy, who view courts as inherently undemocratic.[98] Others, like Eoin Daly, argue that freedom – understood as non-domination – is inconsistent with any concept of rights that aims to identify immunity for individuals, and thus identify in advance those questions that are placed beyond ordinary political contestation, and that the attempt to depoliticise rights by taking them outside the political domain, in fact, amounts to de facto political domination.[99] Indeed, scholars like Jeremy Waldron have structurally argued against the institution of judicial review, as they see it as fundamentally undemocratic.[100] Yet, Daly's point is that even the fiercest opponents of judicial review in the republican camp may, in some instances, agree that judicial review is a good idea. A republican argument is in favour of courts taking account of power differentials in certain contexts while remaining sceptical as to whether judicial power can reduce power differentials in society at large. He argues for a context-based approach, as I understand him, in which it is necessary to pay

[95] Rainer Forst, *Justification and Critique: Towards a Critical Theory of Politics* (Cambridge, Polity Press, 2013).

[96] Franck I. Michelman, "Rawls on Constitutionalism and Constitutional Law" in S Freeman (ed), The Cambridge Companion to Rawls (Cambridge, Cambridge University Press 2003), ch 11 pp 394–425.

[97] Daly (n 9) 289.

[98] Richard Bellamy, *Political Constitutionalism: A Republican Defence of the Constitutionality of Democracy* (Cambridge, Cambridge University Press, 2007). See, also, Jeremy Waldron, *Law and Disagreement* (Oxford, Oxford University Press, 1999).

[99] Daly (n 9) 296.

[100] Bellamy, *Political Constitutionalism* (2007); Waldron, *Law and Disagreement* (1999).

attention to the perceived experience of freedom and unfreedom by citizens.[101] As Daly points out, if rights are understood as channelling the kinds of reasons that governments can invoke when they act in certain arenas, and therefore are not trumps à la Dworkin, but rather its channels and its pointers, this has a republican flavour.

Similarily, Yasmin Dawood has developed a domination-minimising institutional trade-off.[102] The basic idea behind this institutional trade-off is, acccording to her, to prevent the most dominating legislative action by means of the least dominating form of judicial intervention. This trade-off is based in part upon the recognition that court intervention itself can raise the risk of domination. Not only does this trade-off result in an overall net minimisation of domination, it also constrains judicial intervention to the most serious instances of domination. In this way, the anti-domination model guards against the danger of judicial over-reaching.[103] Under the anti-domination model, judicial action is warranted only if the actual and apparent domination that would result from judicial intervention is decisively outweighed by the actual and apparent domination that would result from the legislative action at issue. Not only does this trade-off result in a net minimisation of domination, it also constrains judicial intervention to serious instances of domination.[104] However, not every instance of dominating behaviour by the legislature warrants judicial intervention. Moreover, decisions by courts to intervene should be reconceptualised as domination-minimising institutional trade-offs.

But what would it take for a court to interfere upon the basis of non-domination? What sort of argument would hold in a court? In the EU-AFSJ nexus, this question would seem to turn largely on the elasticity of the proportionality principle as a legal expression of the right to justification. The basic right of due process is, of course, also a guarantee against domination in the courtroom. Moreover, clearly, it could be argued that the rights in the EU Charter of Fundamental Rights and the Convention on Human Rights, by themselves, work as a buffer against state domination of the individual.[105]

As explained above, the idea of the EU constructing an area of freedom and justice while, at the same time, ensuring security might – at first sight – signify a striking imbalance between the different parameters of the promises of freedom, security and justice. The AFSJ is currently one of the most dynamic EU integration areas and, as such, one of the newest EU policy areas, and how it develops in the future is of great importance not only for the Member States but also for the citizens of the EU.

[101] Daly (n 9).

[102] Yasmin Dawood, 'The Antidomination Model and the Judicial Oversight of Democracy' (2008) 96 *The Georgetown Law Journal* 1411–85, with further references.

[103] ibid.

[104] ibid.

[105] Mattias Kumm, 'The Turn to Justification: On the Structure and Domain of Human Rights Practice' in Adam Etinson (ed), *Human Rights: Moral or Political?* (Oxford, Oxford University Press, 2018) 238–61.

VI. TRANSLATING THE 'NON-DOMINATION' QUESTION TO THE SUPRANATIONAL EU LEVEL AND ITS RELEVANCE FOR EU SECURITY REGULATION

It is worth clarifying in brief why the concept of non-domination is a useful one in the area of EU constitutional law, and why it is linked to the idea of legitimacy.[106]

Indeed, the freedom argument coupled to that of non-domination, seems an essential component of the EU legal objectives. While much of the current debate on legitimacy has focused on the notorious democratic deficit within the EU and the need to move away from state templates, EU lawyers have tended to avoid the associated issue of legitimacy as well as the political theory concept of the meanings and critical understanding of freedom as non-domination.

Certainly, as noted above, in a traditional EU constitutionalist world, the EU has its own constitutional structure in its commitment to human rights, democracy and the rule of law, and this commitment would be at its heart. The continuing search for legitimacy then, when related to the political theory debate, seems to turn on the EU's need to reinvent both its ambitions and its narrative. When discussing the EU's legitimacy, the starting-point – from an EU legal perspective – is the democratic credentials of the EU, which are also connected to legitimacy, the latter being a constitutional principle of the EU, as recognised in Article 2 TEU, which is listed as one of the very principles that inspired the creation of the EU. Central to the rule of law is the idea of bounded government restrained by law from acting outside its powers.[107] The rule of law presupposes that both of the criteria of justness/justice and legitimacy in its enactment are fulfilled. Considering this, could it be argued that the rule of law in itself is a more workable concept than the concept of non-domination, and, by extension, the idea of justice seen as non-domination in the AFSJ. For are they not already part the rule of law criteria? The answer, as I see it, is that these concepts, as concretised in the proportionality test (in short, that legal measures or state actions should not be more intrusive than is necessary to achieve their aim), are more concrete in legal practice as representing a contextualised approach to justice as a counter-mechanism to domination, and should be seen in conjunction with the rule of law. This, admittedly, is a very broad view.

And the problem here is what we create from the proportionality test (as a sword or a shield), which will be discussed in further detail in chapter four below. Indeed, it seems close to the heart of any EU constitutional scholar to

[106] On legitimacy in EU law, see, for example, Joseph HH Weiler, 'The Transformation of Europe' (1990–91) 100 *Yale Law Journal* 2400; Paul Craig, 'Integration, Democracy and Legitimacy' in Paul Craig and Gráinne de Búrca, *The Evolution of EU Law* (Oxford, Oxford University Press, 2011) ch 1; and Anthony Arnull and Daniel Wincott (eds), *Accountability and Legitimacy in the European Union* (Oxford, Oxford University Press, 2002).

[107] See Mattias Kumm, 'Constitutionalism and the Moral Point of Constitutional Pluralism' in Julie Dickson and Pavlos Eleftheriadis (eds), *Philosophical Foundations of EU Law* (Oxford, Oxford University Press, 2012) ch 9.

think that the principle of proportionality – understood critically – offers the best available constitutional solution for establishing the idea of solidarity as a workable legal principle through the key of proportionality reasoning.

But, it is submitted, the merits of proportionality outweigh its downsides, as it could help improve the democratic shortcomings in the AFSJ and secure rights where the legislator has failed to do so. But we still need to explain why it is reflected in a non-domination-based view.

VII. INTRODUCTION TO THE LINKS BETWEEN JUSTIFICATION AND PROPORTIONALITY IN THE CONTEXT OF NON-DOMINATION

The question of a common or shared European solidarity (or culture) is a very relevant one for the mission of establishing a common security area. But how can this be achieved in the EU's emergency-driven security legislation, which is to date driven by political considerations, rather than legal concerns? As Mattias Kumm points out, the question of politics is the practice of rights-based justice-seeking through a constitutional framework (among free and equal people) under conditions of reasonable disagreement.[108] It seems to me that the impact of rights-based proportionality in the EU security-regulated context and the notion of solidarity in the EU could play a significant function in the formation of the AFSJ. For Aharon Barak, proportionality links up with the question of justice because: 'There is always law (domestic or international) according to which the state must act. There are no black-holes'.[109]

But, while, in the EU, there currently seems to be a lot of vacuum in the debate, the principle of proportionality allows for some stability, which serves as a rescuer until the real work of legislation and deliberation begins, which seems particularly important in criminal law and security regulation in order to avoid a ticking bomb of state violence against the individual. Hence, as noted, the merits of proportionality outweigh its downsides, as it could help to improve the democratic shortcomings in the AFSJ and secure rights where the legislator has failed to do so, assuming that we agree that this is what a democratic system should do.[110] This question will be explored in further detail in chapter four below.

Since limitations on rights must be 'rationally connected to the objective and not be arbitrary, unfair or based upon irrational considerations',[111] this can be interpreted as a mechanism for ensuring that coercive state interference remains non-arbitrary, in the republican sense, in that it tracks commonly

[108] Kumm, 'Constitutionalism' (2012).

[109] Aharon Barak, 'The Role of a Supreme Court in a Democracy and the Fight Against Terrorism' (2005) 35 *Hong Kong Law Journal* 287.

[110] Mattias Kumm, 'The Idea of Socratic Contestation and the Right to Justification: The Point of Rights-based Proportionality Review' (2010) 4 *Law & Ethics of Human Rights* 141.

[111] Daly (n 9).

avowable public interests. It is true that, in some variants, at least, the proportionality test will effectively require judges to make substantive, even intuitive, appraisals as to the relative merits of competing claims of public and private right, and that this implicates judges in a more far-reaching normative endeavour, which goes beyond a mere assessment as to arbitrariness in its republican sense.[112] However, the more technical aspects of the proportionality doctrine – particularly the requirement of a rational connection between the means and ends of a restriction on rights – helps to show, again, that constitutional rights are just not moral rights which are institutionalised, but are instead controls on the predicates of state power. In turn, this makes rights-based constitutional adjudication quite consistent with a political concept of rights, and accommodates the fact of disagreement about rights.[113]

Again, we will return to these questions and the intriguing, albeit sometimes complicated, relationship between the idea of EU proportionality and the questions of justice and justification, in chapter four below.

VIII. CONCLUSION

This chapter has tried to conceptualise the concept of non-domination in political theory discourse, how it is translated into EU constitutional law, and its relevance for EU security studies with specific focus on the EU policy area of the AFSJ. It has highlighted the long-standing debate in political theory on freedom as non-domination-oriented theories and equality-oriented ones, and explained why this debate has now been re-routed to that of a connection between the neo-republican concept of non-domination and methods against arbitrariness to that of a constitutional right of justification for arbitrary decisions.

The chapter has also attempted to show why the concept of non-domination is highly relevant for the understanding of the security architecture of the constitutional structure for the EU-AFSJ nexus, where the quest for justice and freedom is currently being challenged by the security-focused make-up of the AFSJ. Finally, the chapter has argued that a contextualised approach to non-domination is important where the legislator has failed in its promise to deliver high-quality law which upholds the rule of law and due process rights even in times of emergency.

The next chapter will explore the concepts of justice and justification in further detail, and why those concepts are relevant in an EU security context.

[112] ibid.
[113] ibid, 289.

Part II

3

The Right to Justification, Justice and the Area of Freedom, Security and Justice

I. INTRODUCTION

THIS CHAPTER EXPLORES the idea that there can be such a thing as a right to justification. It builds on chapter two and the question of freedom as non-domination. It takes its starting point in the legal and political theory-bound idea of a right to justification, and assesses it in the context of justice theory, by arguing – and following Rainer Forst in this regard – that the two notions are connected. Non-domination, in this respect and in the specific AFSJ context, is, as this chapter will try to argue, seen as justice. I critically examine and explore the impact of a justice-oriented approach to the AFSJ sphere by linking the long-standing debate on justice to what justification the EU owes to both its citizens and to the Member States when enacting new security-dominated legislation. While justice is a highly controversial notion, for Dworkin, the concept of justice depends on the underlying interpretation and competing rationales behind any conception of it.[1] Therefore, it is not the abstract notion of justice but the particular conception – 'justificatory', as I claim below – that needs fleshing out in the EU context and is particularly important in the framework of the progressing area of EU security regulation.

While the EU's heavy reliance on security as a justificatory tool for the EU's presence both on the internal and the external scene has been criticised by academics in the years following 9/11, as charted in chapter two above, it still plays an important role as the main driving force for the furthering of the EU security agenda.[2] Consequently, as was briefly mentioned in the previous chapters, a large majority of the measures adopted in the EU's suppression of terrorism have been characterised by a strong preventive focus closely related to

[1] Ronald Dworkin, *Law's Empire* (Oxford, Hart Publishing, 1986) 98–99.

[2] See, for example, David Jenkins, Amanda Jacobsen and Anders Henriksen (eds), *The Long Decade: How 9/11 Changed the Law* (Oxford, Oxford University Press, 2014) and Sionaidh Douglas-Scott, 'The Problem of Justice in the European Union' in Julie Dickson and Pavlos Eleftheriadis (eds), *Philosophical Foundations of EU Law* (Oxford, Oxford University Press, 2012) 412–47.

that of market creation. For example, the anti-money laundering scheme – and the question as to why the suppression of financial crimes and terrorism financing is relevant in EU law – offer good examples of a longstanding case of cross-over competences between the AFSJ and the internal market sphere. The EU Security Agenda 2015–2020 tries to address this complex issue by stressing the need for more joined-up inter-agency cooperation and a cross-sectorial approach.[3] In any case, the current EU practices with regard to security cooperation often adopt a precautionary approach to, inter alia, fighting crime and terrorism-related activity through emergency measures. However, from the perspective of justice, such an approach has proven problematical, since the basic due-process fundamentals were not given significant weight in the supranational state of security.

Although justice is a highly contested concept, I try to argue that it is nonetheless still a useful one. After all, how could the EU construct an Area of Freedom, Security and Justice (AFSJ) space without a shared sense of justice? The chapter runs though the main political theory literature on justice, including, among others, John Rawls, Gerald A Cohen, Ronald Dworkin, Michael Walzer, Amartya Sen, Rainer Forst, Thomas Nagel, Simon Caney, John Simmons, Arthur Ripstein and Martha Nussbaum, who are some of the contributors to the contemporary justice theory which will be discussed in this chapter, given their relevance to the argument presented.[4] The chapter specifically looks at how the justice discourse could successfully be transposed to the EU framework by also considering the current EU political debate on justification.[5] Hence, this chapter outlines the main debate (as briefly discussed in chapter one) as well as the question of to what extent we can even debate justice at EU level.[6] In other words, the chapter asks what conception of justice should become an integral part of the EU's constitutional vocabulary. For justice to work as a concept in AFSJ law, we need, however, to establish the extent to which justice can appropriately be debated in the supranational sphere, or whether it is predominantly

[3] COM(2015) 185 final, 'The European Agenda on Security' https://ec.europa.eu/home-affairs/sites/homeaffairs/files/e-library/documents/basic-documents/docs/eu_agenda_on_security_en.pdf.

[4] See, for example, John Rawls, *A Theory of Justice* (Cambridge MA, Harvard University Press, 1971), Gerald A Cohen, *Rescuing Justice and Equality* (Cambridge MA, Harvard University Press, 2008), Ronald Dworkin, *Justice for Hedgehogs* (Cambridge MA, Harvard University Press, 2011), Martha C Nussbaum, *Frontiers of Justice: Disability, Nationality, Species Membership* (Cambridge MA, Harvard University Press, 2007), Amartya Sen, *The Idea of Justice* (Cambridge MA, Belknap Press, 2011), Rainer Forst, *The Right to Justification: Elements of a Constructivist Theory of Justice* (Chicester-New York, Columbia University Press, 2012). Simon Caney, *Justice beyond Borders: A Global Political Theory* (Oxford, Oxford University Press, 2005), Thomas Nagel, 'The Problem of Global Justice' (2005) 33 *Philosophy and Public Affairs* 113–47; see, also, Laura Valentini, *Justice in a Globalized World: A Normative Framework* (Oxford, Oxford University Press, 2011) and Lea Ypi, *Global Justice and Avant-Garde Political Agency* (Oxford, Oxford University Press, 2011), Arthur Ripstein, 'Justice and Responsibility' (2004) 17 *Canadian Journal of Law and Jurisprudence* 361–86.

[5] Jürgen Neyer, The Justification of Europe: A Political Theory of Supranational Integration (Oxford, Oxford University Press, 2012).

[6] Nagel, 'The Problem of Global Justice' (2005), and Caney, *Justice beyond Borders* (2005).

a local (national) phenomenon. As noted in chapter one, Rainer Forst argues that there is good reason to believe that, for example, Rawls' theory of justice could be extended beyond the nation state, providing we have the right toolkit for doing so.[7] There is thus an interesting normative shift in Rawls' move from a domestic theory of justice to an international theory. The normative individualism fundamental to his domestic theory is replaced by a 'communitarianism' of a sort that takes societies or peoples to be the basic subjects of justice. As Simon Caney puts it, ideals of global equality and the principle of not imposing (for example, liberal values on people which they can reject) are not really incompatible on Rawls' own terms.[8]

Moreover, as Shmuel Nili explains, statists already have some problems with justice theory today, about whether a supranational body such as the EU, with its own regulations and coercive framework, produces special political ties and a coercive framework between co-citizens as justifying the limitation of egalitarian concern to compatriots alone.[9]

In the following, I will try to explain why the question of justice is tied to the right to justification and the legitimacy process. This part of the book seeks to scrutinise what it means to speak of an AFSJ area that both respects and fosters a common sense of justice. It does this while acknowledging that justice is an essentially contested concept. The chapter seeks to discuss why justice could nonetheless serve as a device for ensuring non-domination through the framework of constitutionalism.[10] It tries to explain why justice, both in the AFSJ context and beyond, should be seen as a constitutional question, and not merely as an administrative concept of the right to access to justice in concrete court cases.[11] In other words, the chapter argues that justice, as an overall ambition, should be reflected in the overall architecture and structure of the AFSJ project. Such an understanding enhances the robustness of the system. For example, it could be argued that it is not possible to separate procedural and substantive justice in EU law so sharply. After all, the debate on justice in EU law arguably concerns how to justify the EU project, and is, therefore, also a question about equality between the Member States and the quality of the legislation. As explained, applying a Rawlsian account to the theory of justice would imply using reasonableness as an adequate standard for measuring legitimacy at an EU level, and for linking it to the greater debate on justice.

In addition, the chapter discusses the function of justification as an expression of democratic credentials, which are imbued within the AFSJ, as well

[7] Forst, *The Right to Justification* (2012).

[8] Caney (n 4).

[9] Shmuel Nili, 'The Moving Global Everest: A New Challenge to Global Ideal Theory as a Necessary Compass' (2016) 17 *European Journal of Political Theory* 1–22.

[10] On contested concepts and the EU regime, see the contributions in Jürgen Neyer and Antje Wiener (eds), *Political Theory of the European Union* (Oxford-New York, Oxford University Press, 2010).

[11] On critical justice in legal context, see Sionaidh Douglas-Scott, *Law after Modernity* (Oxford, Hart Publishing, 2013) and Andrew Williams, *The Ethos of Europe: Values, Law and Justice in the EU* (Cambridge, Cambridge University Press, 2010); see, also, Forst (n 4).

as the process-based vision of constitutionalism and legitimacy.[12] The right to justification, as developed in political theory, in particular by Forst, is then translated into the constitutional legal framework of the EU. It is suggested that the question of justice and justification is ultimately that of sufficiently good reasons, in which the establishment of the AFSJ is a question of constitutionalism as such. This part of the project looks at the rights of others in an EU-global context, and, by briefly considering Michael Walzer's theory on spheres of justice based upon membership in a community, asks whether his theories work in the EU context of citizenship rights in the AFSJ.[13] It will seek to link the debate on justice and justification to that of legitimacy in an EU constitutional context.[14]

For Walzer, the theory of justice brings with it an account of membership rights, such as security and welfare. Walzer has noted that the concept of justice is a human construction and it is therefore doubtful that it can be used in one single way.[15] Clearly, the idea of justice and how to construct a just society is still a controversial topic. Justice discourse today, and its implications for law, spans from what some would characterise – simplistically summarised here – as 'moralism to realist' views[16] and 'ideal versus non-ideal' theories,[17] to the capability approach advocated by Martha Nussbaum,[18] who argues that what is needed in the debate on justice is a minimum level of justice in accordance with a list of basic capabilities that must be protected.

II. JUSTICE AS A CONTESTED CONCEPT[19]

The quest for justice in any society or organisation is often considered as a self-evident political objective. So it should be for the EU with the rule of law,

[12] Poul F Kjaer, 'Why Justification? The Structure of Public Power in Transnational Contexts' (2017) 8 *Transnational Legal Theory* 8–21.

[13] Michael Walzer, Spheres of Justice: A Defence of Pluralism and Equality (New York, Basic Books, 1983).

[14] Forst (n 4) and Richard Bellamy, *Political Constitutionalism: A Republican Defence of the Constitutionality of Democracy* (Cambridge, Cambridge University Press, 2007).

[15] Walzer, *Spheres of Justice* (1983). Walzer famously addressed the question of membership in a political community for theories of distributive justice (what people owe to one another) as well as for theories of democracy. See, also, the discussion in Seyla Benhabib, *The Rights of Others: Aliens, Residents and Citizens* (Cambridge, Cambridge University Press, 2004) 117.

[16] See Enzo Rossi, 'Justice, Legitimacy and (Normative) Authority for Political Realists' (2012) 15 *Critical Review of International Social and Political Philosophy* 149, *Spheres of Justice* 64.

[17] ibid.

[18] Nussbaum, *Frontiers of Justice* (2007).

[19] This section draws partly on Ester Herlin-Karnell, 'The Domination of Security and the Promise of Justice: On Justification and Proportionality in Europe's "Area of Freedom, Security and Justice"' (2017) 8 Transnational Legal Theory 79–102.

democracy and human rights as its foundational and core values.[20] However, is the concept of justice at risk of losing all its concrete meaning, of becoming no more than a metaphor for the political process? As explained above, given the strong emphasis on security and its current domination in the security sphere, the idea of justice is of crucial importance for shaping the future EU security law.

Essential to the justice toolkit provided by Forst is the conception of context and critical interpretation as the main yardstick for understanding justice. This chapter seeks to elucidate why it is helpful to analyse EU security regulation through the lens of justice as non-domination,[21] and how constitutionalism offers a useful framework for this process. Thus, the chapter is focused on the broader theoretical and normative understanding of the EU security project. In doing so, it explores the link between justice and justification, and explains how a proper understanding of them may enhance the legitimacy of the EU freedom, security and justice project. As explained above, the idea of the EU constructing an area of freedom and justice, while at the same time ensuring security, might signify a striking imbalance between the different parameters of freedom, security and justice. Yet the construction of a true AFSJ space pre-supposes a balance, but how this balance is to be achieved remains a messy task for the EU. Consequently, as noted in chapter two, it could be argued that it is not justice in any administrative sense that is being balanced, but a broader conception of justice as a European notion of fairness. And here, an important component in this project is the question of the right to justification.

While Rawls anchored justice in the basic structure of society as a response to the question of how government action could be justified and designed,[22] a broader discourse on what public reasoning means in the context of the relationship between the individual and the state emerged at transnational level. While justice is often proclaimed to be an essentially contested concept,[23] this chapter argues that it can still be a vital and useful notion for gauging

[20] On justice in the EU context, see, for example, Sionaidh Douglas-Scott, 'Human Rights as a Basis for Justice in the European Union' (2017) 8 *Transnational Legal Theory* 59–78. See, also, Sionaidh Douglas-Scott, 'The Problem of Justice in the European Union: Values, Pluralism, and Critical Legal Justice' in Julie Dickson and Pavlos Eleftheriadis (eds), *Philosophical Foundations of EU Law* (Oxford, Oxford University Press, 2012) ch 16; Dimitry Kochenov, Gráinne de Búrca and Andrew Williams (eds), *Europe's Justice Deficit?* (Oxford, Hart Publishing, 2015), especially the contribution of Neil Walker, 'Justice in and of the European Union' 247–58; Andrea Sangiovanni, 'Solidarity in the European Union' (2013) 33 *Oxford Journal of Legal Studies* 213; Neyer, *The Justification of Europe* (2012). See, also, most recently Floris de Witte, *Justice in the EU: The Emergence of Transnational Solidarity* (Oxford, Oxford University Press, 2016).

[21] On freedom as non-domination, see Philip Pettit, *On the People's Terms: A Republican Theory and Model of Democracy* (Cambridge, Cambridge University Press, 2013).

[22] Rawls (n 4). See, also, Andrea Sangiovanni, 'Justice and the Priority of Politics to Morality' (2008) 16 *The Journal of Political Philosophy* 137–64.

[23] See, for example, contributions in Neyer and Wiener (eds), *Political Theory* (2010).

fairness when applied contextually.[24] This becomes especially evident in legal settings where the level of sophistication of the legal reasoning that grounds each concrete court case reflects the question of how to achieve a just order.[25] As Aharon Barak points out, the idea of fairness is deeply connected to the idea of human dignity as a constitutional value.[26]

One of the most helpful debates on justice in contemporary political thought is between Rawls' justice model and Gerard Cohen's attempt to rescue equality from what he claimed represented a distorted picture of justice. As is well known, Cohen criticised Rawls' model of justice as the structure of society upon the basis that his difference principle would permit inequality.[27] He also rejected Rawls' idea that justice is the basic structure of society by arguing that it is not enough for justice to be built into the institutional design of societies, it must also be an imperative for individuals.[28] For Cohen, there must be pure justice, one that is not mixed with any other components (such as empirical facts). Cohen's theory is idealistic, as his version of justice cannot reflect any other virtue than justice.[29] Others, such as Amartya Sen, attempted to shift attention away from notions of ideal justice to the more practical questions of advancing justice by eliminating at least the worst forms of the existing injustice.[30]

Yet justice is often considered a self-evident political objective. Surely, no civic-minded person would argue against justice as a normative benchmark for a decent society. However, the concept of justice risks losing all concrete meaning, of becoming no more than a metaphor for the political process.[31] Given the EU's prevailing strong emphasis on security, the idea of justice is of crucial importance as EU security law is being shaped for the future. Justice within the AFSJ ought to be seen as an expression of non-domination. Against this background, Rainer Forst has developed a political and critical understanding of justice.[32] In his view, instead of imagining justice as a distribution machine which allocates various goods in a just way, justice allows individuals equality and the right to justification for any decisions that both concern them and form part of the very

[24] See Forst (n 4).

[25] Mattias Kumm, 'The Turn to Justification: On the Structure and Domain of Human Rights Practice' in Adam Etinson (ed), *Human Rights: Moral or Political?* (Oxford, Oxford University Press, 2018) 238–61.

[26] Aharon Barak, *Human Dignity: The Constitutional Value and the Constitutional Right* (Cambridge, Cambridge University Press, 2015).

[27] Cohen, *Rescuing Justice* (2008).

[28] J Donald Moon, 'Cohen vs. Rawls on Justice and Equality' (2015) 18 *Critical Review of International Social and Political Philosophy* 40–56.

[29] Eliane Saadé, The Concept of Justice and Equality: On the Dispute between John Rawls and Gerald Cohen (Berlin-Boston MA, Walter de Gruyter, 2015).

[30] See, also, Douglas-Scott, 'Human Rights' (2017) and Sen, *The Idea of Justice* (2011).

[31] See, for example, Philip Pettit, 'Justice: Social and Political' in David Sobel, Peter Vallentyne and Steven Wall (eds), *Oxford Studies in Political Philosophy, Vol 1* (Oxford, Oxford University Press, 2015) 9–35.

[32] Forst (n 4).

idea of human dignity.[33] This appears similar to the debate in legal discourse on proportionality: both suggest that there can be no simple formula, but that what is required is a multifaceted understanding of justification. However, the picture is more complex and requires a political understanding of the specific context in which it operates. For Walzer, there are different spheres of justice linked to a faithful understanding of the wishes of the members of a society.[34]

According to Sen, though, there can be no liberal justice, and he argues – in essence – that Rawls appears to allow multiple original positions, and that this leaves us without any all-inclusive definition.[35] While different spheres of justice would seem to challenge the idea, or imaginary, of a single culture of justice in the EU domain, this chapter acknowledges these difficulties, but nonetheless argues that justice matters as a multifaceted concept in AFSJ law. The reason for this is that much of EU involvement in AFSJ matters has been built on the concept of European security as a device for achieving further integration across the Member States and through a largely administrative conception of justice. This trend has been visible not only in the EU counter-terrorism action, but also in other areas such as immigration and asylum law, where securitisation has formed much of the main justification for involvement in the AFSJ domain. In the migration context, justice (or the lack of it) may be very relevant in those cases in which the EU invokes criminal sanctions through administrative procedures as a preventive strategy in dealing with migrants placed in detention as part of the securitisation of the AFSJ.[36]

Moreover, conceptions of justice offer a compelling perspective for understanding the wider governance structure of the EU.[37] As already suggested above, rather than merely anchoring the individual's array of legal rights and the access to justice that expresses it – which is a basically administrative concept – justice would then constitute a broader normative as well as institutional principle for arranging the values underlying the EU's AFSJ. Such a conception of the AFSJ would not only value security, but equally strive to ensure freedom and justice – and, in so doing, the overall fairness of the system.

But what conception of justice, to repeat, should become an integral part of the EU's constitutional vocabulary? In line with the Kantian interpretation of justice as fairness and what Rawls refers to as Kantian constructivism, justice is

[33] Rainer Forst, *Justification and Critique: Towards a Critical Theory of Politics* (Cambridge-Malden MA, Polity Press, 2014).

[34] Walzer, *Spheres of Justice* (1983).

[35] Sen (n 4), also discussed in Gerald Gaus, *The Tyranny of the Ideal: Justice in a Diverse Society* (Princeton NJ, Princeton University Press, 2016) 207–08.

[36] See, for example, Jennifer M. Chacón, 'Immigration Detention: No Turning Back?' (2014) 113 *South Atlantic Quarterly* 621–28, and Andrew Ashworth and Lucia Zedner (eds), *Preventive Justice* (Oxford, Oxford University Press, 2014).

[37] On the role of transnational law in this process more generally, see Peer Zumbansen, 'Defining the Space of Transnational Law: Legal Theory, Global Governance and Legal Pluralism' (2012) 21 *Transnational Law and Contemporary Problems* 305–36. For competing notions of justice, see Dworkin, *Law's Empire* (1986) 98–99.

construed as those principles that would be justified to, and accepted by, everyone, under conditions that characterise them as free and equal moral persons.[38] As Samuel Freeman argues, overlapping consensus (that citizens all endorse a core set of laws for different reasons)[39] is, in effect, a hypothesis about the kinds of conceptions of the good that will be fostered by a well-ordered society and central for our understanding of justice. According to Freeman, justice, in a well-ordered society, is not deprived of its finality, but rather it shifts finality to a more restricted domain of public reason.[40]

By his specific conception of justice as fairness, Rawls argues that a political conception of justice for the basic structure of a democratic society stems from fundamental ideas that can reasonably be seen as emanating from the culture of such a society. In the Rawlsian political conception of justice, a set of values is developed from certain fundamental ideas which are seen as inherent in the culture of a democratic society and then transmitted through some form of elaboration or demonstration to a set of principles.[41] Furthermore, in the co-deliberation model, the reasons to be exchanged in co-deliberation need not be essentially general.[42] Instead, on this view, the generality of moral and legal rules is the production of the reciprocal exercise of the right to justification by citizens concerned about the ability to justify their institutions to each other. That is to say, moral and legal rules are general because they must include everyone, be acceptable to everyone, and be the same for everyone. Morality demands that first order reasons, which are primitive in the account, be brought together in the right or correct way; co-deliberation is the specific subject matter of moral reasoning for beings who are both already able to, and conversant with, reasons, in terms of both acting for them and offering them. This is the sense in which any or all generality is the product of the right to justification in the co-deliberation view.[43]

III. JUSTICE AND ON THE CONSTITUTIONAL STRUCTURE

As noted above, while the concept of justice is often proclaimed as an essentially contested concept,[44] this chapter argues that it can still be an essential and

[38] Samuel Freeman, 'Congruence and the Good of Justice' in Freeman (ed), *The Cambridge Companion to Rawls* (Cambridge, Cambridge University Press, 2003) 277–315.

[39] In Rawlsian terms, each citizen supports a political conception of justice for reasons internal to his or her own comprehensive doctrine. See: https://plato.stanford.edu/entries/rawls.

[40] Freeman, 'Congruence' (2003).

[41] Frank I Michelman, 'Rawls on Constitutionalism and Constitutional Law' in Freeman (ed), *Cambridge Companion to Rawls* (2003) 394–425.

[42] ibid.

[43] ibid.

[44] For example, see the contributions in Neyer and Wiener (n 10), especially Mattias Kumm, 'How does European Union Law Fit into the World of Public Law? Costa, Kadi, and Three Conceptions of Public Law' 111–38.

useful notion for gauging fairness when applied in a contextualised manner.[45] This becomes especially evident in legal settings where the question of justification is reflected in the level of sophistication of the legal reasoning that grounds each concrete court case.[46] As Arthur Ripstein points out in advocating the need for constitutional structure, in The Social Contract, Jean-Jacques Rousseau wrote that 'no citizen shall be rich enough to buy another and none so poor as to be forced to sell himself'.[47] For Ripstein, what is needed is a robust public sphere and the proper conditions for participation which relate to the idea of a just system.[48] Such a just system also needs a system of justification. Contemporary states do not always do a good job in guaranteeing adequate rights and opportunities to private citizens. Providing people with a full membership in a society is a matter which Rawls labelled 'background justice', and provides the conditions and need for institutions of background justice as individual transactions would otherwise erode the possibility for everyone to be a full participant in society.[49] For Ripstein, it provides a ground for the moral structure of background justice. But, as he argues, it also pre-supposes what could be dubbed 'foreground justice', a system in which co-operation is voluntary, rather than mandatory, and is pursued by individuals. In his view, the very idea of justification is also connected to the co-deliberation model, and seeks no deeper vindication than its own ability to survive the very process of both giving and demanding reasons in the non-dominating context that it characterises.[50]

Related to this theme, Joseph Raz has argued that the normal justification thesis, which says that a person has authority over another if his or her orders would help that person conform better to the requirements of reason than he or she would otherwise do.[51] The normal justification thesis is a test for the legitimacy of an authority of any sort.[52] Moreover, Raz's theory of justification is a consequentialist theory.[53] The central theme of Raz's theory is the right to justification. For these authors, the Raz model offers an account of legitimacy. While Raz sets aside the Kantian innate right to humanity, it adds a context-sensitive

[45] See Forst (n 4).

[46] Kumm, 'The Turn to Justification' (2018).

[47] Citing Jean-Jacques Rousseau, *The Social Contract* (Harmondsworth, Penguin, 1968) 96.

[48] Arthur Ripstein, *Private Wrongs* (Cambridge MA, Harvard University Press, 2016) citing Jean-Jacques Rousseau, *The Social Contract and Other Later Political Writings* (Cambridge, Cambridge University Press, 1997) 289.

[49] Ripstein, *Private Wrongs* (2016) 291.

[50] Arthur Ripstein, 'The Innate Right of Humanity and the Right to Justification' in Ester Herlin-Karnell and Matthias Klatt (eds), *Constitutionalism Justified* (Oxford, Oxford University Press, forthcoming).

[51] Joseph Raz, *The Morality of Freedom* (Oxford, Oxford University Press, 1988) ch 2.

[52] '[T]he normal way to establish that a person has authority over another person involves showing that the alleged subject is likely better to comply with reasons which apply to him (other than the alleged authoritative directives) if he accepts the directives of the alleged authority as authoritatively binding and tries to follow them, rather than by trying to follow the reasons which apply to him directly.' Raz, *The Morality of Freedom* (1988), and see Stanford Encyclopedia, available at: https://plato.stanford.edu/entries/authority.

[53] See, also, Alon Harel, *Why Law Matters* (Oxford, Oxford University Press, 2014).

judicial principle to which authorities must confirm.[54] Hence, Raz argues, there is no general obligation to obey the law. One should obey the law only if it serves one's autonomy, and, then, one obeys it because of its content, not because it is the law.[55] For Raz, a political authority is legitimate when – and only when – it serves the interests of those subject to it, and these conditions are established by a liberal account of individual autonomy.[56]

Others like Dworkin (and regardless of disagreement between him and Raz[57]) famously linked the general justification for the exercise of the coercive power of state with that of the moral obligation of citizens to obey the law. Thus, every conception, in Dworkin's terms, faces the same dilemma, as it asks the question of whether anything can justify coercion in ordinary politics? Rawls' notion of justification is, instead, a justification of coercion coupled to the question of the extent to which coercion is a necessary price to pay for people living in a state together.[58] Against this backdrop and given the strong emphasis of security for the construction of the AFSJ, we need to pause and reflect upon the level of justice (we can call it a culture of fairness) that could be achieved.

As was suggested in Chapter 2, one question that arises when discussing the EU's security mission is how it is related to the identity of the AFSJ, and the extent to which this identity mission is more broadly tied to the EU's symbolic function. After all, just like 'security', terms such as 'symbolic' run the risk of being used in an overly broad way. As was mentioned above, there is the tendency for ill-defined legislation, and concealment[59] in the EU-legislative process, which arguably constitute domination at the expense of an adequate high level of human rights protection. Again, it is suggested here that a critical notion of justice within the AFSJ is therefore linked to the basic right of justification as a counter-measure to domination.

A. The Concepts of Justice and Dignity: Kantian Themes

For Forst, justice is not only a matter of which goods, for which reasons, and in what circumstances, and in what amounts it should be allocated to whom – he argues that it is about how these goods come into the world in the first place, and of who decides on their allocation, and how this allocation is made.

[54] Evan Criddle and Evan Fox-Decent, *Fiduciaries of Humanity: How International Law Constitutes Authority* (Oxford, Oxford University Press, 2016) 35.

[55] David Dyzenhaus, 'Consent, Legitimacy and the Foundation of Political and Legal Authority' in Jeremy Webber and Colin M McLeod (eds), *Between Consenting Peoples: Political Community and the Meaning of Consent* (Vancouver, UBC, 2010) 163–87.

[56] Raz, *The Morality of Freedom* (1988) ch 2.

[57] See eg Scott J Shapiro, 'The "Hart-Dworkin" Debate: A Short Guide for the Perplexed' in Arthur Ripstein (ed), *Ronald Dworkin* (Cambridge, Cambridge University Press, 2007) 22–55.

[58] Sangiovanni, 'Justice' (2008).

[59] See for example, Deirdre Curtin, 'Overseeing Secrets in the EU: A Democratic Perspective' (2014) 52 *Journal of Common Market Studies* 684–700.

For him, justice pre-supposes an autonomous, reflexively grounded theory of justice that rests on no other values or truths than the principle of justification itself.[60] It is not merely a discursive principle (a justification without any substance) but is, in his view, a Kantian theory.[61] The autonomy and dignity that consists in being subject to no norms or structures other than those that can be justified towards the individual. This dignity is violated when individuals are regarded as merely the recipients of redistributive measures and not as independent agents of justice. As Barak has pointed out, citing Dworkin, 'because we honour dignity, we demand democracy'.[62] It should be recalled that, according to Dworkin, human dignity is an organising idea, as it brings ethical principles together under the one roof of human dignity.[63] For Barak, Dworkin did not, however, understand dignity as a constitutional value, but as one of self-respect, similarly to that of Forst. Others, such as Daniel Statman, emphasise that dignity is not simply the Kantian moral paradigm, but, in contrast, that dignity has a clear-cut message in insisting on non-humiliating treatment.[64]

It is against this background that Rainer Forst has developed a political and critical understanding of justice.[65] For him, the core idea of justice is avoiding arbitrariness. As Forst explains, 'there is at least one fundamental moral demand that no culture or society may reject: the unconditional claim to be respected as someone who deserves to be given justifying reasons for the actions, rules, or structures to which he or she is subject'.[66] Under this theory, these justifications are to be structured by considerations of reciprocity and generality as explained in chapter two. In the context of the connection between justice and justification, Forst argues that there are two pictures of justice which add to the grammar. First, there is 'normal' justice with regard to what is generally accepted as justified in a given social setting.[67] Second, there is 'reflexive' justice, which primarily asks whether the current terms of the justification of justice are truly justifiable for those subjected to them.[68] The rationale of the reciprocity view is that responsibility is an issue because people are required to treat each other in certain ways. Indeed, as Ariel Zylberman pointed out, reciprocity is a basic deontic norm that avoids circularity, as it acknowledges the whole system of human rights.[69]

[60] Rainer Forst, *Normativity and Power: Analyzing Social Orders of Justification* (Oxford, Oxford University Press, 2017) ch 1.

[61] ibid.

[62] Barak, *Human Dignity* (2015) 108, citing Ronald Dworkin, *Life's Dominion: An Argument about Abortion, Euthanasia and Individual Freedom* (New York, Alfred Knopf, 1994) 239.

[63] Dworkin, *Hedgehogs* (2011).

[64] Daniel Statman, 'Two Concepts of Dignity' (2001) 24 *Tel Aviv University Law Review* 541–604 (Heb), discussed in Barak (n 26) 119.

[65] Forst (n 4).

[66] Rainer Forst, cited in Criddle and Fox-Decent, Fiduciaries of Humanity (2016).

[67] Forst, *Justification and Critique* (2014).

[68] ibid 83.

[69] Ariel Zylberman, 'Why Human Rights? Because of You' (2016) 24 *The Journal of Political Philosophy* 321–43.

While Michael Walzer's model of different spheres of justice would seem to challenge the idea, or imagination, of a single culture of justice in the EU domain, this chapter acknowledges these difficulties and nonetheless argues that justice matters as a concept in AFSJ law.[70] The reason for this is that much of the EU involvement in AFSJ matters has been built on the concept of European security as a device for achieving further integration across the Member States. This trend has been visible not only in the EU counter-terrorism fight, but also in other areas such as immigration and asylum law, where securitisation has formed much of the main justification for involvement in the AFSJ domain. In the migration context, justice (or the lack of it) may be very relevant in those cases where the EU invokes criminal sanctions through administrative procedures as a preventive strategy in dealing with migrants placed in detention as part of the securitisation of the AFSJ.[71]

Moreover, in the EU setting, conceptions of justice offer a compelling perspective for understanding and conceiving of the wider governance structure of the EU.[72] Again, the concept of justice would then constitute a broader normative, as well as institutional, principle for arranging the several values underlying the AFSJ.

IV. THE IDEA OF JUSTIFICATION, DEMOCRACY AND THE QUESTION OF LEGITIMACY

For Forst, although every political philosophy raises the question of the legitimation of legitimate rule, very few lend it a reflexive turn and take the principle of justification itself as a principle of discursive practice as their theoretical foundation.[73] Although the question turns on who has a right to justification and who has the authority to answer it. Moreover, Forst, a conception of justice must contain a practice of public justification while avoiding arbitrariness.[74] In sum, he argues that the first task of justice is to establish a basic structure of justification that facilitates a reflexive practice of critique and construction by according roughly equal justificatory power to all those subjected to it. As noted in chapter two, and as pointed out by Yasmin Dawood, and, in the context of the link between justification and non-arbitrariness, in the

[70] Walzer (n 13).

[71] For example, Chacón, 'Immigration Detention' (2014) and Ashworth and Zedner, *Preventive Justice* (2014).

[72] Peer Zumbansen, 'Defining the Space of Transnational Law' (2012), available at: https://digitalcommons.osgoode.yorku.ca/cgi/viewcontent.cgi?referer=https://www.google.com/&httpsredir=1&article=1758&context=scholarly_works.

[73] Forst (n 33) 5. For a critique of the idea of justification, see Sameer Bajaj and Enzo Rossi "Noumenal Power, Reasons and Justification: A Critique of Forst" chapter in E Herlin-Karnell and M Klatt (eds), Constitutionalism Justified (Oxford, Oxford University Press 2019), forthcoming.

[74] Forst (n 4) chs 1 and 2.

Federalist Papers, James Madison was aware that the continued stability of the republic rested upon public confidence in the structures of government. The appearance of domination, even in the absence of actual domination, diminishes democratic legitimacy and integrity, and hence concomitantly diminishes public confidence in governing institutions and actors.[75] If the state's actions create the appearance or notion that the state has the capacity to interfere arbitrarily, then the citizen has no way of verifying whether or not his or her perception is accurate. In other words, for the citizen, the appearance of state domination amounts to actual domination. For Dawood, to minimise domination, the state must also minimise the appearance of domination, and this increases its legitimacy.

Likewise, Allen Buchanan argues that international human rights institutions have important epistemic functions in that they contribute to the specification of the content of human rights norms by providing a public deliberative forum for their ongoing development and interpretation.[76] In line with this, Evan Criddle and Evan Fox-Decent have recently argued that the fiduciary model (closely associated with non-domination) can bring democratic deliberation into its fold. In doing so, they adopt Forst's model of the basic right to justification. For the fiduciary theory, public deliberation performs an important function within the state-subject fiduciary relation as an expression of the state's respect for its dignity and independent agency.[77] In their view, deliberative inquiry would be guided by the substantive principles that are constitutive of the state–subject fiduciary relation itself.[78]

A. Justification, Public Reason and Fiduciary Law

As Seyla Benhabib points out, the question of normative justification is also about democratic legitimacy, since the transnational law project cannot sacrifice discursive deliberation.[79] For her, human rights are most central to a public vocabulary of political justice and this designates a special and narrow class of moral rights. She emphasises that the question of human rights protection is very complex in the democratic context and that it is too simple to refer to the authorship of laws.[80] To solve this problem, Benhabib has developed ideas on democratic iterations, by which she means the complex processes of

[75] Yasmin Dawood, 'The Antidomination Model and the Judicial Oversight of Democracy' (2008) 96 *The Georgetown Law Journal* 1411–85.

[76] Forst (n 4); Allen Buchanan, 'Human Rights and the Legitimacy of the International Order' (2008) 14 *Legal Theory* 39–70.

[77] Criddle and Fox-Decent (n 55) 105.

[78] ibid.

[79] Seyla Benhabib, 'Democratic Sovereignty and Transnational Law. On Legal Utopianism and Democratic Skepticism', available at: http://papers.ssrn.com/sol3/papers.cfm?abstract_id=2455436.

[80] ibid, at 23.

public argument, deliberation and exchange through which universalist rights claims are contested and contextualised, invoked and revoked, posited and positioned throughout legal and political institutions as well as in the associations of civil society. In constitutional democracies, the interaction between domestic norms, on the one hand, and transnational ones, on the other, do not take place in courts alone, but also through, for example, NGOs such as Amnesty International and Human Rights Watch, organisations that can produce expert reports and thereby mobilise public opinion around controversial norm interpretation and implementation.[81] At the core of the issue is, as Benhabib expresses it, the dichotomy between self-determination and values of sovereignty and global constitutionalism, and the need to reconcile legal pluralism with legal cosmopolitanism.

The idea of public reason entails a particular version of democratic deliberation, one in which citizens and public officials only support political decisions when they sincerely believe that these decisions can be justified by appeal to considerations that each person can reasonably endorse in their capacity as a free and equal citizen, that is, that they only support laws that can be justified by appeal to public reasons.[82] Thus, the idea of justification, which is traditionally state-bound, has now become a transnational question. As noted by Poul Kjaer, the question of justification has largely become one of a substitute debate for democracy beyond the state proper.[83] Moreover, theories such as fiduciary law and the trusteeship of humanity advocated by Eyal Benvenisti, Fox-Decent and Criddle have developed an understanding of obligations and a duty of justification to outsiders.[84] For Fox-Decent and Criddle, under the Kantian theory of fiduciary obligations, individuals have the right to freedom in as much as it can be reconciled with the freedom of others. Public institutions are necessary to vindicate this right because, in their absence, individuals would be subject to the continual threat of unilateral and arbitrary interference from others, and

[81] ibid.

[82] ibid. See, also, John Rawls, ' Lecture VI: The Idea of Public Reason' in Rawls, *Political Liberalism* (New York-Chicester, Columbia University Press, 1993) 212–54; and Rawls, 'The Idea of Public Reason Revisited' in John Rawls, *Collected Papers*, Samuel Freeman (ed) (Cambridge MA, Harvard University Press, 1999) 573–615.

[83] Poul F Kjaer, 'The Function of Justification in Transnational Governance', WZB Berlin Social Science Center Discussion Papers, SP IV 2015-808 (2015). For Kjaer, the turn to justification reflects a temporalisation of the social world, where reality is constituted in the distinction between past and future. This again implies that within the never-ending stream of political and administrative decisions every decision could have been different. According to him, it is a move which not only reflects the structural foundation and functional orientation of transnational processes but also implies a fundamentally different kind of law and politics, as the foundation of transnational law and politics in contrast to national law and politics are given ex post rather than ex ante.

[84] Criddle and Fox-Decent (n 55); Eyal Benvenisti, 'Sovereigns as Trustees of Humanity: On the Accountability of States to Foreign Stakeholders' (2013) 107 *American Journal of International Law* 295–33.

fiduciary theory entrusts this power to the state. Moreover, as they point out, international law requires states to act as the guardians of rights, so that no individual is able to instrumentalise or dominate others with impunity.[85] According to this model, the state is accountable under international law for safeguarding equality and freedom. For both Benvenisti, and Criddle and Fox-Decent, a state is still (in the Hobbesian tradition) necessary for ensuring this. Transnational law then mediates not only between states, but also between states and their own people.[86] Fiduciary theories were also central to John Locke,[87] who used the claim that men are naturally free and equal as part of the justification for understanding legitimate political government as the result of a social contract in which people in the state of nature conditionally transfer some of their rights to the government in order to ensure better, more stable, comfortable enjoyment of their lives, liberty and property.[88] However, Criddle and Fox-Decent argue that fiduciary law is more complex than traditional natural law theories.

Thus, the fiduciary principle entrusts public power to the state in order to secure against domination. As is well known, Rawls famously defined legitimacy in terms of what is justifiable to the citizen.[89] As mentioned above, according to his liberal principle of legitimacy, the use of political power is fully proper only when 'it is exercised in accordance with a constitution the essentials of which all citizens as free and equal may reasonably be expected to endorse in light of the principles and ideals acceptable to their common human reason'.[90] A European notion of legitimacy must surely subscribe to societal concerns *à la* Max Weber, who suggested that constituent power derives from the emergence of the concept of what he referred to as rational legitimacy.[91] As he saw it, rational legitimacy is the belief in the rightful nature of a ruler to make law and presents itself as a modern, rational concept.[92]

When discussing ideas of justice and justification, one could be forgiven for thinking that it is an overly tilted towards an 'ideal theory' picture of justice which is difficult to realise in real life. The next section will tentatively address this question.

[85] Criddle and Fox-Decent (n 55) 26.

[86] ibid 29.

[87] John Locke, An Essay Concerning Human Understanding: Second Treatise of Civil Government (Ware, Wordsworth Editions, 2014).

[88] Alex Tuckness, 'Locke's Political Philosophy', *The Stanford Encyclopedia of Philosophy* (Spring 2016 edition), Edward N Zalta (ed), available at: https://plato.stanford.edu/archives/spr2016/entries/locke-political.

[89] Rawls, Political Liberalism (1993).

[90] ibid.

[91] Joel Colón-Ríos, 'The Legitimacy of the Juridical' (2010) 48 *Osgoode Hall Law Journal* 199–246.

[92] Max Weber, *The Vocation Lectures*, David Owen and Tracy B Strong (eds) (Cambridge, Hackett, 2004), cited in Matt Sleat, 'Legitimacy in Realist Thought: Between Moralism and Realpolitik' (2014) 42 *Political Theory* 314–37.

V. THE IDEAL AND NON-IDEAL PICTURE OF JUSTICE

'A map of the world that does not include Utopia, is not even worth glancing at,' states Gerald Gaus, citing Oscar Wilde, at the start of his recent book, *The Tyranny of the Ideal: Justice in a Diverse Society*.[93] Is a theory of justice a theory of utopia? In defending Rawls against Amartya Sen, John Simmons captures what Shmuel Nili has labelled the 'ideal compass' view as follows: 'We don't need to know all that ideal justice requires in order to compare … our policy options here and now, any more than we need to know that Everest is the highest mountain in the world before we can compare the heights of lesser peaks …'[94]

Much on the debate on global justice is concerned with ideal justice. According to Avery Plaw, the main focus of Rawls' writing is defining 'a perfectly just basic structure' assuming 'favorable circumstances' and the 'strict compliance' of citizens to the demands of justice. Rawls prioritises ideal theory because it helps us to see the long terms goals 'that we should achieve if we can', and thus provides guidance to non-ideal theory. Isaiah Berlin, by contrast, is clearly engaged in non-ideal theory, beginning from circumstances as they are.[95]

As cautiously noted above, it could be asked why justice should be debated at EU level at all, rather than in the different justice spheres of the individual Member States. Is justice at the EU and global level the paramount example of ideal theory of something that will not be realised in practice? The question is similar to the issue of democracy beyond the nation state and to what extent the EU has to live up to the same standards as the Member States (the no demos question, etc).[96] This is developed further in the section on public justifications below. It is true that, when constructing his basic structure of society, Rawls did not explicitly discuss justice in the global or even in the international arena.[97] In fact, Rawls rejected the concept of global distributive justice firstly upon the basis that a duty of humanitarian assistance is already required by the Law of the Peoples as part of non-ideal theory, and thus global principles of distributive justice would be redundant and, secondly, that global distributive principles would have unacceptable results.[98] As Plaw suggests, Rawls prioritises ideal theory because it helps us to see the long-terms goals 'that we should achieve if we can', and thus provides guidance to non-ideal theory.[99] Berlin, by

[93] Gaus, *The Tyranny of the Ideal* (2016).

[94] Discussed in Shmuel Nili, 'Between Domestic and Global Justice' (2015) 12 *Journal of Moral Philosophy* 55–81.

[95] Avery Plaw, 'Does Justice Stand Alone?' (2015) 18 *Critical Review of International and Social Philosophy* 57–73.

[96] See, for example, Jürgen Habermas, *The Crisis of the European Union* (Cambridge, Polity Press, 2012); Neyer (n 5).

[97] Rawls (n 4).

[98] Kok-Chor Tan, *Justice without Borders: Cosmopolitanism, Nationalism and Patriotism* (Cambridge, Cambridge University Press, 2004) 66.

[99] Plaw "Does Justice stand alone?" (2015) 57–73.

contrast, is clearly engaged in non-ideal theory, beginning from circumstances as they are.[100] As noted by Kok-Chor Tan, the principles in Rawls' *The Law of Peoples* are explicitly principles of justice, as the work is a theory of justice for the society of peoples.[101] But as he asks, if Rawls is right that there is no place for distributive principles in the global setting, how does he reach that conclusion? Rawls rejected an extension of domestic egalitarianism to the global level, inter alia, because of the existence of special political ties and a coercive framework between co-citizens as justifying the limitation of egalitarian concern to compatriots only.[102] As a consequence for Rawls there is a lack of an international basic structure.[103] Yet, as many global justice theorists argue, a global egalitarian can easily allow that global principles have different content from domestic egalitarian principles since the practices and institutions that global principles are meant to regulate are quite different from domestic ones.[104] Why, one may legitimately ask once again, is this relevant in an EU context? In the EU setting the ideal theory debate is largely reflected in the EU integration debate and the question as to why he EU should regulate justice questions. As was mentioned above, for example, Forst has argued that there is reason to believe that we can extent the Rawlsian framework for justice providing we have the right toolkit for doing so.[105] As was also suggested above, essential to such a toolkit is the conception of 'context' and the right to justification. Likewise, for Bertjan Wolthuis, for instance, while Rawls argued that social justice only apply within the nation state, statists are wrong not to adapt to the contemporary political landscape, which in the case of the EU includes now also the economic union of societies.[106] This is relevant for the wider picture of justice, and even though this chapter is primarily concerned with the notion of public justice, as manifested in the AFSJ. Within this complex area of multiple conceptions of justice at the Member State–EU level, the question is to what extent an ideal theory view is then automatically integrated into the non-ideal picture when it comes to the empirical reality of enforcing EU values.

According to Tan, while a duty of humanity would work towards improving the situation of societies that are burdened by unfavourable circumstances, such assistance is not required as part of an ideal theory in which all societies are assumed to have attained the basic developmental level requisite for a decent society. A principle of distributive justice, on the other hand, is an

[100] ibid.

[101] Tan, *Justice without Borders* (2004), discussing Rawls, *The Laws of Peoples* (Cambridge, Harvard University Press, 1999).

[102] Nili, 'Between' (2015).

[103] Michael Blake and Patrick Taylor Smith, 'International Distributive Justice', *The Stanford Encyclopedia of Philosophy* (Spring 2015 edn), Edward N Zalta (ed): https://plato.stanford.edu/archives/spr2015/entries/international-justice.

[104] Kok-Chor Tan, *What is this thing called Global Justice?* (Abingdon, Routledge, 2017) 29.

[105] Forst (n 4).

[106] Bertjan Wolthuis, 'Principles of Economic Union: An Extension of John Rawls's Theory of Justice' (2017) 23 *European Law Journal* 454–66.

integral part of ideal theory, and thus would apply as long as there are inequalities between societies, even 'after the duty of assistance is fully satisfied'.[107] Rawls' own followers have long argued that the cosmopolitan view follows naturally from Rawls' own fundamental commitments.[108] But as Tan and Simon Caney and others ask, what justifies the global justice model?

More specifically, they point out that, as a philosophical inquiry, global justice involves an investigation into what a just global order would look like.[109] Roughly, cosmopolitans argue that the scope of justice is global, and that distributive patterns should apply to all individuals regardless of their state membership.[110] Moreover, justice among states will require some justification which must presume a global institutional order which, according to Tan, encounters the problem of coercion. Statists hold, inter alia, that states are the primary subject of international justice, where justice is best understood as justice between states, while the cosmopolitan view takes individuals as the ultimate unit of concern and global justice. As Fox-Decent and Caney clarify, the generality condition stipulates that, 'in moral contexts', the community of justification may not be arbitrarily restricted, but rather must include all those affected by actions or norms in morally relevant ways. In this way, the right to justification seems similar to the question of freedom as non-domination. Moreover, according to Fox-Decent, given the entrenched nature of the domination that pervades contemporary border regimes, borders are a moral context to which the duty of justification applies, and thus it applies to all who are affected, including outsiders. Significantly, the duty is borne by the state, since the state produces the moral context of domination typical of border regimes.[111] This is particularly important in the EU transnational context, and we will return to this question in chapter five below.

VI. CONSTITUTIONAL ESSENTIALS, PUBLIC REASON AND JUDICIAL REVIEW

Against this background, we need to explore the link between justice and justification further. It is sometimes suggested that, for Rawls, the commitment to the public justification of political power lies at the heart of his vision of a just and stable society.[112] Moreover, it is often said that you are not engaged in

[107] ibid.

[108] Tan (n 101).

[109] Kok-Chor Tan, 'Why Global Justice Matters' (2014) 10 *Journal of Global Ethics* 128–34.

[110] Cécile Laborde and Miriam Ronzoni, 'What is a Free State? Republican Internationalism and Globalisation' (2015) 64 *Political Studies* 279–96.

[111] Evan Fox-Decent, 'Constitutional Legitimacy Unbound' in: David Dyzenhaus and Malcolm Thorburn (eds), *Philosophical Foundations of Constitutional Law* (Oxford University Press, 2016) 119–40.

[112] Jonathan Quong, 'On the Idea of Public Reason' in Jon Mandle and David A Reidy (eds), *A Companion to Rawls* (Chichester, Wiley, 2014) 265–80.

the practice of public reason unless you offer a reason or argument that will be acceptable to everyone in their capacity as free and equal citizens.[113] Public reasons, on this Rawlsian approach, are thus shared reasons. It provides justification in terms of legal reasoning for decisions taken and the different but related classic questions of the obligations to state reason. Indeed, as Dworkin argued, judges should decide hard cases by interpreting the political structure of their community by trying to find the best justification that they can in principles of political morality for the structure as a whole.[114] According to Forst, human rights exhibit a certain grammar of justice and non-domination which excludes any ethno-centric determination of such rights. Autonomy understood in the sense of having a right to justification is a basis to individual self-understanding and self-respect.[115] As explained above, in his view instead of imagining justice as a distribution machine which allocates various goods in a just way, justice allows individuals equality and the right to justification for any decisions that concern them, and thus form part of the very idea of human dignity.[116] As also suggested above, this appears similar to the debate in legal discourse on proportionality: both suggest that there can be no simple formula, but that what is required is a multifaceted understanding of justification. While the legal technicalities of proportionality will be explored further in chapter four, this chapter will now turn to explore the meaning of the constitutional essentials for our understanding of justice and justification in the AFSJ.

For Jonathan Qoung, the content of Rawlsian public reason is provided by the political conception of justice, or principles which are meant to provide citizens and public officials with reasons that they can appeal to when deliberating and voting on political matters – reasons that will be acceptable to others in their capacity as free and equal citizens. Second, there are the commonly accepted methods of inquiry and rules of reasoning that are acceptable, and to which any public justification must adhere. Rainer Forst, for example, argues for a context-based approach in which it is necessary to pay attention to the experience of freedom and un-freedom that is perceived by citizens.[117] As Eoin Daly points out, if rights are understood as channelling the kinds of reasons that governments can invoke when they act in certain arenas, and therefore are not trumps *à la* Dworkin, but rather its channels and its pointers, this has a republican flavour and helps to ensure non-domination.[118]

For Rawls, the right to justification is about the limits of public reason. The idea of public reason serves to identify the grounds on which valid justifications

[113] See, for example, Martin Shapiro, 'The Giving Reasons Requirement' (1992) 8 *The University of Chicago Legal Forum* 179–220, and Arthur Ripstein, *Force and Freedom: Kant's Legal and Political Philosophy* (Cambridge MA, Harvard University Press, 2009).

[114] Ronald Dworkin, "Hard Cases" Harvard Law Review (1975), pp 1057–1109.

[115] Ripstein, *Force and Freedom* (2009) 124.

[116] Forst (n 33).

[117] Forst (n 4).

[118] Eoin Daly, 'Freedom as Non-domination in the Jurisprudence of Constitutional Rights' (2015) 28 *Canadian Journal of Law and Jurisprudence*, 289–316.

are to be discriminated from invalid ones, and thus it essentially operates as an extension of the idea of 'the original position', as it is fundamental to Rawls' original *A Theory of Justice*.[119] Mattias Kumm, too, in the context of judicial review, stresses that: 'the right to justification in the same way that institutionalizing fair and open elections is connected to the right to democratic participation.'[120]

Kumm also explains that it is implausible to claim that the right to justification is taken seriously without the appropriate institutionalising of a procedure that allows acts of public authorities to be subjected to impartial review in a way that provides the unduly burdened individual with an effective remedy. In Rawlsian political liberalism, the reference to reasonable disagreement does not imply that we must view those who disagree with us as justified.[121] It only implies that, given the burdens of opinion, we must expect that the exercise of human reason under conditions of liberty will always produce disagreement about certain matters such as religion and human flourishing. Others may disagree with us, but we must recognise that their disagreement need not be 'rooted solely in ignorance or perversity, or else in the rivalries for power, status, or economic gain'.[122]

Moreover, as he argues,

> 'Reasonable pluralism, for Rawls, thus does not entail any particular thesis with regard to what comprehensive doctrines other people are justified in believing. Rather, reasonable pluralism alerts us to the fact that free and equal people, sincerely exercising their powers of reason under liberal conditions, will always disagree about certain issues.'

For Rawls, political liberalism thus strives 'for publicly based justifications for questions regarding the constitutional essentials and matters of basic distributive justice but not in general for all the questions to be settled by the legislature within a constitutional framework'.[123] According to Quong, though, the basic structure argument fails to justify the restriction of public reason to constitutional essentials because it cannot tell us why it is either undesirable or unattainable to apply the norms of public reason to the problems of everyday democracy.[124]

[119] Ben Crum, 'Multi-layered Justice and Public Reason' (2017) 8 *Transnational Legal Theory* 42–58.

[120] Mattias Kumm, 'Alexy's Theory of Constitutional Rights and the Problem of Judicial Review' in Matthias Klatt (ed), *Institutionalized Reason: The Jurisprudence of Robert Alexy* (Oxford, Oxford University Press, 2012) 201–17.

[121] ibid.

[122] ibid.

[123] ibid.

[124] Quong, ' Public Reason' (2014).

VII. SAME FOR STATES AND CITIZENS? THE EU CONTEXT

For scholars such as Kumm, Alexy and Barak, for example, judicial review is about democratic deliberation. But the commitment to legally institutionalised judicial review reflects as basic a commitment as an equal right to vote, and is, to a certain extent, immune to outcome-related critiques, much like the commitment to an equal right to vote which is connected to competitive elections.[125]

When there are no shared understandings, 'no solution can possibly be just', according to Walzer.[126] Interestingly, Ripstein has tied this to the question about the justification of arguments. As he explains, for Hobbes, for example, in combining explanation and justification as he does, Hobbes sets up parallel burdens of proof,[127] in which the burden of explanation is to show how artificial social institutions could arise upon the basis of asocial human nature. The burden of justification is to show that the resulting institutions would be agreeable to asocial creatures,[128] and thereby aims at uniting institutions with the citizens.

As will be discussed in greater detail in chapter four, with regard to the contours of proportionality, it is sometimes said that justification is harder in a legislative assembly than in a court – simply because of the numbers of people involved – but (the argument goes) it would be a mistake to think that, for this reason alone, the court is better placed to make decisions than the legislature.[129] Yet for an individual the right to claim a right to justification through the judiciary system seem essential, if on subscribes to a context based vision of justice. The basic claim of this book is that a turn to justice theory in the specific AFSJ context helps to frame the questions that the EU ought to be asking. The contention is that what is needed in the current debate on the future of the AFSJ includes a query into the nature of the EU constitutional canon that is currently forming the AFSJ as well as a foray into the extent to which justice could operate as a golden rule for bridging the AFSJ policy field with the rest of the constitutional landscape. But justice brings its own problems, as it casts light on some burning, albeit difficult, governance questions in the EU. More specifically, and as indicated above, the notion of justice illuminates the difficulty of reconciling the issue of how to solve the democratic deficit with the EU's greater aspiration of becoming a just, modern and effective actor on the international scene.

[125] Kumm 'Alexy's Theory' (2012).

[126] Walzer (n 13); also discussed in Scott J Shapiro, 'The " Hart-Dworkin" Debate: A Short Guide for the Perplexed' in Arthur Ripstein (ed), *Ronald Dworkin* (Cambridge, Cambridge University Press, 2007) 22–55.

[127] Arthur Ripstein, 'Foundationalism in Political Theory' (1987) 16 *Philosophy and Public Affairs* 115–37.

[128] ibid.

[129] I thank the reviewer for pointing this out.

This chapter will now end with a practical example before discussing the notion of proportionality in further detail in the next chapter. Consider, for instance, the notion of data protection: is the very idea of data protection a manifestation of justice as balance?

As mentioned earlier, Rawls famously identified reasonableness as a good yardstick for a just (albeit utopian) legal system.[130] An increasingly sensitive testing field for the enterprise of ensuring a just EU space is that of data protection, which must address the need for the increasing threat posed by cyber-related criminality and the apparent need to safeguard security to be balanced against the need to protect fundamental rights. The EU has become an active player in fighting criminality in the digital space, following the increased cyber-security threat and recent bugging (electronic surveillance) scandals. The recent Directive designed to deal with attacks against information systems seems closely linked to the EU's fight against organised crime.[131] This Directive is based upon Article 83(1) TFEU, which covers computer crime in a broad sense.[132] For the past ten years, the EU has been making significant efforts to develop a framework capable of dealing with cyber security in the EU space. At the core of the debate, however, is the sensitive relationship between the protection of human rights and the effective fighting of crime. Is there a right to justification for a breach of data protection? Data protection is a fundamental EU right as is stated in Articles 7–8 Charter of Fundamental Rights, Article 16 TFEU and also in Article 8 European Convention on Human Rights.

If the EU Court is to develop criteria for the increasing use of proportionality as a balancing principle in connection with the Charter of Fundamental Rights, this will arguably confirm a tentative version of a contextual justice approach and a right to justification. We just have to make sure that it lives up to a critical and holistic view of this. This question will be explored in further detail in chapter four.

VIII. CONCLUSION

This chapter has explored the connection between the concepts of justice and justification, and investigated their relevance for non-domination theory. The chapter has also discussed the question of legitimacy, democratic values and dignity-oriented views. The challenge has been to link and bridge the political

[130] John Rawls, *Justice as Fairness: A Restatement*, 2nd edn (Cambridge MA, Harvard University Press, 2001).

[131] Directive 2013/40/EU. See, also, EU Commission report on necessary measures adopted by the Member States. COM(2017) 474 final; see also the European Security Agenda 2015–2020.

[132] Directive on attacks against information systems and repealing Council Framework Decision 2005/222/JHA.

theory debate with the EU and transnational law project (in the security context). The next chapter will explore the right to justification when applied in the legal context and through a proportionality test. We will thus turn to the empirical reality of security regulation in contemporary EU law, and how the right to justification could be identified both in the proportionality test and in the links to the project of ensuring the legitimacy and robustness of the AFSJ regime. The question of 'good' justifications are then answered through the proportionality test in legal practice, giving rise to a whole host of questions. The next chapter will seek to explore what precisely the terms 'good enough' or 'sufficient justification' actually mean.

4

Proportionality and Reasonable Disagreement in the Area of Freedom, Security and Justice

I. INTRODUCTION

WHILE CHAPTER THREE surveyed the right to justification and its links to justice theory and what public reason means in this context, the idea of this chapter is to make the case that, in order to give the notion of justification concrete meaning in a legal context, we need to understand the principle of proportionality.[1] This is because the principle of proportionality is an expression of the right to justification and could be connected to the European formation of justice and the bigger issue of good governance both in and of the AFSJ. Examples will be drawn from EU AFSJ law, as an expression of how legal practice matters, is dependent on the use of proportionality and, arguably, is reflected in the constitutional theory debate on the right to justification.[2] By looking at the meaning of 'non-domination' as a realisation of justice, as I argued in chapter two above, this will help us to link the rather abstract

[1] See, for example, Aharon Barak, *Proportionality: Constitutional Rights and their Limitations* (Cambridge, Cambridge University Press, 2012), Matthias Klatt and Moritz Meister, *The Constitutional Structure of Proportionality* (Oxford, Oxford University Press, 2012), Jud Mathews and Alec Stone Sweet, 'All Things in Proportion? American Rights Doctrine and the Problem of Balancing' (2010) 60 *Emory Law Journal* 797–875, Kai Möller, *The Global Model of Constitutional Rights* (Oxford, Oxford University Press, 2012), Moshe Cohen-Eliya and Iddo Porrat, *Proportionality and Constitutional Culture* (Cambridge, Cambridge University Press, 2013), and the contributions in: Grant Huscroft, Bradley W Miller and Grégoire Webber (eds), *Proportionality and the Rule of Law: Rights, Justification, Reasoning* (New York, Cambridge University Press, 2014), Grégoire Webber, *The Negotiable Constitution: On the Limitation of Rights* (Cambridge, Cambridge University Press, 2009), Robert Alexy, *A Theory of Constitutional Rights* (Oxford, Oxford University Press, 2002), Jacob Weinrib, *Dimensions of Dignity: The Theory and Practice of Modern Constitutional Law* (Cambridge, Cambridge University Press, 2016) ch 7.

[2] On the right to justification, Rainer Forst, *The Right to Justification: Elements of a Constructivist Theory of Justice* (New York-Chichester, Columbia University Press, 2012).

right to justification to the more graspable proportionality test, and will confirm the need for both ex ante and ex post checks of the legislative domain.[3] At present, much of the thinking in the AFSJ is currently dominated by security, as is witnessed by many of the recent EU security measures in the area and the EU Security Agenda 2015,[4] and the non-domination and justification through the principle of proportionality serves the purpose of ensuring constitutional rights protection at both the abstract and the concrete level. This chapter asks how the principle of proportionality as a legal tool is reflected in the rather abstract political theory debate on the right to justification. And with concreteness, there is a need to pay more attention to the balancing question in practice through the CJEU assessment of public reason in the courtroom.

From a historical point of view, the talion principle – an 'eye-for-an-eye'– is one of the oldest legal principles in western legal history. As such, it is often seen as a revenge principle, but this is a misunderstanding of its broader meaning. At the heart of this principle lies the foundation of what is now known as the proportionality principle: that legal measures or state actions should not be more intrusive than is necessary to achieve their aim. Proportionally has always had a huge impact in EU law. It was referred to in the early days by the CJEU and was closely linked to the creation of human rights protection across Europe. Hence, proportionality developed as a means of ensuring the credibility of EU integration pertaining to national law. One of the benefits of proportionality is that it could enhance judicial reasoning by clarifying justifications for limitations on freedoms. As Vicki Jackson argues, proportionality might also improve the outcomes of adjudication by bringing constitutional law closer to what she described as the varied conceptions of justice, in ways consistent with the demands of effective government.[5]

This chapter starts by setting out the basics of proportionality and the constitutional questions which it raises. Thereafter, the aim is to explain why proportionality is so important in EU law, and especially in the AFSJ. The chapter traces the meaning of proportionality as a constitutional value and its implications in EU law and the specific context of mutual recognition and AFSJ law. Here, however, I am not so much concerned with the well-known question of proportionality as a legislative question in EU law-making.[6] Rather, the chapter explores proportionality as an overarching principle for understanding the

[3] And I adopt the view that proportionality is, in fact, democratic if used in a contextualised manner. For recent studies of proportionality (both for and against it), see n 1 above.

[4] See eg COM(2015) 185 final, European Agenda on Security, Directive 2017/541 on combating terrorism and replacing Council Framework Decision 2002/475/JHA, amending Council Decision 2005/671/JHA, OJ L 88, 31.3.2017.

[5] Vicki C Jackson, 'Constitutional Law in an Age of Proportionality' (2015) 124 *Yale Law Journal* 3094–196. See also Cohen-Eliya and Porat, *Proportionality* (2013) 103–32.

[6] On this, see, for example, Takis Tridimas, *General Principles of EU Law* (Oxford, Oxford University Press, 2012).

constitutional conundrums facing the AFSJ with regard to judicial co-operation and the constitutional structure of the AFSJ. In this regard, proportionality represents a mechanism for understanding good governance as well as the many layers which comprise the AFSJ.

In doing so, the chapter investigates what it is we are actually referring to when we discuss proportionality reasoning, and how it could be linked to the basic right to justification. The chapter also seeks to tie the question of justification and proportionality to the question of the debate on public reason. It will explore what values are utilised in the proportionality test, and why it is a concrete manifestation of freedom as non-domination in that the Court is asked to assess whether the justification offered by the legislator is 'good enough'.

This chapter seeks to demonstrate how constitutional law institutionalises a right to justification, which is reflected in the general proportionality test in EU law.[7] Indeed, proportionality was referred to in the early days by the CJEU and was closely associated with creation of human rights protection in the EU.[8] Moreover, in classic free movement law, the concept of proportionality controls the degree to which the Member States may derogate from their EU law obligations. While much of the discussion on proportionality concerns the merits of this principle as either an addition to human rights protection, or a threat to it when used by authorities to minimise rights in the name of derogations from rights,[9] my understanding of proportionality is that it is a tool for legal reasoning, which is preferable to no check at all. Despite its flaws and the critique of proportionality as being a too-vague concept and indirectly eroding human rights, I believe the proportionality principle has more to offer and can be used effectively to guarantee rights.

This, of course, becomes all the more complex in sensitive areas such as those pertaining to the AFSJ, since, here, proportionality has at least two different implications. One reflects the need to balance the application and enforcement of, for example, penalties and the criminalisation of conduct in itself (so as to avoid using arrest warrants for minor offences, for example). The other reflects the need to combine effectiveness and human rights protection.[10] Clearly, the idea of balance may sometimes prove problematical. Yet, if the EU wants to make a difference, as I have previously suggested in an article with Massimo Fichera, a uniform approach to safeguards at the highest level might be worth

[7] Mattias Kumm, 'Democracy is not Enough: Proportionality and the Point of Judicial Review', NYU School of Law, Public Law Research Paper No 09-10, available at: http://ssrn.com/abstract=1356793; Paul Craig, 'The Nature of Reasonableness Review' (2013) 66 *Current Legal Problems* 131–67; Möller, *Global Model* (2012); Cohen-Eliya and Porrat (n 1).

[8] For example, Paul Craig, 'Proportionality, Rationality and Review' (2010) *New Zealand Law Review* 265–301.

[9] Barak, *Proportionality* (2012).

[10] Massimo Fichera and Ester Herlin-Karnell, 'The Margin of Appreciation Test and Balancing in the Area of Freedom Security and Justice: A Proportionate Answer for a Europe of Rights?' (2013) 19 *European Public Law* 759–87.

the price of allowing for less flexibility for Member State derogations in, for example, criminal law-related area.[11]

II. PROPORTIONALITY IN THE AFSJ AND BEYOND

The AFSJ offers an excellent example, in contemporary EU law, of the tensions with the rule of law in the security and emergency context. In the legal context, an effective way of dealing with reasonable disagreement is through the proportionality test, which is a legal construction tool. It is also, as Aharon Barak explains, a more specific methodological device.[12] The concept of proportionality is made up of four components: proper purpose; rationale connection; necessary means; and a proper relation between the rationale gained by realising the proper purpose and the harm caused to the constitutional right.[13] The core message is that the limiting law must uphold these four components in order to pass constitutional muster.[14] The use and importance of proportionality in EU law is, of course, far from new, and has constituted one of its driving principles since the early days of the EU. But the AFSJ seems to have been largely excluded from it, as the preventive approach has often outweighed other values, such as, most prominently, the basics of due process and the full package of defence rights for those accused of terrorism and other security-related offences.[15]

The AFSJ is a clear example of how one of the most significant challenges faced by EU law consists of identifying criteria for proportionality based upon some common standards, criteria which permit a degree of flexibility without endangering human rights. Proportionality is therefore also part of the wider governance structure regarding how to construct an AFSJ space which contributes to justice through a sufficiently high level of human rights protection at EU level which breeds fairness in the system, or at least has the potential to do so. In the EU–AFSJ context, this question would seem to turn largely on the elasticity of the proportionality principle as a legal expression of the right to justification. The basic right of due process is, of course, also a guarantee against domination in the courtroom. Moreover, it could be argued that the rights in both the EU Charter of Fundamental Rights and the Convention on Human Rights, by themselves, work as a buffer against state domination of the individual.[16]

[11] ibid.

[12] Barak (n 1).

[13] ibid.

[14] ibid, 131.

[15] For example, the debate on the European Arrest Warrant and counter terrorism measures, E Herlin-Karnell, "On Constitutional Law Parameters and EU Security Regulation" *Boston University International Law Journal*, forthcoming, 2018.

[16] Mattias Kumm, 'The Turn to Justification: On the Structure and Domain of Human Rights Practice' in Adam Etinson (ed), *Human Rights: Moral or Political?* (Oxford, Oxford University Press, 2018) 238–61.

And the problem here, as mentioned above, is arguably what we make of the proportionality test (as a sword or a shield). The idea of mutual recognition in the EU context is that states should mutually trust one another in Europe, and recognise, inter alia, a judgment, product, qualification or arrest warrant from another EU state.[17] The application of mutual recognition and trust in the AFSJ raises familiar questions about the implications of free movement within the area of EU criminal law co-operation as well as the constitutional dimension of citizenship in EU criminal law. It could, perhaps, be argued that the most essential aspect has been of a symbolic nature, ie, simply recognising the relevance of citizenship. After all, it could be argued that there was a need to recognise that a system based upon enforcement and mutual recognition also needed the other side of the coin, namely, substantial principles of non-discrimination and the recognition of citizenship rights as well as a general proportionality assessment.

The widespread use of proportionality in various legal systems, most prominently in Germany, the EU, Israel, Canada and South Africa is well known.[18] Common to all approaches to explaining the proportionality phenomenon is functional, political stability, efficiency, judicial legitimacy, or simply judicial power.[19] The UK also has a strong tradition of a reasonableness test, which roughly resembles that of the proportionality test.[20] In the UK, the Wednesbury test helped to define the boundaries of reasonableness in administrative law, and the courts were hesitant to intervene unless the unreasonableness was extreme.[21] Specifically, a decision is unreasonable when it contains 'something so absurd that no sensible person could ever dream that it lay within the powers of the authority'.[22] With the UK joining the EU and ECHR membership, the reasonableness test become essentially streamlined with the proportionality test and, in a sense, constitutionalised.[23] The point of proportionality-based judicial review is that it institutionalises a right to justification that is connected to a particular conception of legitimate legal authority: that law's claim to legitimate authority is plausible only if the law is demonstratively justifiable to those burdened by it in terms that people who are free and equal can accept.[24] As Kumm emphasises: 'Besides the requirement of legality – any limitations suffered by the individual must be prescribed by law – the proportionality requirement lies at the heart of determining whether an infringement of the scope of a right is justified.'

[17] See for example *Advocaten voor de Wereld* [2007] ECR I-3633 and COM (2014) 144 final, 'The EU Justice Agenda for 2020 – strengthening trust, mobility and Growth within the Union'.

[18] Barak (n 1).

[19] Cohen-Eliya and Porrat (n 1) 11.

[20] Paul Craig, 'Proportionality and Judicial Review: A UK Historical Perspective' in Stefan Vogenauer and Stephen Weatherill (eds), *General Principles of Law: European and Comparative Perspectives* (Oxford, Hart Publishing, 2017) 9105–148.

[21] Barak (n 1) 373. *Associated Provincial Picture Houses v Wednesbury Cooperation* [1948] 1 KB 223. And contributions in: Giovanni Sartor, Giorgio Bongiovanni and Chiara Valentini (eds), *Reasonableness and Law* (Dordrecht-Heidelberg-London-New York, Springer, 2009).

[22] Barak (n 1) 375 discussing the *Wednesbury* case (ibid).

[23] My reading of Craig, 'Proportionality and Judicial Review' (2017) and Barak (n 1).

[24] Mattias Kumm, 'The Idea of Socratic Contestation and the Right to Justification: The Point of Rights-based Proportionality Review' (2010) 4 *Law & Ethics of Human Rights* 141–75.

For Malcolm Thorburn, the proportionality test merely provides a structure for the demonstrable justification of an act in terms of reasons that are appropriate in a liberal democracy.[25] For him, it provides a structure for the justification of an act in terms of public reason. The global spread of proportionality is therefore explained by the global spread of a constitutional culture which puts justification at its centre.[26] In short, the main difference between reasonableness and proportionality is that proportionality is structured, transparent and focused on the justifications for the limitation at stake.[27]

Proportionality is the central legal device that ensures the flourishing of a constitutional legal culture.[28] Through this legal culture, proportionality offers a procedure through which the state is required to make explicit precisely how its conduct is consistent with our best conception of the rights in a democratic society.[29] Yet, as this chapter will explain, while proportionality has been largely absent from the debate on the future of AFSJ law, it is now a central component in the EU's structuring of the area, and one that is crucial both for its progress and for the balance of freedom, security and justice.

Furthermore, constitutional rights are often said to function as a filtering mechanism through which we can determine what sort of treatment of persons by the state is consistent with their status as free and equal bearers.[30] In the relation between the CJEU and the national courts, the free and equal paradigm should, perhaps, fall within the national margin of appreciation (both ECHR and EU law proportionality).[31] Since limitations on rights must be 'rationally connected to the objective and not be arbitrary, unfair or based on irrational considerations', this can be interpreted as a mechanism for ensuring that coercive state interference remains non-arbitrary in the republican sense, in that it tracks 'commonly avowable' public interests.[32] As Barak explains, the central or hard core component of proportionality is proportionality *stricto senso*. At the heart of that component lies the notion of balancing between conflicting principles. According to the *stricto sensu* test a proper relation should exist between the benefits gained by fulfilling the purpose and the harm caused to a constitutional right from obtaining that purpose.[33]

[25] Malcolm Thorburn, 'Proportionality' in David Dyzenhaus and Malcolm Thorburn, *Philosophical Foundations of Constitutional Law* (Oxford, Oxford University Press, 2016) 305–22.

[26] For example, Cohen-Eliya and Porrat (n 1).

[27] ibid.

[28] ibid.

[29] Thorburn, 'Proportionality' (2016).

[30] ibid.

[31] On the margin of appreciation, see, for example, Yuval Shany, 'Toward a General Margin of Appreciation Doctrine in International Law?' (2005) 16 *European Journal of International Law* 907–40.

[32] Philippe Pettit, *On the People's Terms: A Republican Theory and Model of Democracy* (Cambridge, Cambridge University Press, 2013), chs 4 and 5.

[33] Barak (n 1) 340; for an extensive discussion of balancing, see 340–70. See, also, Dieter Grimm, 'Proportionality in Canadian and German Constitutional Jurisprudence' (2007) 57 *University of Toronto Law Journal* 383–97, discussed in Barak.

So while the exact difference between proportionality and reasonableness might be rather complex, according to Barak, in the relationship between the means limiting a constitutional right and the law's purpose for which they were chosen, there is no significant difference, as both are concerned with balancing.[34] However, as Barak notes, the idea of reasonableness is open-ended and does not exclude a more holistic view of it, thereby bringing it more in line with proportionality.[35]

III. PROPORTIONALITY DISCOURSE: INTRODUCTORY REMARKS TO A GRAND DEBATE

Before looking at the zone of proportionality specifically at the AFSJ judicial space, we need to ask what proportionality is proper. It is often said that the concept of proportionality constitutes the doctrinal core of any transnational constitutionalism.[36] Generally, proportionality in EU law is taken to mean balancing the means and ends, in which the notion of appropriateness constitutes the golden thread for deciding on the desirability and need for EU action in a given area. As Bernard Schlink states: 'Once it is understood that an authority's reach is extensive but also limited, without the limits being specified, the principle of proportionality serves as an instrument for reconciling both: the extensive reach with the unspecified limits.'[37]

However, for Barak, the boundaries of the zone of proportionality are the lines separating the legislator from the judge, which is connected to the question of the separation of powers. The zone of proportionality is the legislator's kingdom, while keeping the boundaries intact, is that of the judge.[38] For him, the judge's only role is to maintain the boundaries of proportionality and to prevent the selection of disproportional means.[39] The setting of the national policy and its enactment into legislation is the role of the legislative branch; the review of the constitutionality of the legislation and whether it is proportional is a legal construction tool. It is a methodological tool. The limiting law must uphold these four components in order to pass constitutional muster.[40] That way, the proportionality test is not a specific feature of rights reasoning, but bears upon more fundamental characteristics of a shared practice of reasoning in general.[41] In short, for Robert Alexy who, like Barak, is an authority

[34] Barak (n 1) 378.
[35] ibid, 377.
[36] Mathews and Stone Sweet, 'All Things in Proportion?' (2010).
[37] Bernhard Schlink, 'Proportionality in Constitutional Law: Why Everywhere but Here?' (2012) 22 *Duke Journal of Comparative and International Law* 291–302.
[38] Barak (n 1).
[39] ibid.
[40] ibid, 131.
[41] Matthias Klatt, 'Robert Alexy's Philosophy of Law as System' in Klatt (ed), *Institutionalized Reason: The Jurisprudence of Robert Alexy* (Oxford, Oxford University Press, 2012) 1–27.

on proportionality reasoning in legal scholarship, proportionality consists of three sub-principles: the principle of suitability; the principle of necessity; and that of proportionality in the narrower sense. For him, proportionality is about correctness at its core.[42] Any normative speech act needs a justification and needs to follow the procedural rules of practical discourse.[43] According to Alexy, legal argumentation is characterised by a claim to correctness.[44] He argues that proportionality is a formal structure that can be captured in abstraction from a substantive moral theory.[45]

Specifically, for Alexy, in line with Jürgen Habermas, law is part of discourse theory and the critical dimension of law. The moral dimension, according to Alexy, of the claim to law establishes the necessary connection between law and universalistic morality. But proportionality is, for him, amoral. This has famously been criticised by Habermas, who argued, on the one hand, that one cannot separate law from morals and, on the other, that one cannot explain the rightness of cases along the line of correctness, as it is dependent on sociological parameters.[46]

As to the links between proportionality and the idea of reasonableness, for Alexy, the reasonableness test is something different from that of proportionality, and is similar to an absurdity test.[47] And yet reasonableness is not sufficient, according to Alexy, in that there are cases which require a much closer review than an absurdity test can provide.[48] In addition, proportionality, for Alexy, is also about how to create a European culture as a judicial weighing mechanism. Therefore, for him, correctness as a regulatory idea means that it is open to future argumentation and strives towards the dimension of the absolute. As Kumm points out, for Alexy, 'the core claim relating to the structure of rights is that constitutional rights are principles and that proportionality analysis is necessarily at the heart of reasoning about what principles require in real contexts'.[49]

[42] Robert Alexy, 'The Absolute and the Relative Dimensions of Constitutional Rights' (2017) 37 *Oxford Journal of Legal Studies* 31–47.

[43] Giorgio Bongiovanni, Antonino Rotolo and Corrado Roversi, 'The Claim to Correctness and Inferentialism: Alexy's Theory of Practical Reason Reconsidered' in George Pavlakos (ed), *Law, Rights and Discourse: The Legal Philosophy of Robert Alexy* (Oxford, Hart Publishing, 2007) 275–300.

[44] Maeve Cooke, 'Law's Claim to Correctness' in Pavlakos (ed) (ibid) 225–48, and Matthias Klatt, 'Positive Rights: Who Decides? Judicial Review in Balance' (2015) 13 *I-CON* 354–82.

[45] See discussion in Jacob Weinrib, *Dimensions of Dignity: The Theory and Practice of Modern Constitutional Law* (Cambridge, Cambridge University Press, 2016) 239–41.

[46] Jürgen Habermas, Between Facts and Norms: Contributions to a Discourse Theory of Law and Democracy (Cambridge-Malden MA, Polity Press, 1996) 226.

[47] On the difference between reasonableness and proportionality, see Craig (n 8), and Klatt, 'Positive Rights' (2015).

[48] Robert Alexy, 'The Absolute and the Relative Dimensions of Constitutional Rights' (2017) 37 *Oxford Journal of Legal Studies* 31–47.

[49] Mattias Kumm, 'Alexy's Theory of Constitutional Rights and the Problem of Judicial Review' in Klatt, *Institutionalized Reason* (2012) 201–17.

Generally, the proportionality justification addresses three concerns. The first is whether the party infringing the constitutional right actually had the proper standing to claim a justification. As Thorburn argues, courts address this question by asking whether the infringement was prescribed by law, and whether it was undertaken in furtherance of a legitimate state purpose. These considerations play an essential part in the justification process. Taken together, they mean that no one can use the powers of the state to infringe constitutional rights on his or her own private say-so (where the act was not prescribed by law) or for his or her own private purpose (rather than a legitimate public purpose). Furthermore, the requirement of a legitimate state purpose also excludes any purpose that is at odds with the regime of constitutional rights.[50]

In the following, I examine the practical implications of justice as reflected in the legal right to justification as manifested in the proportionality test. In doing so, it is fitting to turn to what Mattias Kumm has referred to as 'Socratic contestation', which refers to the practice of critically engaging authorities in order to assess whether the claims that they make are based upon good reason.[51]

As Kumm argues: 'One important function of proportionality analysis is to function as a filter device that helps to determine whether illegitimate reasons might have skewed the democratic process against the case of the rights-claimant'.

Before analysing the question of proportionality reasoning further and its links to the right to justification, let me first explain the great use of proportionality in EU law and the margin of appreciation in European Convention on Human Rights law.

IV. AN UMBRELLA PRINCIPLE OF PROPORTIONALITY IN EU LAW

The importance of the principle of proportionality as an EU constitutional principle is a well-known and frequently told story. The assumption is that interference with EU law rights should be kept to a minimum, in which the test is to ascertain whether it has been manifestly disproportionate to interfere with these rights. But it also constitutes one of the leading principles for deciding on whether EU legislative competence is warranted (Article 5 (paragraphs 1 and 4) TEU) at all. Alongside the principle of non-discrimination, it is one of the most important principles for the law of free movement.[52] Clearly, the principle of proportionality can be viewed as pointing in the same direction as reasonableness. Alongside the principles of non-discrimination, effectiveness and loyalty,

[50] Malcolm Thorburn, 'Proportionality' in David Dyzenhaus and Malcolm Thorburn, *Philosophical Foundations of Constitutional Law* (Oxford, Oxford University Press, 2016) 305–22.

[51] Mattias Kumm, 'The Idea of Socratic Contestation and the Right to Justification: The Point of Rights-based Proportionality Review' (2010) 4 *Law & Ethics of Human Rights* 141–75.

[52] For example, Tridimas, *General Principles* (2012) chs 3–5, and Paul Craig, *EU Administrative Law* (Oxford, Oxford University Press, 2012).

proportionality is one of the most important principles both for the law of free movement and, beyond that, both in internal market law and in the AFSJ. The CJEU will inquire as to whether the measure was suitable or appropriate to achieve the desired result or whether this could have been attained by a less onerous method. Proportionality is therefore a general review in EU law that is applicable to test the legality both of EU action, and of Member State action when the latter falls within the ambit of the Treaty.[53]

Thus, proportionality is a classic in EU law and is one of the most crucial general principles, one which is used both as a sword and as a shield, usually in the context of to what degree the Member States could derogate from their EU law obligations. But it also constitutes one of the leading principles for deciding on whether EU legislative competence is warranted. In this regard, any legislative action must be reasonably effective to achieve the aim for which the competence has been granted. Secondly, the exercise of competence has to be necessary and indispensable. And, thirdly, such exercise of competence has to be proportionate in the strict sense. However, the CJEU's approach to the proportionality analysis remains strangely abstract with general invocations of the limits of judicial review and the political nature of social and economic choices.[54]

This, then, seems particularly important in the transnational EU context, and is of particular relevance for the AFSJ, where the concept of democracy, as noted, has always been a strained notion, and where security since the 9/11 attacks has dominated the agenda. As discussed in chapter three, the point of justification is that individuals have a right to reasoned decisions, and the function of courts is to assess whether the public authority taking the decision in question can be justified by public policy. Thus, the question of 'good reason' is perhaps most clearly identified in the principle of proportionality, which functions as a justification tool.[55] But, who decides which reasons are good enough? For Rainer Forst, citing Charles Taylor, 'good reasons are not to be found in ethical principles alone, but in an evaluative space of communal values and self-understanding'.[56] In this way, discourse truly articulates what belongs to the character of the community. For Forst, this means that a good reason is a substantive one and is, as such, ethical, as a citizen needs to understand himself or herself as part of a community which is internally connected to the common good. Forst anchors this in the idea of legitimacy. But, as Forst argues, the main commitment would not be to democracy itself, but to the values that

[53] Craig (n 8).

[54] Craig, *EU Administrative Law* (2012) chs 19–20 for an extensive overview of the notion of proportionality in EU law.

[55] For a recent studies of proportionality, see Barak (n 1), Jackson, 'Age of Proportionality' (2015), Klatt and Meister, *Constitutional Structure* (Oxford, Oxford University Press, 2012), Mathews and Stone Sweet (n 1), Möller (n 1), and the contributions in Huscroft et al, *Proportionality and the Rule of Law* (2014).

[56] Forst, *The Right to Justification* (2012) 172, discussing Taylor's work; see, for example, Charles Taylor, *The Ethics of Authenticity* (Cambridge MA, Harvard University Press, 1992).

a community holds dear, meaning that democracy is not autonomous, but is itself ruled by communal values.[57]

A legal way out of this well-known problem from the perspective of law would be to anchor these 'good' reasons in the Charter of Fundamental Rights and the ECHR. Indeed, the principle of proportionality appears to play a key role with regard to both the scope and the limit of the EU Charter of Fundamental Rights.

In the preceding chapters of this book, I discussed the notion of justice as a structuring principle for understanding AFSJ law and its constitutional make-up. The notion of justice is, however, not simply a theoretical concept, but one to be found in the Charter of Fundamental Rights, which sets out a very ambitious plan for human rights protection in the AFSJ. Apart from Article 47 and its general insistence on the right to an effective remedy, the impact of the Charter as a justice tool has, arguably, a larger impact for the architecture of the AFSJ. It consequently represents by far the most important justice document drawn up by EU institutions in the history of the EU.

It would seem, then, that for the AFSJ to constitute a justice space, it requires a critical reading of not only justice, but also proportionality (as the right to justification) in order not simply to constitute a utopian concept, but one that adds to the real lives of the citizens of Europe. As Sionaidh Douglas-Scott so elegantly put it, justice is part of the rule of law.[58] With David Beatty and Barak and others, proportionality is also intrinsic to the rule of law.[59] So, a general adherent to justice would mean that there are limits to what the Member States may deny their citizens upon the basis of proportionality. Of course, in the EU context, the Member States also have a right to justification if they adhere to the basics of power which allow Union action. The notion of proportionality in EU law in general is certainly a well-explored legal axiom, but the Socratic model adds to this well-trodden debate by going one step further and investigating the actual impact of requiring reasoned action from both the EU and the Member States. Proportionality then is a true umbrella concept underlying all Union activity in all fields of law, and points in the direction of a federal balance.

While the principle of proportionality is part of the EU's arsenal for deciding on legislative authority for the EU legislator, it is also a principle that is addressed to individuals in the freedom of movement context. This is usually called the strict proportionality test of the otherwise rather state-centric proportionality test. Hence, the individual plays an increasingly important role in the EU context. For example, Article 3 TFEU makes it clear that not only is the Union to aim to promote the well-being of its peoples, but it is also to offer its

[57] ibid, 173.

[58] Sionaidh Douglas-Scott, 'The Problem of Justice in the European Union' in Julie Dickson and Pavlos Eleftheriadis (eds), *Philosophical Foundations of EU Law* (Oxford, Oxford University Press, 2012) xx–yy.

[59] David M Beatty, The Ultimate Rule of Law (Oxford, Oxford University Press, 2005) 56; Barak (n 1).

citizens an area of freedom, security and justice without internal frontiers, in which the free movement of persons is ensured in conjunction with appropriate measures with respect to, among other things, the prevention and combating of crime. This implies a balance not only vis-à-vis the EU and its Member States, but also between the individual and the EU.[60]

The CJEU will inquire as to whether the measure was suitable or appropriate to achieve the desired result or whether this could have been attained by a less onerous method. The assumption is that interference with EU law rights should be kept to a minimum where the test is whether it has been manifestly disproportionate to interfere with those rights. But it also constitutes one of the leading principles for deciding on whether EU legislative competence is warranted. In this regard, any legislative action must be reasonably effective to achieve the aim for which the competence has been granted – secondly that the exercise of competence has to be necessary and indispensable, and, thirdly, the exercise of such competence has to be proportionate in the strict sense – the adverse effect(s) on other interests must be weighed against the positive effect(s) that the exercised competence entails for the objective pursued by it.[61]

Nevertheless, the high legal goals, as set by the EU in the preamble of the Lisbon Treaty, as well as in the Charter have several consequences from the perspective of sovereignty. The relationship between the EU and the Member States is often described in terms of balancing: the EU only has the powers allocated to it by the Member States. Nonetheless, pinning down these boundaries set by the proportionality principle is sometimes challenging, where proportionality has also formed the *leitmotiv* in European law in a more general sense without actually generating any actual bite. After all, it is also a general principle of EU law that has to be taken into account in all actions of EU law, such as the creation and management of the internal market, as well as the operation of the Treaty freedoms.[62]

V. PROPORTIONALITY ON THE EU LEGISLATIVE TABLE

As noted, the principle of proportionality constitutes one of the leading principles for deciding on whether EU legislative competence is warranted and justified.[63]

[60] Craig (n 49) chs 19–20, for an extensive overview of the notion of proportionality in EU law. See, also, Paul Craig and Gráinne de Búrca, *EU Law, Text, Cases and Materials* (Oxford, Oxford University Press, 2012), Stephen Weatherill, *Law and Values in the European Union* (Oxford, Oxford University Press, 2016), and, for example, Tridimas (n 6) chs 3–5.

[61] Linda Senden, *Soft Law in European Community Law* (Oxford, Hart Publishing, 2004) 88.

[62] For example Tridimas, General Principles (n 6).

[63] The discussion concerning subsidiarity has always started from the assumption that it is too political as a legal notion. Proportionality in EU law has always been taken for granted and singled out as a more successful path to EU integration. See the discussion in for example, Weatherill "Law and Values" (n 57).

In this regard, any legislative action must be reasonably effective to achieve the aim for which the competence has been granted. In addition, the exercise of competence has to be both necessary and indispensable. This is the 'manifestly inappropriate' template as applied by the Court. There is thus a cost–benefit aspect to proportionality. However, the cost–benefit or utility of EU action aspect is usually discussed in the framework of subsidiarity. This is reflected in the so-called efficiency check of proposed legislation, which requires a comparative evaluation of the costs and benefits of action at EU and national level. This better criteria analysis is thus commonly described as the comparative efficiency test,[64] where EU action must be, to put it simply, more effective than action at national level. More specifically, the Union should act only if the action in question cannot be achieved by the individual Member States, and the EU can achieve the desired result because of its effects or scale.

Accordingly, again, the principle of proportionality is generally regarded as a very wide principle. But unlike the principle of subsidiarity, proportionality also applies to areas under the exclusive competence of the Union as stipulated in Article 5 TEU. Moreover, according to this provision, the institutions of the Union are to apply the principle of proportionality as laid down in the Protocol on the application of the principles of subsidiarity and proportionality.

Furthermore, the principle of proportionality plays an important role in the context of the reach of the EU Charter.

A. Charter of Fundamental Rights and Proportionality

Proportionality appears to play a key role with regard to the Charter of Fundamental Rights, both in its scope and in its application. The point of justification as explored above, is that individuals have a right to reasoned decisions, and the function of courts is to assess whether the public authority taking the decision in question can be justified by public policy. Thus, the question of good reason is perhaps most clearly identified in the principle of proportionality, which functions as a justification tool.[65] But, as was asked above, who decides which reasons are good enough? One legal way out of this well-known problem would be to anchor these good reasons in the Charter. Indeed, the principle of proportionality appears to play a key role with regard to both the scope and the limit of the Charter. Nonetheless, Article 52(1) of the Charter sets out some important exceptions to the application of the Charter as a whole. This provision makes it clear that:

> Any limitation on the exercise of the rights and freedoms recognised by this Charter must be provided for by law and respect the essence of those rights and freedoms.

[64] See, for example, Gráinne de Búrca, 'The Principle of Subsidiarity and the Court of Justice as an Institutional Actor' (1998) 36 *Journal of Common Market Studies* 217–35.

[65] For recent studies of proportionality, see Barak (n 1), Jackson (n 5), Klatt and Meister (n 1), Matthews and Stone Sweet (n 1), Möller (n 1) and the contributions in Huscroft et al (n 1).

> Subject to the principle of proportionality, limitations may be made only if they are necessary and genuinely meet objectives of general interest recognised by the Union or the need to protect the rights and freedoms of others.

Admittedly, such a limitation is not unique to the EU: Article 5 ECHR has a similar limitation of the presumption of freedom based upon when it is necessary.

The notion of proportionality is therefore somewhat adaptable, and thus it is often criticised by scholars who think that proportionality is a dangerous concept, which will be discussed in further detail below.[66]

Furthermore, the Member States could invoke proportionality to derogate from the rights guaranteed in the Charter since Article 52 applies to all rights. The explanatory memorandum on the Charter confirms that these exceptions are based upon the Court's well-established case law, which shows that restrictions may be imposed on the exercise of fundamental rights. The explanatory notes also make it clear that the reference to the general interests recognised by the Union covers both the objectives mentioned in Article 3 TFEU and other interests protected by specific provisions of the Treaties provided that those restrictions do, in fact, correspond to objectives of general interest of the EU. Moreover, these explanatory notes state that such restrictions may not, with regard to the aim pursued, be disproportionate or cause unreasonable interference which would undermine the very substance of any Charter rights.[67] So, unlike the ECHR, which limits derogations from certain rights, the Charter does not appear to recognise absolute rights in the sense that all rights may be derogated from, in accordance with Article 51(1) Charter.[68] Yet, the Charter refers to the ECHR in Article 52(3) in pointing out that the ECHR is always the minimum standard of protection.

An example of the use of the Charter in the context of strict liability and the question of proportionality can be found in the case of Åkerberg Fransson, which concerned the compatibility with the *ne bis in idem* principle of a national system involving two separate sets of proceedings to penalise the same wrongful conduct.[69] Advocate General Cruz Villalón stated, in his opinion, that Article 50 of the Charter did not preclude the Member States from bringing criminal proceedings relating to facts in respect of which a final penalty has already been imposed in administrative proceedings.

The Advocate General put his trust in the hands of a stringent application of proportionality here in the national courts. The CJEU in turn, did not elaborate on this aspect of proportionality, but adopted a very broad reading of the Charter. It held that, although the national rules in questions did not *stricto sensu* involve any implementation, it was clear from Article 325 TFEU that the

[66] See, for example, Webber, The Negotiable Constitution: On the Limitation of Rights (2009).
[67] The Explanations relating to the Charter of Fundamental Rights, [2007] OJ C83/2.
[68] Fichera and Herlin-Karnell, 'The Margin of Appreciation Test' (2013).
[69] Case C-617/10, *Åkerberg Fransson*, judgment of 26 February 2013 nyr.

Member States are required to fight fraud against the EU and thereby supply the same level of penalties for EU fraud and domestic fraud respectively. Moreover, the Court observed that EU law precludes a judicial practice which makes the obligation for a national court to disapply any provision contrary to a fundamental right guaranteed by the Charter conditional upon that infringement being clear from the text of the Charter or the case law relating to it. According to the Court, such an interpretation would withhold from the national court the power to assess fully whether the provision in question was compatible with the Charter.[70]

Yet, as already noted, some rights are absolute and thereby holy or sacrosanct according to the ECHR. Interestingly, as indicated, the Charter does not seem to recognise absolute rights in the sense that all rights may be derogated from, in accordance with Article 52 Charter and proportionality. Thus, there is scope for a sophisticated debate here about what this means and why it should be so, as well as what the general impact of the ECHR in this area actually is, so as to safeguard that notion of an absolute right. As all the Member States – but not the EU – are members to the ECHR, the question might be of theoretical, rather than practical, importance. Moreover, in Opinion 2/13, the Court held that the principle of mutual trust requires, particularly with regard to the AFSJ, 'each of those States, save in exceptional circumstances, to consider all the other Member States to be complying with EU law and particularly with the fundamental rights recognised by EU law'.[71] Hence, the EU's accession to the ECHR was seen as potentially weakening the EU enforcement project. This unilateral approach may appear to be a contradictory message against the background of the struggle to achieve better enforcement in AFSJ matters.

B. Margin of Appreciation and the ECHR

The margin of appreciation test, as developed by the European Court of Human Rights (ECtHR), is similar to the EU proportionality test, but is directed to the state, and thus is different from proportionality, which goes in both directions, ie, also concerns the relationship between the individual and the state. It provides a margin of appreciation to the state vis-à-vis the international fora. As Barak stresses, both the proportionality principle and the margin of appreciation deal with the possible limitations of rights by focusing on normative and factual circumstances. Likewise, both proportionality and the margin of appreciation doctrine deal with the relative importance of the marginal social

[70] Paragraph 48 of the judgment.

[71] Opinion 2/13 Accession to the ECHR, 18 December 2014.

benefit added by fulfilling the law's purposes in relation to the marginal social benefit of preventing the harm caused to the constitutional right.[72]

The margin of appreciation test has always played a pivotal role in the case law of the ECtHR. It allows Member States to derogate from their Treaty obligations with a given margin, or area, of discretion upon the basis of their moral preferences as reflected in their national constitutions. In EU law, the notion of a margin of appreciation has always been reflected in the free movement rules and the possibilities of derogation under the Treaty, where the EU principle of proportionality draws up the exact contours for the scope of such derogations. The margin of appreciation test has, however, also constitutional implications in that it regulates the Member States' leeway in applying their own national standards. The doctrine of the margin of appreciation has been extended to other sensitive areas, such as freedom of expression, privacy, fair trial and freedom of religion.[73] The strategy of the ECtHR normally consists in allowing a restricted margin when a wide consensus among the Member State parties exists. But the margin of appreciation is very much political and the Court has narrowed it down considerably, when the right at issue was considered fundamental to democracy.[74] At the same time, the Court seems often wary of interfering in national sovereignty even when it would be necessary in order to uphold human rights and the rule of law.

Interestingly, the margin of appreciation test was developed in parallel with the emergency provision of Article 15 ECHR where authorities should be able exercise a certain measure of discretion in assessing the extent strictly required by the exigences of the situation.[75] The ECHR commission maintained that it was competent to decide whether a derogation from the Commission was justified and whether the state's measures were strictly required by the exigences of the situation.[76] As, for example, both Eval Benvenisti and Andreas Føllesdal explain, the margins doctrine initially responded to concerns of national governments that international policies could jeopardise their national security.[77]

The EU also has the possibility of derogating from EU law obligations upon the basis of public security. Yet, unlike the EU law rights framework, the ECHR

[72] Barak (n 1) 420. See, also, for example, the contributions in: Eva Brems and Janneke H Gerards (eds), *Shaping Rights in the ECHR: The Role of the European Court of Human Rights in Determining the Scope of Human Rights* (Cambridge, Cambridge University Press, 2014) and see Shany, 'General Margin' (2005).

[73] See, for example, *Handyside v United Kingdom*; Application no 5493/72 ECtHR; *Klass v Germany*; Application no 65655/01 ECtHR; *Lautsi v Italy*; Application no 30814/06 ECtHR).

[74] Shany (n 28) and Eyal Benvenisti, 'Margin of Appreciation, Consensus and Universal Standards, International Law and Politics' (1999) 31 *New York University Journal of International Law and Politics* 843–54.

[75] For example, Andreas Føllesdal, 'Appreciating the Margin of Appreciation' in Adam Etinson (ed), *Human Rights: Moral or Political?* (Oxford, Oxford University Press, 2018) 269–94, discussing the 1958 *Cyprus* case, Application nos 1976/56 and 299/57.

[76] ibid.

[77] Benvenisti, 'Margin of Appreciation' (1999) and Føllesdal, 'Appreciating' (2018).

does not address individual rights, but whether the state is granted a certain margin of appreciation. As will be explained below, in the EU context, the question of to what extent Member States have a margin of appreciation, and how the balancing test is applied in security cases, is very pertinent. As will be shown, proportionality has a huge impact in AFSJ law and is directly addressed to the individual's right to justification.

VI. THE NEW CONTOURS OF PROPORTIONALITY WITHIN THE AFSJ: CASE LAW

This section will now look at the impact of proportionality reasoning in AFSJ law. With regard to the possible usefulness of balancing in concrete cases and of applying Barak's view of proportionality as inherent in the balancing test, it is useful to turn to the mutual recognition arena.[78] The notion of trust has been crucial for the development of mutual recognition ie, that no additional barriers should exist between the Member States in AFSJ law,[79] the assumption being that Member States trust each other sufficiently, and regard each other as equals,[80] so as not to insist on additional legal safeguards or checks. By investigating the impact of proportionality in the context of mutual recognition, this chapter seeks, in particular, to demonstrate the force and power of proportionality as a governing principle, and why it is needed as a device for constructing the AFSJ space. As mentioned above, remarkably, the proportionality principle has not been applied to any great extent in the legally thorny terrain of the AFSJ, with its complex ties between the EU, the Member States, and their citizens, despite this being an area that is closely connected to national sovereignty and the protection of human rights. Important legal measures in this area include the European Arrest Warrant (EAW), which introduced the concept of mutual recognition in the fight against crime, which seem to have been excluded from such a proportionality test.[81]

With regard to the possible usefulness of balancing in concrete cases and of applying Barak's view of proportionality as inherent in the balancing test, it is useful to turn to the mutual recognition arena.[82] The most radical example of this is, of course, the EAW, which still poses controversies in the national legal systems, as it abolished the requirement of dual criminality as a pre-condition

[78] Barak (n 1).

[79] See, for example, Christine Janssens, *The Principle of Mutual Recognition in EU Law* (Oxford, Oxford University Press, 2013).

[80] For example, Koen Lenearts, 'The Principle of Mutual Recognition in the Area of Freedom, Security and Justice' (Sir Jeremy Lever Lecture 2015, Oxford University, Oxford, 30 January 2015), available at: www.law.ox.ac.uk/sites/files/oxlaw/the_principle_of_mutual_recognition_in_the_area_of_freedom_judge_lenaerts.pdf.

[81] The European Arrest Warrant, 584/JHA [2002] OJ L190/1 Council Framework Decision.

[82] Barak (n 1).

for extradition. As one Advocate General put it: 'the principle of mutual recognition which lies at the heart of the mechanism behind the European arrest warrant cannot conceivably be applied in the same way as it is in the case of the recognition of a university qualification or a driving licence issued by another Member State.'[83] The Court confirmed this view in, inter alia, Lopes Da Silva Jorge, by asserting that there is no absolute obligation to execute arrest warrants, while, at the same time, emphasising the duty of national courts to ensure the full effectiveness of the actual application of the EAW framework decision.[84]

The crucial point here is that the proper application of proportionality functions as a rebuttal of the previous assumption that there were no, or very few, limits to mutual recognition in this area. When human rights are at stake, there needs to be a good justification for relying on trust. The following section aims to draw on some further examples from practice, and argues that these examples represent an important testing ground for the resilience of justice-based reasoning, and explains why this matters in the context of security. Admittedly, as already mentioned, such a limitation is not unique to the EU: Article 5 ECHR has a similar limitation of the presumption of freedom based upon when it is necessary. The key point is that, although it is necessary to maintain a secure society, the security agenda can be easily manipulated always to fit what is needed in a democratic society.[85]

In any case, it is clear that the Charter offers itself as an important trendsetter with regard to proportionality as a balancing mechanism and its future scope as a constitutional principle in the AFSJ. Specifically, it has had a huge impact on the emerging EU criminal law principles of procedural law. With respect to due process rights, Article 49 provides for the guarantee of legality and proportionality in a more extensive way than the ECHR. Article 47 of the Charter also guarantees the right to an effective remedy, while Articles 48 and 49 stipulate the presumption of innocence and the right of defence.[86] The latter provision also makes it clear that the severity of penalties must not be disproportionate to the criminal offence.

Thus, the scope of EU human rights protection in legal terms seems to turn on the elasticity of the proportionality principle, an argument which is easily accused of paving the way for circular reasoning. So, a general adherent to justice would mean that there are limits to what the Member States may deny

[83] Case C-42/11, *Lopes Da Silva Jorge*, judgment 5 September nyr, opinion delivered by AG Mengozzi on 20 March 2012, para 28.

[84] ibid.

[85] See, for example, Cian C Murphy, *EU Counter Terrorism Law: Pre-emption and the Rule of Law* (Oxford, Hart Publishing, 2012) 229–30.

[86] In her opinion delivered on 18 October 2012 in *Radu* C-396/11 (para 103), AG Sharpston discusses the boundaries of Article 49 of the Charter by stipulating that it would be interesting to explore the boundaries of these provisions in the context of Article 3 ECHR in which the ECtHR has held that a sentence that is grossly disproportionate could amount to ill-treatment contrary to Article 3 ECHR. The Court did not elaborate on this issue.

their citizens upon the basis of proportionality. Of course, in the EU context, the Member States also have a right to justification if they adhere to the basics of power which grant Union action. The notion of proportionality in EU law in general is certainly a well-explored legal axiom, but the Socratic model adds to this well-trodden debate by going one step further and investigating the actual impact of requiring reasoned action from both the EU and the Member States. It is a true umbrella concept underlying all Union activity in all fields of law, and points in the direction of a federal balance.

The problem is that the AFSJ seems to have been largely exempted from this golden rule of balancing. As a result, in an attempt to address this deficit, the Commission published an evaluation of the implementation of the EAW framework decision in 2011.[87] The Commission points out that the systematic issue of EAWs for the surrender of persons has undermined the application of the EAWs, which are often sought in respect of very minor offences. In addition, the Commission states that there is a need to apply a proportionality test to make sure that offences which, even if they fall within the scope of Article 2(1) of the EAW, are not serious enough to justify the measures and co-operation which the execution of an EAW requires. In particular, the Commission stipulates that the handbook on the EAW needs to be adjusted in order to comply with proportionality. The amended handbook now sets out the factors to be assessed when issuing an EAW and the possible alternatives to be considered before issuing an EAW.[88] This is thus an example of where the proportionality principle could have crucial impact.

Moreover, for example, in the *ZZ* judgment,[89] regarding restrictions to free movement upon the basis of public security concerns (Article 27 Citizenship Directive 2004/38),[90] and the right to information of disclosed procedures (Article 31 Citizenship Directive), the proportionality principle in the Charter as a derogating principle was explicitly linked to the general right to effective judicial protection, Article 47 of the Charter.[91] The Court stated that, if it turns out that state security does stand in the way of disclosure of the grounds to the person concerned, judicial review must be carried out in a procedure which strikes an appropriate balance between the requirements flowing from state security and the requirements of the right to effective judicial protection whilst limiting any interference with the exercise of that right to that which is strictly necessary.[92]

More specifically, the Court held that any limitation upon the basis of proportionality must respect the essence of free movement rights, the principle

[87] COM(2011) 175 final 'On the implementation since 2007 of the Council Framework Decision of 13 June 2002 on the European arrest warrant and the surrender procedures between Member States'.

[88] ibid.

[89] Case C-300/11, *ZZ*, judgment of 4 June 2013.

[90] Directive 2004/38, OJ L 158/77.

[91] *ZZ* (n 80). See, also, *Kadi II*, Joined Cases C-584/10P, C-593/10P and C-595/10P, judgment of 18 July 2013.

[92] *ZZ* (n 80), para 64.

of proportionality, and that the limitation must be necessary and genuinely meet the objectives of general interest recognised by the EU, but that very essence is still largely unexplained.[93] In *Kadi II*, the Court adopted a restrictive reading of the proportionality requirement when used as a derogation possibility under Article 52 of the Charter. The General Court of the EU had held that the restrictive measures adopted against Mr Kadi had been implemented without any real safeguards which would have enabled the applicant to put his case to the competent authorities, and therefore amounted a breach of proportionality.[94] The Court, in turn, focused on the need to ensure a fair balance between the maintenance of international peace and security, and the protection of the fundamental rights and freedoms of the person concerned, those being shared values of both the UN and the EU.[95] For this reason, it concluded that there had been no violation of the proper legal safeguards in question.

Therefore, it could be argued that the scope of EU human rights protection under the Charter turns on the width of the proportionality principle.[96] Although the Member States could invoke proportionality to derogate from the rights guaranteed in the Charter, since Article 52 applies to all rights, there are limits in the light of dignity and the rule of law (EU law principles). Nonetheless, the explanatory memorandum on the Charter confirms that these exceptions are based upon the Court's well-established case law that restrictions may be imposed on the exercise of fundamental rights.[97] The explanatory notes also make it clear that the reference to the general interests recognised by the Union covers both the objectives mentioned in Article 3 EU and other interests protected by specific provisions of the Treaties provided that those restrictions do, in fact, correspond to the objectives of general interest of the EU. Moreover, these explanatory notes state that such restrictions may not, with regard to the aim pursued, be disproportionate or cause unreasonable interference, thereby undermining the very substance of any Charter rights.[98] So, as previously mentioned but deserves repeating unlike the ECHR, which limits derogations from certain absolute rights, the Charter does not appear to recognise absolute rights in the sense that almost all rights may be derogated from in accordance with Article 51(1) Charter. However, the Charter refers to the ECHR in Article 52(3), in pointing out that the ECHR is always the minimum standard of protection.

In the much debated *Melloni* ruling,[99] concerning the validity of the amendments made to the EAW by Framework Decision 2009/299/JHA,[100] and addressing

[93] Paragraphs 64–69 of the judgment.
[94] Case T-85/09, 30 September 2010.
[95] Joined Cases C-584/10P, C-593/10P and C-595/10P, judgment of 18 July 2013.
[96] Fichera and Herlin-Karnell (n 10).
[97] The Explanations relating to the Charter of Fundamental Rights, [2007] OJ C83/2, see, also, the discussion in Craig (n 49) 473–74.
[98] ibid.
[99] Case C-399/11 Criminal proceedings against Stefano Melloni.
[100] Council Framework Decision 2009/299/JHA.

the application of the principle of mutual recognition to trial in absentia, the Court stated that, where an EU legal act calls for national implementing measures, national authorities and courts remain free to apply national standards of protection of fundamental rights, provided this does not compromise the level of protection provided for by the Charter, as interpreted by the CJEU, and the primacy, unity and effectiveness of EU law.[101] It could be argued, though, that Article 53 also enables the EU to adopt a higher standard if it wants to do so. If the national constitution provides for a higher standard, and if the objective of the EU is to establish an AFSJ with a high level of human rights protection, then the interesting question in the present context is what would happen if the ECHR provided for a higher standard with regard to human rights protection? The disappointing news is that it does not seem to allow for a broader protection. Yet, this insistence on not allowing the Charter a character as a derogation tool from EU law obligations seems to run counter to the *NS*[102] case in the context of the EU asylum system, where the CJEU asserted that, if there are substantial grounds for believing that there are systematic flaws in the asylum procedure in the Member State responsible, then the transfer of asylum-seekers to that territory would be incompatible with the Charter.

Nevertheless, it could be argued that the scope of EU human rights protection in legal terms turns on the elasticity of the proportionality principle. It seems, then, that, for the AFSJ to constitute a justice space, it requires a critical reading of not only justice, but also proportionality (as the right to justification). As stated above, I have, so far, put my trust in the principle of proportionality as a balancing mechanism which readily requires good enough justifications for any intrusion in the public sphere of due process rights, and I have argued that such justifications are particularly linked to the possibilities of the EU creating a successful justice space which lives up to the EU endeavour and promise of good governance. And yet, as explained below, the principle of proportionality is far from one-sided, and the Member States could invoke proportionality to derogate from the rights guaranteed in the Charter, since Article 52 applies to all rights.

Indeed, if the Court is to develop criteria for the increasing use of proportionality as a balancing principle in connection with the Charter, this will arguably confirm a tentative version of a contextual justice approach. We will just have to make sure that it lives up to a critical and holistic view of this. It seems clear that balancing in this context is what the creation of fairness in AFSJ law is about, which is not about a trade-off, but about ensuring a balanced system in which there is both security and justice and freedom.

Yet, in *Aranyosi* and *Căldăraru*,[103] the Court held that the executing judicial authority had to postpone its decision on the surrender of the individual

[101] Case C-399/11 Criminal proceedings against Stefano Melloni, para 60.

[102] C-411/10 and C-493, judgment of 21 December 2011.

[103] Joined Cases C-404/15 and C-659/15 PPU, *Aranyosi* and *Căldăraru*, Judgment of the Court of Justice (Grand Chamber) of 5 April 2016.

concerned until it obtained the supplementary information that would allow it to exclude the existence of such a risk. This approach was also confirmed in, for example, the *CK* judgment in the context of asylum law and the transfer of seriously ill applicant and the risk of him being subject to torture. In particular, the question at stake was whether the idea of mutual recognition is contingent on what is meant as exceptional circumstances.[104]

The Court has interwoven the AFSJ and the different areas that it entails. In the project of asylum law, the judgment of *El Dridi* (Case C-61/11) is instructive here, as the Court held that the principle of proportionality must be complied with when deciding on the return procedure. In this case, the principles of proportionality and effectiveness were relied upon by the CJEU to define the competence and margin of appreciation of Member States concerning the coercive measures that they can implement in the context of the procedure for the return of illegally staying third-country nationals.[105] The first principle was employed by the Court to examine the lawfulness of such measures (which include, for example, detention in a facility and deportation) (Case C-61/11). The second principle restricted national competence in the sense that the Member State must not prevent the achievement of the objectives of the Return Directive,[106] with regard to the implementation of an efficient policy of removal and repatriation of irregularly staying third-country nationals. The obligation to ensure compliance with EU law implies that the national court has the power to refuse to apply a custodial sentence which is imposed for the mere reason that the third-country national continues to stay in the territory of the Member State after the expiry of the period established for him or her to leave the country.

While the principle of proportionality is part of the EU's arsenal for deciding on the legislative authority for the EU legislator, it is also a principle that is addressed to individuals in the free movement context. This is usually called the strict proportionality aspect of the otherwise rather state-centric proportionality test. The problem – for a long time – has been that the AFSJ seems to have been largely exempted from this golden rule of balancing. Despite this being an area closely connected to national sovereignty and the protection of human rights. As explained, important legal measures in this area with regard to arrest warrants, which introduced the concept of mutual recognition in the fight against crime, seem previously to have excluded such a proportionality test.[107] As noted, in the recent joined case of *Aranyosi* and *Căldăraru*,[108]

[104] Case C-578/16 PPU, *CK*, judgment delivered on 6 February 2017, nyr.
[105] See to this regard points 13 and 16 Preamble and Article 8(4) of the Directive 2008/115/EC of the European Parliament and of the Council of 16 December 2008 on common standards and procedures in Member States for returning illegally staying third-country nationals, OJ L 348, 24.12.2008.
[106] Directive 2008/115/EC (ibid).
[107] European Arrest Warrant, 584/JHA [2002] OJ L190/1, Council framework decision.
[108] Joined Cases C-404/15 and C-659/15 PPU, judgment of 5 April 2016. See, also, Case C-578/16 PPU.

the CJEU stated that the judicial authority which executes an arrest warrant must respect the requirement of proportionality, laid down in Article 52(1) of the Charter, with respect to the limitation of any right or freedom recognised by the Charter. The Court of Justice held that 'The issue of a European arrest warrant cannot justify the individual concerned remaining in custody without any limit in time'.[109] The Court also stated that the consequence of the execution of such a warrant must not be that the individual in question suffers inhuman or degrading treatment. This sounds self-evident, but the case was handed down in 2016, indicating the somewhat bizarre situation with regard to arrest warrants in Europe for a long time.

Despite the seemingly bleak picture painted above, there is reason to be hopeful regarding the potential of the CJEU to be a successful guardian of the AFSJ and the fostering of justice. After all, the recent case of *Digital Rights*,[110] and the *Schrems* and *Tele 2 Sverige* cases are instructive as a touchstone of justice-inspired reasoning in the Court. In *Digital Rights*, the Court annulled the 2006 Data Retention Directive, which was aimed at fighting crime and terrorism, and which allowed data to be stored for up to two years. It concluded that the measure breached proportionality on the grounds that the Directive had too sweeping a generality and therefore violated, inter alia, the basic right of data protection as set out in Article 8 of the Charter. The Court pointed out that access by the competent national authorities to the retained data was not made dependent on a prior review carried out by a court or by an independent administrative body whose decision sought to limit access to the data to what was strictly necessary for the purpose of attaining the objective pursued. Nor did it lay down a specific obligation on Member States designed to establish such limits. The EU legislator had provided insufficient justification – it was simply not good enough from the perspective of EU fundamental rights protection. The approach was confirmed in *Schrems*[111] and *Tele 2 Sverige*, where the Court held that:

> [L]egislation not providing for any possibility for an individual to pursue legal remedies in order to have access to personal data or to obtain the rectification or erasure of such data, does not respect the essence of the fundamental right to effective judicial protection, as enshrined in Article 47 of the Charter.

These findings were also confirmed in the recent Opinion 1/15 where the Court annulled a pending Agreement between Canada and the EU on the transfer and processing of Passenger Name Record (PNR) data.[112] The Court held that the Agreement granted too sweeping a purpose of fighting terrorism without concrete justification in the individual case just simply a general concern

[109] ibid, paras 101–03 of the judgment. See also *Schrems* and *Tele 2 Sverige*.

[110] Case C-293/12, opinion of AG Cruz Villalón delivered on 12 December 2013, judgment of 8 April 2014.

[111] Case C-362/14, *Schrems*, judgment delivered on 6 October 2015, nyr.

[112] Opinion 1/15, judgment of 26 July 2017.

of public security and without respecting private life and data protection (Articles 7 and 8 of the Charter, Article 16 TFEU) and proportionality (Article 52 of the Charter).The PNR Agreement would have permitted data retention for up to five years.[113] The Court specifically stated that the Agreement needs to limit the retention of passenger name record after departure to that of passengers in respect of whom there is objective evidence from which it may be inferred that they may present a risk in terms of the fight against terrorism.[114]

The crucial point here is that the proper application of proportionality functions as a rebuttal of the previous assumption that there were no, or very few, limits, to mutual recognition in this area. When human rights are at stake, there needs to be a good justification for relying on trust. The following section aims to draw on some further examples from practice, and argues that these examples represent an important testing ground for the resilience of justice-based reasoning, and explains why this matters in the context of security.

As explained above, much of AFSJ law is contingent on the proportionality principle, as it is concerned with constitutional and human rights: it could be argued that the scope of EU human-rights protection under the Charter seems to turn on the width of the proportionality principle. After all, the Member States could invoke proportionality to derogate from the rights guaranteed in the Charter and this applies to all rights. Again, the explanatory memorandum on the Charter confirms that these exceptions are based upon the Court's well-established case law that restrictions may be imposed on the exercise of fundamental rights.[115] So to sum up the explanatory notes also make it clear that the reference to the general interests recognised by the Union covers both the objectives mentioned in Article 3 TEU and other interests protected by specific provisions of the Treaties provided that those restrictions do, in fact, correspond to the objectives of general interest pursued by the Community and do not constitute, with regard to the aim pursued, disproportionate and unreasonable interference which undermines the very substance of those rights.[116] Indeed, as mentioned, the Charter refers to the ECHR in Article 52(3) in pointing out that the ECHR is always the minimum standard of protection.

VII. CRITIQUE AND APPRAISAL OF THE PROPORTIONALITY PRINCIPLE

Regardless of its attractiveness as a judicial principle, proportionality is often attacked on the grounds that it involves judicial weighing of incommensurables, and thereby erodes rights. Moreover, it is often accused of being far too

[113] Paragraphs 154–78.

[114] Para 232.

[115] The Explanations relating to the Charter of Fundamental Rights, [2007] OJ C83/2; see, also, the discussion in Craig (n 49) above 473–74.

[116] ibid.

pragmatic and thus simply too mechanical as a legal principle. The argument hinges on the concern that moral values cannot be adequately balanced, as the interests at stake cannot actually be weighed on any sort of scale.[117] In short, critics argue that there is too much ambiguity with the pathologies of the proportionality test, and that it fails to deliver what it promises, namely, that, contrary to what some scholars argue, it increases neither transparency nor rationality, and thus has no legitimacy. Another critique is that often not enough information is, empirically speaking, available in the proportionality cases, which makes it difficult to rule on the facts and strike a balance.[118] Justice, in our case then, just like the principle of proportionality, is vulnerable to the critique that its political dimension means that it is not amenable to judicial review.[119]

As Douglas-Scott has observed, it can be doubted whether international courts such as the CJEU or ECtHR are better suited than national policy-makers to decide on the public reason.[120] Judges are not philosopher kings or Herculian experts, so why should they be better at judging empirical facts?

So, despite its attractiveness as a judicial principle, proportionality is often attacked on the grounds that it involves judicial weighing of incommensurables, that it is too pragmatic, and simply too mechanical as a legal principle, and that it gives judges too much power. The argument hinges on the concern that moral values cannot be adequately balanced, as the interests at stake cannot actually be weighed on any sort of scale.

For example, Timothy Endicott claims that it is not possible to value human rights equally and thus they are not amenable to the proportionality test.[121] As Malcolm Thorburn explains, 'proportionality justification is sometimes described as a triumph of expediency over principle, for it allows the state to infringe constitutional rights whenever they get in the way of its pursuit of important policy goals'.[122]

Yet is it not unavoidable that Courts make these deliberations? The common criticism is that balancing between competing interests is the legislator's job, and that by ruling on the appropriateness of the legislation trespasses on this.[123]

Why should we grant so much power to unelected judges to allow them to decide upon the appropriateness of a legal measure? As already indicated, they may not be fit to make these decisions. One reason for doing so is the right to justification, as discussed above. The point of justification, with Kumm, is that individuals have a right of reason, and the function of courts is to assess

[117] Timothy Endicott, 'Proportionality and Incommensurability', Oxford Legal Research Papers, Paper No 40 (2012), and Webber (n 1).

[118] Schlink, 'Proportionality in Constitutional Law (2012).

[119] See, for example, Paul Craig, 'Subsidiarity: A Political and Legal Analysis' (2012) 50 *Journal of Common Market Studies* 72–87.

[120] Sionaidh Douglas-Scott, *Law After Modernity* (Oxford, Hart Publishing, 2013) 321.

[121] Endicott, 'Proportionality' (2012).

[122] Thorburn (n 25).

[123] Barak (n 1) 490–91.

whether the public authority taking the decision in question can be justified on public-policy reasons.[124] As Kumm argues and as already mentioned above as it is central to this chapter: 'One important function of proportionality analysis is to function as a filter device that helps to determine whether illegitimate reasons might have skewed the democratic process against the case of the rights-claimant.'

As Ripstein points out, proportionality figures prominently in many areas of practical thought, not only legal discourse. He demonstrates that many accounts of the moral emotions and of virtue incorporate ideas of proportionality.[125] And the idea of judicial review is commonly seen as the hallmark of a constitutionalist way of thinking about law.[126] A common republican argument in favour of courts taking account of power differentials in certain contexts would remain sceptical as to whether judicial power can reduce power differentials in society at large.[127] Moreover, according to Daly: 'the more technical aspects of the proportionality doctrine – particularly the requirement of a rational connection between the means and end of a restriction on rights – helps to show that constitutional rights are not moral rights, institutionalised, but rather, controls on the predicates of state power.'[128]

What sort of claim would hold in a court in the AFSJ context and its emphasis on security? And, again, what justifies giving so much power to courts? With Matthias Klatt, in order to determine more precisely when the competence of courts is supported by democratic legitimacy, we may employ the three key values of democracy: accountability; participation; and equality.[129] As Klatt has described it: 'The more serious a limitation of rights is, the more intense should be the review engaged in by the court.'[130]

As indicated in chapter three, courts provide individuals with an opportunity to raise their grievances and challenge what the individuals perceive (justifiably or unjustifiably) as a violation of their rights.[131] In this way, courts engage in reasoned deliberation and provide an explanation for the alleged violation. Institutions that operate in this way thereby inevitably become institutions that operate in a judicial manner.[132] In the EU–AFSJ context, as already noted, this

[124] Mattias Kumm, 'Alexy's Theory of Constitutional Rights and the Problem of Judicial Review' in Matthias Klatt (ed), *Institutionalized Reason: The Jurisprudence of Robert Alexy* (Oxford, Oxford University Press, 2012) 201–17.

[125] Arthur Ripstein, 'Reclaiming Proportionality' (2017) 34 *Journal of Applied Philosophy* 1–18.

[126] Alon Harel, *Why Law Matters* (Oxford, Oxford University Press, 2014) ch 2.

[127] Eoin Daly, 'Freedom as Non-domination in the Jurisprudence of Constitutional Rights' (2015) 28 *Canadian Journal of Law and Jurisprudence* 289–316.

[128] ibid.

[129] Klatt (n 41).

[130] ibid.

[131] Harel, *Why Law Matters* (2014) ch 2. And draft paper 'Robust Constitutionalism' (on file with the author).

[132] Daly, 'Freedom' (2015).

question would seem to turn largely on the scope of the proportionality principle as a legal expression of the right to justification. The basic right of due process is, however, also a guarantee against domination in the courtroom. Moreover, it could be argued that the rights in the EU Charter and the Convention on Human Rights, by themselves, work as a buffer against state domination of the individual.[133] And the problem here is, arguably, what we make of the proportionality test.

As Barak has put it: 'Real democracy is not just the law of rules and legislative supremacy. Democracy is a multi-dimensional concept. It requires recognition of the power of the majority and limitations on the power of the majority.'[134] For him, proportionality serves as a tool, one which ensures that law is upheld even in the worst of times. Therefore, proportionality can be interpreted as a mechanism for ensuring that coercive state interference remains non-arbitrary in the republican sense.[135]

As explained above, proportionality has, of course, always played a pivotal role in EU law (both legislative and judicial) law, and rule-making. The Treaty of Lisbon makes it clear that: 'The Union is founded on the values of respect for human dignity, freedom, democracy, equality, the rule of law and respect for human rights, including the rights of persons belonging to minorities' (Article 2 TEU). But how this is achieved at EU level is trickier. And this is where the role of national courts is both interesting and important.

After all, as Barak makes clear, the development of common law is nothing but the continuous historical process of balancing between competing principles.[136] According to him, proportionality does not lack rationality and it has a sufficiently rigorous criterion, mainly because the alternatives are no better, and there is no universal definition of the core of rights. Hence, put simply, for Barak, proportionality works as a mediator. Most of the critics are united in the view of proportionality as a legislative principle but admit that there are dangers in allowing courts this degree of discretion.[137] But, as David Beatty notes: 'Although it would seem to count in favour of the proportionality principle that it satisfies Dworkin's twin criteria of "fit" and "value" better than any rival theory, some may worry that its empirical and moral claims leave it open to a fundamental, potentially fatal objection.'[138]

In line with such a proposition, Grégoire Webber argues that constitutional rights scholarship should seek to cleanse itself of the burden of the contemporary cult of rights reasoning and aspire to struggle more explicitly with the

[133] Kumm, 'The Turn to Justification' (2018).

[134] Aharon Barak, 'The Role of a Supreme Court in a Democracy and the Fight Against Terrorism' (2005) 35 *Hong Kong Law Journal*, 287–308.

[135] Daly (n 127).

[136] Barak (n 1).

[137] ibid, 483–84, with further references.

[138] Beatty, 'The Ultimate Rule of Law (2005)176; Ronald Dworkin, *Law's Empire* (Oxford, Hart Publishing, 1998).

moral and political reasoning inherent to all rights. What then, if anything, is wrong with proportionality? Webber argues, in line with the global theory put forward by Möller,[139] that, instead of excessively focusing on balancing, one should engage in a sophisticated reading of all the moral values at issue. Proportionality properly understood is then reasoned proportionality.

Clearly, the debate is connected to the classic debate in constitutional theory about the legitimacy of judicial review.[140] It is sometimes stated that the Anglo-Saxon concept of reasonableness review does not suffer from these shortcomings because it does not entail consideration of weight and balance. However, it is often argued that reasonableness is distinct from proportionality review. According to Paul Craig, reasonableness review is concerned with the weight accorded by the primary decision-maker to factors that have been, or can be, deemed to be relevant and whether they are reasonable, so there is balancing here too.[141]

As Yutaka Arai-Takahashi states, the idea of a 'justification-blocking function' of human rights is akin to Dworkin's view of human rights as trumps that can be deployed against policy arguments in legal discourse.[142] He points out that 'Rawls argues that: "Each person possesses an inviolability founded on justice that even the welfare of society as a whole cannot override".'[143] Also, Jürgen Habermas cautions against reducing the idea of human rights to policy arguments, observing that: 'if in cases of collision all reasons can assume the character of policy arguments, then the fire wall erected in legal discourse by a deontological understanding of legal norms and principles collapses.'[144]

Moreover, as noted by Malcolm Thorburn, 'Dworkin and many others have argued that constitutional rights must not be amenable to the balancing of interests. Instead, they must act as firm and impenetrable constraints (variously described as "side constraints" or "trumps" or "shields" or "firewalls") on the ordinary logic of state action.'[145]

The worry is that fundamental rights would be downgraded to the level of policies, sustained or refused by policy arguments, thereby losing their normative power. It has been pointed out that Dworkin describes a principle as 'a standard that is to be observed, not because it will advance or secure an economic, political, or social situation deemed desirable, but because it is a requirement of justice or fairness'.[146]

[139] Möller (n 1).
[140] Webber (n 1).
[141] Craig (n 8).
[142] Yutaka Arai-Takahashi, 'Proportionality' in Dinah Shelton (ed), The Oxford Handbook of International Human Rights Law (Oxford, Oxford University Press, 2013) 446–68.
[143] ibid.
[144] Habermas, *Between Facts and Norms* (1996) 258–59, also discussed in Arai-Takahashi, 'Proportionality' (2013) and in Robert Alexy, *A Theory* (2002) 388.
[145] Thorburn (n 23).
[146] Kai Möller, VU-CELS presentation 16 November 2016, 'Dworkin's Theory of Rights in the Age of Proportionality' (on file with the author).

Furthermore, other commentators, such as Jacob Weinrib, stress the proportionality test has many similarities with Dworkin's appeals to reasoning about the moral complexity of constitutional conflicts and orders them into a sequence of conditions that government must satisfy in order to justify the limitation of a constitutional right.[147] For this reason, he argues that the doctrine of proportionality offers more than the famous 'rights as trumps' thesis offered by Dworkin. He also points out that Dworkin never explicitly discussed the notion of proportionality, and, instead, dismissed limitation clauses on human rights as the product of political compromises.

However, Kai Möller has recently argued that we are mistaken in seeing Dworkin's theory as being in opposition to proportionality; instead, his theory of trumps as rights is largely influenced by the multifaceted function of proportionality.[148] As Möller argues, it is remarkable that Dworkin never seems to have written about proportionality as a doctrine of constitutional law (maybe because it is not used in the US, which is the jurisdiction that he was most familiar with and wrote about regularly).[149] For Möller, we ought to add Dworkin's conception of rights and dignity to these existing attempts to make sense of proportionality as being both related and different from the 'rights as trumps' discussion.[150] In his view, Dworkin's insights should be integrated with the currently dominant, proportionality-oriented discourse about rights.[151] This could be seen as being linked to the Rawlsian conception of the basic structure of society and constitutional essentials, and what reasonable disagreement is among free and equal citizens.

The next section will bring together these insights and connect the proportionality principle to the bigger question of reasonable disagreement. In our context, perhaps this insight results in an obligation, a fiduciary obligation, on the part of the EU and constitutional courts to ensure a right to justification and thereby guarantee a just construction of the AFSJ and engage in argumentation. In the legal context, the question of justification is also one of practice-dependence and the question of 'good enough' justification.

VIII. THE TURN TO JUSTIFICATION: PROPORTIONALITY AS REASONABLE DISAGREEMENT

Political theory concepts such as reasonableness and reciprocity, which are often given loose context-dependent definitions, seem inherently complex.

[147] Weinrib, *Dimensions of Dignity* (2016) ch 6.
[148] Kai Möller, 'Dworkin's Theory of Rights in the Age of Proportionality' (2018) 12 *Law & Ethics of Human Rights*, forthcoming.
[149] ibid.
[150] ibid.
[151] ibid.

As explained in chapter three above, for Rawls, a contractualist conception of justice is based upon a notion of public justification.[152] Again, and as already discussed, according to this view, the use of political power is fully proper only when 'it is exercised in accordance with a constitution the essentials of which all citizens as free and equal may reasonably be expected to endorse in light of the principles and ideals acceptable to their common human reason'. In this view, a well-ordered society is a fair system of social and political co-operation which is effectively regulated by a public conception of justice. But, as argued by Wilfried Hinsch, the requirement of public justification means that the basic norms of a well-ordered society must secure the consent of citizens, whose moral, philosophical and religious views are, at least partially, incompatible. It is, therefore, not inconceivable that no publicly justified political principles can be found. There will always be reasonable disagreement in some areas, and the AFSJ seems likely to belong to such an area due to its sensitive subject matter.

It has been suggested that reasonable disagreement, the lifeblood of ordinary politics, appears to be right at the heart of reasoning about rights.[153] Arguably, the question of the EU's political structure is, deep down, a question concerning the common good and a too security-dominated system goes against this idea. Thus, the justice movement, and the basic right to justification, is readily transferable to the transnational level, since it concerns a political concept of justice. In the EU context, justice must be politically grounded, assuming that we start from a common justice platform where fundamental rights are fully respected in practice. As argued above, it could be argued that it is not possible to separate procedural and substantive justice in EU law so sharply. After all, the debate on justice in EU law arguably concerns how to justify the EU project, and is, therefore, also a question about quality. In addition, and as already mentioned above, applying a Rawlsian account to the theory of justice would, in any case, imply using reasonableness as an adequate standard for measuring legitimacy at EU level and linking it to the broader debate on justice. Proportionality reasoning is then connected not only to the question of the quality of arguments, but also to the question of reasonable disagreement. As noted above, proportionality is a yardstick for legal reasoning that is arguably reflected in the question of justification. So proportionality constitutes an important value in AFSJ law by insisting on a common-sense element in the law. At a more theoretical level, the very notion of proportionality – the question of balance – is about ensuring fairness. Moreover, as is well known, Rawls constructed justice as fairness upon the basis of fundamental ideas that he believed are generally accepted in contemporary liberal democracies.[154] Indeed, 'reasonable disagreement' has become the

[152] John Rawls, *Political Liberalism* (Ithaca NY, Columbia University Press, 1993), discussed in Wilfried Hinsch, 'Justice, Legitimacy, and Constitutional Rights' (2010) 39 *Critical Review of International Social and Political Philosophy* 39–54, and see Wojciech Sadurski, 'Reason of State and Public Reason' (2014) 27 *Ratio Juris* 21–46.

[153] Kumm (n 15).

[154] John Rawls, *Justice as Fairness: A Restatement* (Cambridge MA, Harvard University Press, 2001).

guiding dictum for deciding when something is just and thereby connected to the basic right of justification.

In the legal context, an effective way of dealing with reasonable disagreement is through the proportionality test, which is a legal construction tool. It is also, as Aharon Barak explains, as already noted, a more specific methodological device.[155] The concept of proportionality is made up of four components: proper purpose; rationale connection; necessary means; and a proper relation between the rationale gained by realising the proper purpose and the harm caused to the constitutional right.[156] The core message is that the limiting law must uphold these four components in order to pass constitutional muster.[157] Yet, as explained above, the AFSJ seems to have been largely excluded from this, as the preventive approach has outweighed other values, such as, most prominently, the basics of due process and the full package of defence rights for those accused of terrorism and other security-related offences.

IX. PROPORTIONALITY AND JUSTICE AS A FORCE FOR GOOD AFSJ STRUCTURE?

One important reason for appreciating the legal principle of proportionality – as noted above – is the right to justification. Another reason is to accept that, despite its flaws, it is inherent in any court-based system and thereby better than the alternative of no check at all. Furthermore, Vicki Jackson argues that proportionality, in the US constitutional context, serves an important function for ensuring good governance.[158]

Hence, as explained above, Kumm has tied the discussion on proportionality to the right to justification and the democratic question in human rights law.[159] Another reason is its identity-building function. By requiring the EU to think through its AFSJ vision and to guarantee its citizens a right to good governance (eg, Article 41, The Charter of Fundamental Rights), justice serves not only a political function but also provides a legal method. This appears particularly important in the flexibility scenario, as mentioned above, where an individual could be deprived of his or her basic legal rights depending on what Member State he or she is located in and where the Charter will serve the function as a balancing mechanism for ensuring a high AFSJ standard through the Union. The debate on the future of AFSJ law begs the fundamental – yet difficult – question of what exactly is Europe's *raison d'être* with regard to the AFSJ? While this question remains largely unanswered, the commitment to consistency

[155] Barak (n 1).
[156] ibid.
[157] ibid, 131.
[158] Jackson (n 5).
[159] Kumm (n 120).

between the EU's pursuit of justice is often considered to be a paramount concern in the European process.

As has hopefully been shown in the previous chapters, serious attention to justice as a critical legal concept could add democratic credibility to the AFSJ by reading it as a basic right of justification which safeguards due process rights and helps the EU to achieve its agenda in this policy field successfully. Its usefulness thus lies in its potential to place the individual at the centre of the stage and by requiring a sufficiently coherent system which guarantees adequate human rights protection in an area where it is most needed.

Accordingly, applying a Rawlsian account to the question of proportionality would imply using reasonableness as an adequate standard for measuring legitimacy at EU level.[160] Regardless of whether one agrees with all the technicalities in Rawls' argument and the question of public reason, this chapter looks at the practical legal implications of a right to justification – in terms of public reason – in a legal context.

But does dignity decide the ambit of proportionality? For Dworkin, human dignity is an organising idea, as it brings ethical principles under the one roof of human dignity.[161] For Avishai Margalit, dignity is what it means to have a decent society. Limiting the dignity of a person leads to his or her humiliation. Barak, in turn, has emphasised the multifaceted structure of dignity. As Barak points out, most constitutional rights are relative and may be limited. Yet, in determining the proportionality of the limiting right, the constitutional value of human dignity plays an important role.[162]

Human dignity is also a value in European law. Both the margin of appreciation test and the proportionality test will always operate within the ambit of the constitutional value of dignity.[163] The idea of due process, then broadly painted, is an innate right to dignity, which is institutionalised.

As just mentioned and is worth repeating, human dignity is a value in European law. Both the margin of appreciation test, concerning what national discretion states have when implementing convention rights, and the proportionality test will always operate within the ambit of the constitutional value of dignity.[164] The value of dignity is always at the heart of any discussions of what forms the constitutional law process. For example, the criminal law process seeks to guarantee justice and fairness and dignity is an umbrella concept in this regard.

Dignity is also central to Rainer Forst's theory on the right to justification, justice allows individuals equality and the right to justification for any decisions

[160] Rawls, *Justice as Fairness* (2001).

[161] Ronald Dworkin, *Justice for Hedgehogs* (Cambridge MA, Harvard University Press, 2011).

[162] Aharon Barak, *Human Dignity: The Constitutional Value and the Constitutional Right* (Cambridge, Cambridge University Press, 2015) 112–13.

[163] ibid. See, also, the contributions in Christopher McCrudden (ed), *Understanding Human Dignity* (Oxford, Oxford University Press, 2013).

[164] ibid.

that concern them and form part of the very idea of human dignity.[165] This appears once again similar to the debate in legal discourse on proportionality: both suggest that there can be no simple formula, but that what is required is a multifaceted understanding of justification. According to some scholars, such as Yasmin Dawood, courts could use a reasonable person standard in order to assess the appearance of domination from an objective perspective.[166] Though, as Alexy noted, and as mentioned above, the reasonableness test is more of an absurdity test than a proportionality test proper. Dawood replies to her critics by arguing that we need to be legitimately concerned that what appears to be dominating to one person may not appear to be dominating to another. Moreover, she argues that the anti-domination approach could be applied more generally to other concrete problems in the judicial oversight of democratic politics.

This seems to be captured by the proportionality test in constitutional law and by the right to justification, which focuses on avoiding arbitrariness.

X. CONCLUSION: NON-DOMINATION UTILISED THROUGH PROPORTIONALITY?

This chapter has sought to provide an overview of the landscape of proportionality in EU law and its wider implications for the discussion on the theory of balancing in the AFSJ. It has been necessarily open-ended and aimed at introducing the reader to the complex issues under consideration in this book. Specifically, it acknowledged the vague and contested meaning of proportionality, but pointed to its function as a principle for ensuring that EU law is applied in a just way. In addition, it has opened up the debate on just what proportionality and justification mean, why it has been given so much importance in mainstream EU law, and why it ought to be applied in the AFSJ.

It could then be asked whether non-domination is utilised in law through a proportionality test.

The question of common European solidarity (or culture) is a very relevant one for the mission of establishing a common security area. But how can this be done in the EU's emergency-driven security legislation, which is driven by political considerations rather than legal concerns? As Kumm points out, the question of politics is the practice of rights-based justice-seeking through a constitutional framework (among free and equal people) under conditions of reasonable disagreement.[167] It seems to me that the impact of rights-based proportionality in the EU security-regulated context and the notion of solidarity in the

[165] Forst (n 2).

[166] Yasmin Dawood, 'The Antidomination Model and the Judicial Oversight of Democracy' (2008) 96 *The Georgetown Law Journal* 1411–85, with further references.

[167] Kumm (n 16).

EU could play a significant function in the formation of the AFSJ. For Barak and as also noted in chapter two, proportionality links up with the question of justice because 'There is always law (domestic or international) according to which the state must act. There are no black-holes'.[168] To repeat: the EU, however, is not a state. But, while, in the EU, there currently seems to be a lot of vacuum in the debate, the principle of proportionality allows for some stability, a rescuer until the real work of legislation and deliberation begins, and this seems particularly important in criminal law and security regulation in order to avoid a ticking bomb of state violence against the individual. Hence, the merits of proportionality outweigh its downsides, as it could help improve the democratic shortcomings in the AFSJ and secure rights where the legislator has failed to do so, assuming that we agree that this is what a democratic system should do.[169] It seems to be close to the heart of any EU constitutional scholar to think that the principle of proportionality, understood critically, offers the best available constitutional solution for establishing the idea of solidarity as a workable legal principle through the key of proportionality reasoning.

Finally, for republicans, and to connect to chapter two above, non-dominating interference must pursue a legitimate aim connected to a common public good, and this concern is captured, at least in part, in the existing methodologies of constitutional and human rights courts.[170] As discussed above, in some variants, at least, the proportionality test will effectively require judges to make substantive, evaluations of the various claims and that this implicates judges in a more far-reaching normative endeavour which goes beyond an assessment as to arbitrariness in its republican sense.[171] In turn, this makes rights-based constitutional adjudication quite consistent with a political concept of rights, and accommodating of the fact of disagreement about rights.[172]

The next chapter will test the normative reasoning and doctrinal points as outlined in the previous chapters and look at both the EU fight against terrorism and the migration crisis by exploring the right to justification further.

[168] Barak, 'Role of a Supreme Court' (2005).
[169] Kumm, Socratic Contestation (2010).
[170] Daly (n 127).
[171] ibid.
[172] ibid.

Part III

5

The Right to Justification, Territoriality and Migration, Refugees and Terrorism

I. INTRODUCTION

THIS CHAPTER AIMS to adopt a more hands-on approach and thereby seeks to concretise some of the rather abstract findings in the previous chapters. It scrutinises two areas – highly dynamic fields – of particular importance: the EU's response to the refugee and migration crisis; and the ongoing EU fight against terrorism, both of which represent crisis-driven and emergency-related legislation. The preceding chapters in this book have tried to discuss the broad question as to what, if any, justification the EU offer its citizens and those entering its territory in submitting them to its current forms of regulation. The chapters have also discussed the implications of a non-domination test for understanding justice within the AFSJ. Specifically, chapter four looked at the link between justice and justification and how it could be identified in the legal proportionality principle as an institutionalised way of gauging both reasons and the assessment as to what should be deemed to be 'good enough' justification. However, as cautiously touched upon above, the idea of justification tests, perhaps, the question as to why the EU needs to offer a justification in the first place. Could one reasonably claim that this right to justification merely amounts to 'a right to due process and to be treated fairly'? The question would seem to be highly relevant, as, increasingly, the EU invokes criminal sanctions as a preventive strategy in dealing with migrants, who are put into detention as part of the securitisation of the AFSJ as discussed below.

This chapter combines the normative approach to constitutionalism with a more descriptive approach. There are good reasons for doing this, as AFSJ law is being designed by a number of policy developments and empirical dimensions but still has a clear lack of normative discussion about the shaping of security law for Europe. While the preceding chapters have intended to provide an in-depth analysis of the impact of non-domination reasoning for understanding justice within the AFSJ, as well as the implications of a right to justification, this chapter turns to the practices of a right to justification, and seeks to elucidate these questions further by explaining how justice seen as non-domination works here in concrete empirical examples. The concrete examples of legislative action will serve to illustrate to what extent there is an intrinsic value of constitutionalism within the AFSJ and the implications of a conception of justice which fully integrates the Treaty values of justice and fundamental rights protection into legal practice.

The chapter is structured as follows. First, the main problems and questions with regard to EU security regulation are discussed. I call this the status quo of security in AFSJ law. Next, the chapter focuses on two case studies, zooming in on both the migration crisis and the fight against terrorism respectively, and testing the impact of a right to justification. The chapter begins by discussing the migration crisis that started to become increasingly serious from 2015 onwards. Thereafter, it moves on to scrutinise the fight against terrorism, and security pitted against justice. In testing the propositions outlined in this project on the meaning of non-domination and a right to justification, the book turns to the two areas as useful testing grounds for the implications of constitutional justice in the AFSJ.

A. Status Quo and Security

The security threat in Europe is so severe that the threat of terrorism has been described as the new normal. Kaarlo Tuori has argued that the emergency vocabulary that took shape in the wake of the terrorist attacks in the USA on 11 September 2001 (9/11) was always discussed in terms of security regulation in the EU context.[1] It is true that security has largely shaped the formation of the AFSJ, and, as I have previously argued, that (in-)security became part of the EU *acquis communitaire*.[2] In addition, the AFSJ is defined by a need to ensure a high level of security, as is stipulated in Article 67 TFEU. Thus, in the EU context, the vocabulary has focused more on risk regulation than on emergency regulation, although, admittedly, the two are very difficult to separate.

What, precisely, are the implications of a right to justification with regard to the construction of the AFSJ as a justice space, when we are discussing humanitarian questions such as the ongoing migration crisis? Although some have disputed whether this really was a crisis, it nonetheless represents unprecedented challenges to some of the EU Member States on how to integrate a huge influx of asylum-seekers and other categories of migrants. Is it even legitimate that the EU sets out to establish the AFSJ with an emphasis on justice within the

[1] Kaarlo Tuori, 'A European Security Constitution?' in David Jenkins, Amanda Jacobsen and Anders Henriksen (eds), *The Long Decade: How 9/11 Changed the Law* (Oxford, Oxford University Press, 2014) 103–19.

[2] Ester Herlin-Karnell, 'The Development of EU Precautionary Criminalization' (2011) 2 *European Criminal Law Review* 149–69. Ester Herlin-Karnell, *The Constitutional Dimension of European Criminal Law* (Oxford, Hart Publishing, 2012).

EU territory? What does it tell us about the EU's obligations towards outsiders?[3] While these questions are indeed huge issues, both practically and philosophically, they still need to form the backbone of what we are discussing in the AFSJ. Should we accept a cosmopolitan claim of a duty of justice towards outsiders?[4] While (and as mentioned in chapter one) it would seem politically utopian to claim cosmopolitan-based justice when some 'old' Member States still have problems with the 'new' Member States, the conception of justice could still inform the European Treaty-based interpretation of what it means to refer to solidarity. Increasingly, the EU and its Member States invoke criminal sanctions as a preventive strategy in dealing with migrants, who are placed in detention as part of the securitisation of the AFSJ.[5]

Yet the EU itself does not have an emergency provision; instead, it has the public security derogations within the internal market framework (eg, Article 36 TFEU) while national security is a competence for the Member States (Article 4 TEU). The ECHR emergency provision, Article 15, allows state signatories to derogate from their human-rights obligations under states of emergency. A core set of the Convention's provisions is, however not derogable, and are absolute, such as the right to life, and the right not to be subjected to torture. These days it is not only the threat of terrorism but also unauthorised migration and cross-border travel that are perceived as security risks to mainland Europe. As explained in chapter one, while the EU was, in the early days, an economic endeavour to unite Europe through co-operation and trade as a mechanism designed to prevent the possibility of another war on the continent, it rapidly became a lot more ambitious than merely limiting itself to regulating free movement and economics.[6] To date, it has evolved as an enterprise of risk regulation, one which has been largely influenced and shaped by the administrative practices and market-construction ambitions of the EU.[7] While security is predominantly a national competence (Article 4 TEU, which states that national security remains the responsibility of each Member State), the EU has, in fact, adopted a number of security measures that severely blurs the distinction

[3] Ian Ward, 'Identifying the European Other' (2002) 14 *International Journal of Refugee Law*, 219–37, 221.

[4] On cosmopolitan law, see, for example, Mattias Kumm, 'The Cosmopolitan Turn in Constitutionalism: An Integrated Conception of Public Law' (2013) 20 *Indiana Journal of Global Legal Studies* 605–28, and Alexander Somek, *The Cosmopolitan Constitution* (Oxford, Oxford University Press, 2014). See, also, Ulrike Beck and Edgar Grande, *Cosmopolitan Europe* (Cambridge, Cambridge University Press, 2007).

[5] See eg Daniel Wilsher, Immigration Detention, Law History Politics (Cambridge, Cambridge University Press 2012) 171–206.

[6] See, for example, from a legal perspective, the introductory chapters in Paul Craig and Gráinne de Búrca (eds), The Evolution of EU Law, 2nd edn (Oxford, Oxford University Press, 2011) and Robert Schütze, From Dual to Cooperative Federalism: *The Changing Structure of European Law* (Oxford, Oxford University Press, 2013).

[7] See Stephen Weatherill, *Law and Values in the European Union* (Oxford, Oxford University Press, 2016).

between the EU and national security, and even global security.[8] Consequently, the EU is currently facing numerous interrelated challenges, and needs to deal with a broad range of issues ranging from how to tackle the growing national populism movements, ie, the emergence and rise of anti-EU parties, and the concomitant associated fears of disintegration, to European citizens joining terror organisations outside Europe's borders, which poses yet another terrorist threat for the EU to deal with. The European Agenda on Migration 2015[9] focuses on solidarity and humanity as the key words here. The Agenda makes it clear, among other things, that the EU should fight criminal smuggling networks. It is stated that the EU has a duty to contribute its share in helping displaced persons in clear need of international protection, and that smugglers already ought to be criminalised before they reach the shores of Europe. This duty for the Member States is framed in the solidarity and multilateral action of the EU, rather than individual Member State action. In addition, the EU Security Agenda in 2015 sets out the actions necessary to deliver a high level of internal security in the EU. It is stated that the AFSJ must be a shared agenda.[10] Its successful implementation depends on the political commitment of all the actors concerned to do more and to work better together. The Security Agenda does not deal with the classic EU law idea of subsidiarity, ie, local level first, but instead highlights the importance of solidarity and the need for joint action when fighting terrorism and other transboundary crimes.

As also outlined in chapter one, the AFSJ is, in itself, a very broadly defined field of law dealing with a wide EU policy area that ranges from security and criminal law to border control and civil law co-operation. Although the AFSJ is identified as one policy area, it is quite obvious that the task of identifying the underlying values in this divergent area and how these values drive the development of an AFSJ is of paramount importance in which the concept of justice ought to guide the EU as a constitutional compass. Before exploring these two empirical areas of AFSJ security regulation in further detail, let me say something briefly about the idea of a decent society and what the implications are for the question of border controls. The idea of a decent society, it seems, is connected to what Kant saw as the civil condition and the need to leave the state of nature.[11] The civil condition as a possible right to freedom is now widely

[8] Directive 2017/541 on combating terrorism, and replacing Council Framework Decision 2002/475/JHA and amending Council Decision 2005/671/JHA. See, also, Directive of the European Parliament and of the Council on the Prevention of the Use of the Financial System for the Purpose of Money Laundering and Terrorist Financing, Directive (EU) 2015/849, Directive 2013/40/EU, L 218/8 Directive on attacks against information systems.

[9] European Agenda on Migration, COM(2015) 240 final.

[10] COM(2015) 185 final, The European Agenda on Security (see, also, the EU Global Strategy, available at: https://eeas.europa.eu/archives/docs/top_stories/pdf/eugs_review_web.pdf.

[11] Claudio Corradetti, 'Constructivism in Cosmopolitan Law: Kant's Right to Visit' (2017) 6 *Global Constitutionalism* 412–41.

recognised as basic to Kant's position in the Doctrine of Right.[12] Central for Kant is the requirement of a rightful condition.[13] As Arthur Ripstein explains, for Kant, the citizens of a state are governed by the public right of the state. People who are not citizens are governed by a 'cosmopolitan right'. However, for Kant, the cosmopolitan right amounts to a right to visit, and citizens who get to another state must take account of its status as a rightful condition.[14] As Ripstein elucidates, the idea of the rightful condition is the idea of the original contract, that is, to make its institutions through law, in which no private person is subject to the determining choice of another.[15] Central to this idea is the idea of freedom (or independence, as Ripstein uses) as non-domination, as discussed in chapter two above.

II. THE DECENT SOCIETY AND ITS BORDERS: SOME KEY DEBATES EXPLORED

The debate about the construction of the European AFSJ is, deep down, also a question about the contours of a just and decent society. As this book has attempted to argue in the preceding chapters, non-domination seen as justice has important implications for how we understand the AFSJ. As Avishai Margalit argues, a decent society is a just society both to its members and its non-members.[16] It is a society that treats humans as humans, without humiliating them, and a society where dignity is the core.[17] Moreover, Margalit claims, while the ideals of a decent and a just society are optimistic ones, in that they describe a situation that is better than the existing one, being optimistic about the ideal does not necessarily mean being optimistic about its realisation. Instead, vital to an understanding of this is sensibility.[18] As I understand him, he also argues that the debate on ideal or non-ideal is not very fruitful, for what is needed is reasonableness and contextualisation.

In the framework of a decent society and the EU, it is interesting to look at the idea of membership in a society. This section elaborates on the question of inclusion and exclusion in the context of Michael Walzer's theory of membership, and the meaning of both terms in the security context.

[12] Katrin Flikschuh, 'A Regime of Equal Private Freedom? Individual Rights and Public Law in Ripstein's Force and Freedom' in Sari Kisilevsky and Martin J. Stone (eds), *Freedom and Force: Essays on Kant's Legal Philosophy* (Oxford, Hart Publishing, 2017) 55–74.

[13] Arthur Ripstein, *Force and Freedom: Kant's Legal and Political Philosophy* (Cambridge MA, Harvard University Press, 2009) 268.

[14] ibid, 296–97.

[15] Kant sees the states as in a 'state of nature' in relation to each other and treats them as private individuals as against each other.

[16] Avishai Margalit, *The Decent Society* (Cambridge MA, Harvard University Press, 1998).

[17] In the context of criminal law, see Lindsay Farmer, *The Making of Modern Criminal Law: Criminalization and Civil Order* (Oxford, Oxford University Press, 2016) on the civilising process.

[18] ibid, 290.

As Walzer notes, what is at stake when discussing membership and justice is not just the question of sovereignty, of acting in the world, and pursuing national interests: the shaping of a community, in which exclusion and admission are at the core and where the idea of self-determination is not absolute, is also at stake. Instead, self-determination in terms of the consent requirement in international law is, as Kumm argues, contingent on the type of externalities, in which state consent has a different role to play in trade law, human rights, or law relating to the use of force.[19] As Kumm points out, focusing on the conditions under which justice can be established between free and equal persons is the core preoccupation of constitutionalist thinking in the tradition of the French and American Revolutions.[20] But as Hannah Arendt famously stated in *The Origins of Totalitarianism*, the problem and core question was the relationship between the citizen and the human. For her, as long as human rights were grounded in the social contract, there could be no structural commitment to humans per se.[21] The basis for international law instruments is still that of state consent.[22] As Itamar Mann argues, in contemporary law, human-rights law is revealed as a thin, but firm, modicum of legal responsibility towards all other individuals.

All states are required by international law to respect, protect and fulfil the human rights of those subject to their jurisdiction.[23] Moreover, Anna Stilz has argued that territorial jurisdiction is the right to establish or maintain a distinct system of law on part of the Earth's surface and claim resource rights in the said territory. Moreover, states claim the right to control borders and to regulate the movement of people and goods across their territory.[24] So, in the context of territoriality, what is debated is, perhaps, a general right to justice in Kantian cosmopolitan terms, substantiated in a due process right, rather than a right to relocation, as such.

But what justifies the coercive force of a state that someone might encounter at the border? As Ripstein has noted, a cosmopolitan right is a right to be greeted with hospitality, or, more specifically, a right to be treated with 'universal hospitality'. For Kant, everyone has the right to occupy the surface of the Earth, and, since the surface itself is a closed sphere, everyone, ie, all human beings, must put up with being close to one other.[25] As Ripstein states, by restricting the cosmopolitan right to visit, Kant rejected the colonial tendency. But a state

[19] Mattias Kumm, 'Sovereignty and the Right to be Left Alone: Subsidiarity, Justice-sensitive Externalities and the Proper Domain of the Consent Requirement in International Law' (2016) 79 *Law and Contemporary Problems* 239–58.

[20] Mattias Kumm, 'Constitutionalism and the Cosmopolitan State: An Integrated Conception of Public Law' (2013) 20 *Indiana Journal of Global Legal Studies* 605–28.

[21] Discussed in, Itamar Mann, *Humanity at Sea: Maritime Migration and the Foundations of International Law* (Cambridge, Cambridge University Press, 2016), and Ruti Teitel, *Humanity's Law* (Oxford, Oxford University Press, 2011).

[22] Teitel, ibid.

[23] Kumm, 'Sovereignty and the Right to be Left Alone' (2016).

[24] Anna Stiltz, 'Nations, States and Territory' (2011) 121 *Ethics* 572–601.

[25] Ripstein, *Force and Freedom* (2009) 296.

can only turn a visitor away if it can do so without destroying him or her. If you have no other place to go, any power exercised over you must be consistent with your innate right of humanity in which the right to refuge is a right either of or to world citizenship.[26] Furthermore, the right to be your own master, which embodies the Kantian idea of an innate right to humanity, is elaborated by Ripstein.[27] As he explains, the conception of an innate right is a system of equal freedom and shows how coercion, like domination, is a hindrance to freedom. Kant's account identifies a right with a restriction on the conduct of others 'under universal law'.[28]

Moreover, as Kumm stresses, the claim to sovereignty over territory by 'We the People' can be and has been analogised to the right to property over land by individuals.[29] As he notes, outsiders have a right not to be unjustly harmed by a state, but those governing themselves within the framework of a state have a right not to be required to make themselves a mere instrument of the well-being of others. A state is under a positive duty to ensure that there are no dangers or harm emanating from its territory. Justice concerns, as Kumm argues, are not merely raised by negative externalities of state action, but also by omissions that result in the failure to realise positive externalities when the state has a responsibility to act. This could, for example, include a failure to undertake adequate counter-terrorism measures by effectively granting safe harbour to terrorist organisations or failing to crack down on other forms of organised crime with potential cross-border effects.[30]

Famously, for Walzer, there are different spheres of justice linked to a faithful understanding of the wishes of the members of a society.[31] Walzer is often noted as one of the defenders of the state's right to control admissions.[32] In the EU context, the migration crisis and the increased security threat caused by terrorism in the recent years has brought the Schengen border system to a crisis.[33] This new reality begs the question of just what it actually means to refer to a Europe of solidarity and justice. While the idea of open borders may be one of the hallmarks of EU integration, as established by the Schengen Agreement

[26] ibid, 298–99.

[27] Ripstein (n 13); and see Aravind Ganesh, 'Rightful Relations with Distant Strangers: A Kantian Critique of the Law of the European Union in the Wider World' unpublished PhD thesis draft (2018).

[28] ibid, 34–35.

[29] Arthur Ripstein, 'Property and Sovereignty: How to Tell the Difference' (2017) 18 *Theoretical Inquiries in Law* 243–68.

[30] Kumm (n 19) 253.

[31] Michael Walzer, *Spheres of Justice: A Defense of Pluralism and Equality* (Chichester, Wiley-Blackwell, 1983).

[32] See the discussion in Joseph H Carens, *The Ethics of Immigration* (Oxford, Oxford University Press, 2013) 12.

[33] See Regulation No 1987/2006 of the European Parliament and of the Council and Article 46(8) of Council Decision 2007/533/JHA on the establishment, operation and use of the second generation Schengen Information System. In December 2016, the Commission proposed to extend and improve the use of this database by enriching the data it contains with new alert categories. See https://ec.europa.eu/home-affairs/sites/homeaffairs/files/what-we-do/policies/european-agenda-security/20180612_agenda-on-security-factsheet-sis_en.pdf.

of 1985, its future is currently uncertain and hotly debated. The argument for open borders is the idea that the Earth is the common property of all.[34] According to David Miller, a global version of the equal opportunity principle fails to give us a good reason for abandoning controls on immigration. The state's legitimacy depends on its ability to protect the human rights of all those who are present on its territory.[35] As he further notes, the question of whether the jurisdiction of a state includes the right to control the inflow of people is contingent on the argument about self-determination, when it takes a democratic form about deciding on policy choices and when it does not, to the detriment of the human rights of those that it chooses to admit in order to justify the right to close its borders. Miller grounds this in the idea that it gives us the possibility to control membership, and what happens in the political community cannot be required to fuse its citizen body with that of its neighbour(s). With Jeremy Waldron, though, one reason for thinking that a sovereign state needs a justification for excluding outsiders from its territory is that such an exclusion is coercive, and all coercion requires justification.[36]

As Waldron points out, it may seem strange that no one asks whether it is permissible for the sovereign to exclude foreign people.[37] Waldron poses the interesting question of whether the right to exclude pre-supposes a state-based system, or whether it simply pre-supposes a community of people, which also holds for stateless societies.[38] But excluding immigrants amounts to coercion and calls for a special justification. Thus, according to Miller, actual coercion needs to be distinguished from prevention. Specifically, he argues that, if border controls were coercive, they would be hard to justify. Instead, and in the light of the refugee crisis, which started to become serious in 2015, emergency-driven events formed the different categories between different groups of immigrants: refugees; economic migrants; and temporary workers. Miller makes a comparison with the case of burglary: if you prevent someone from entering your home, that person has other options. But if you force or coerce people rather than preventing them, you remove the autonomy and freedom of those people. What those other options are remains somewhat unclear.[39] Miller concludes that the Walzerian position is that only full citizenship to everyone who enters a given society can avoid the risk of domestic tyranny. In this view, when it comes to perceived risks, the majority of the cases are still economic and a burden on society therefore cannot be totally ruled out.[40]

[34] David Miller, *Strangers in our Midst: The Political Philosophy of Immigration* (Cambridge MA, Harvard University Press, 2016) ch 3.

[35] ibid, 61.

[36] Jeremy Waldron, 'Exclusion: Property Analogies in the Immigration Debate' (2017) 18 *Theoretical Inquiries in Law* 469–89.

[37] ibid, 484.

[38] ibid, 485.

[39] Miller, *Strangers in our Midst* (2016) 172–73.

[40] Miller (n 34), also discussed in Mann, *Humanity at Sea* (2016).

For Lea Ypi, justice in immigration must also be seen in the context of justice of emigration. Specifically, she argues that justice in emigration requires limiting the outflow of more productive groups, since it is precisely their exit which will most likely affect the sending societies negatively.[41] If one subscribes to this approach, the question seems ultimately to be a question of global justice and the extent to which states can exclude and to what extent individuals can choose where to live. To date, however, political philosophers have, for the most part, not examined the moral basis for the distinction between citizens and foreigners, even when they have argued that citizens and foreigners are morally equal.

The refugee status is, however, rather straightforward, as defined by the Geneva Convention of 1951: it concerns the well-founded fear of persecution for reasons of race, religion, nationality or membership of a particular social group. But not all interpretations as to who is a refugee are consistent. Specifically, a discussion has emerged as to whether those who are refugees and granted asylum should also be granted full and permanent membership in the receiving society, whereas those who are forced to leave, for example, for economic reasons should be granted temporary residence rights. Yet, it has been argued that the problem is that states, while not merely reflections of the relations of power and the strength of particular interests in society, are nonetheless substantially precisely that.[42] To the extent that individuals engage with any society for the first time through a confrontation with the state, they are more likely to be met with hostility than hospitality.

As Chandran Kukathas points out, citing Rousseau, 'Wherever strangers are rare, they are welcome'.[43] Nothing makes one more hospitable than seldom needing to be. In addressing the right of outsiders, Seyla Benhabib has pleaded for moral universalism with Kant and cosmopolitan federalism. Thus, she does not argue for open borders, but rather for porous borders.[44] Transformations of citizenship, through which rights are extended to individuals by virtue of residency, rather than cultural identity, is a clear indication of a cosmopolitan norm.[45] But, as she says, the Kantian right to universal hospitality is sacrificed on the altar of state interest.[46] For Benhabib, though, crossing borders does not automatically grant citizenship, as democratic people will still have to devise rules of membership at national, sub-national and regional level, and so on. The treatment of outsiders is inexorably connected with the moral conscience as well

[41] Lea Ypi, *Global Justice and Avant-Garde Political Agency* (Oxford, Oxford University Press, 2011) 409.

[42] Chandran Kukathas, 'Are Refugees Special?' in Sarah Fine and Lea Ypi (eds), *Migration in Political Theory: The Ethics of Movement and Membership* (Oxford, Oxford University Press, 2016) 249–68.

[43] ibid.

[44] Seyla Benhabib, *The Right of Others: Aliens, Residents, and Citizens* (Cambridge, Cambridge University Press, 2004).

[45] ibid, 176–77.

[46] ibid.

as the political reflexivity of liberal democracies.[47] Moreover, for her, the crucial point is that a democratic people considers itself to be bound by certain guiding norms and principles, which it appropriates and reinterprets, thus showing itself to be not only the subject of, but also the author of, the laws.[48]

According to Itamar Mann, a central question here is the duty to rescue migrants, which is particularly relevant in the EU context.[49] In the context of migrants fleeing on sea vessels, it is interesting to put it in the context of the law of the sea, where there is a specific duty of rescue at sea.[50] However, it has been suggested that extending such a duty of rescue at sea cannot automatically be extended to refugee emergencies.[51] The question hinges primarily on whether it is possible to translate the abstract morality of rescue in a limited social context into a complex international environment, one in which, arguably, states have no moral principles, but only political, pragmatic interests.[52] The problem is, according to Jean-François Durieux, the 'refugee box', which, according to the Geneva Convention of 1951 points at solidarity rather than duty. Thus, rescue is both admission and burden-sharing in the same breath.[53] For him, a collective duty to rescue offers a more helpful lens than the traditional pathway of development assistance into the impasse in which it struggles to survive.[54]

For David Miller, there is, in principle, no unilateral way of distributing responsibilities that are collectively shared.[55] Precisely because of this difficulty, Kok-Chor Tan has argued that a way of addressing this question is by assigning an imperfect duty by institutionalising the responsibility of states. Tan's argument chiefly concerns humanitarian intervention, and the duty to rescue.[56] An institutionalised vision would then mean the creation of an institutional role or office with its own force to deal with these questions.[57] In many ways, it could be said that the EU has, to a large extent, institutionalised these questions within the EU territory.[58]

Indeed, political and constitutional theory has for a long time been absorbed with the discussion of the question of outsiders and justification in the context of the Kantian idea of a cosmopolitan right that requires those who arrive in the territory of a foreign state to be received without hostility or discrimination. From a practical point of view, one can hardly claim that the EU has effective

[47] ibid, 178.
[48] ibid, 181.
[49] Mann (n 21).
[50] Jean-Francois Durieux, 'The Duty to Rescue Refugees' (2016) 28 *International Journal of Refugee Law* 637–55. See, also, Mann (n 21).
[51] ibid.
[52] ibid.
[53] ibid, 643.
[54] ibid, 655.
[55] David Miller, 'Distributing Responsibility' (2001) 9 *The Journal of Political Philosophy* 453–71.
[56] Kok-Chor Tan, 'Humanitarian Intervention as a Duty' (2015) 7 *Global Responsibility to Protect* 121–41, 134, discussed in Durieux, 'Refugees' (2016).
[57] ibid.
[58] See, for example, Ganesh, 'Rightful Relations with Distant Strangers' (2018).

control of its external borders, so how can it ground jurisdiction? According to the CJEU, border and migration enforcement activities can stretch beyond the actual, territorial border of Member States.[59] Does it mean that the EU asserts universal jurisdiction? More crucially, it asks the question of whether the EU is following a natural conception of human rights or a more positivistic view with regard to the relationship between moral and positive legal obligations.

A. The Right to Justification: Theory and Human Rights

In the context of the normative foundation for human rights, and as briefly mentioned in chapter one above, Allen Buchanan has asked what it would take to produce reliable factual information of the sort that is likely to be relevant for specifying and justifying claims about human rights.[60] Specifically, he asks what justification, if any, there is for having a system of international legal human rights. As Buchanan stresses, the term 'human rights' is sometimes used to refer to the rights of all humans by virtue of their humanity and in ways that do not pre-suppose the existence of the state system. Moreover, there is more than one valid use of the term 'human rights', and, in international human rights practice, it is often used in ways that are captured by the political view.[61] As Andrea Sangiovanni explains, Buchanan represents the legal view, while scholars such as Joseph Raz and Charles Beitz have focused on the political aspect, and John Tasioulas sees human rights as grounded entirely in moral rights.[62] Sangiovanni states that 'human rights are moral rights whose violation makes various forms of international interference permissible that would have otherwise been impermissible.[63]

Yet, as Buchanan emphasises, a system of international legal human rights can also contribute to legitimacy in the sociological sense. If citizens know that, when it comes to the legal claims that they make against their state, the state is not the final arbiter in its own case, this can bolster the belief that the state is legitimate.[64] For Stephen Gardbaum, international human rights law may have an enforcement problem, and perhaps an specification problem, but not a general legitimacy problem.[65] What, then, are the benefits of having a system

[59] *Melki* and *Abdeli*, Joined Cases C-188/10 and C-189/10 (22.06.2010), and *Adil*, Case C-278/12 PPU.

[60] Allen Buchanan, 'Human Rights and the Legitimacy of the International Order' (2008) 14 *Legal Theory* 39–70.

[61] Idem, 'Why International Legal Human Rights?' in Rowan Cruft, S Matthew Liao, and Massimo Renzo (eds), *The Philosophical Foundation of Human Rights* (Oxford, Oxford University Press, 2015) 244–62.

[62] Charles R. Beitz, *The Idea of Human Rights* (Oxford, Oxford University Press, 2009).

[63] Andrea Sangiovanni, 'Human Rights, Interests, and Variation' in Ester Herlin-Karnell and Matthias Klatt (eds), *Constitutionalism Justified* (Oxford, Oxford University Press, forthcoming).

[64] ibid. See, also, Alon Harel, *Why Law Matters* (Oxford, Oxford University Press, 2014).

[65] Stephen Gardbaum, 'Human Rights as International Constitutional Rights' (2008) 19 *European Journal of International Law* 749–68.

of international human rights? Realists like Günter Frankenberg have suggested that:

> On the one hand, the claim of human rights law to neutrality underscores its legitimacy. On the other hand, this very neutrality – based on legal formalization in abstract and universal terms, recognized in court as entitlements, and implemented, and their violations remedied depending on the inherent command – masks the political power at play in legislation and application.[66]

The EU and its Member States have so far mainly used the criminal law model to fight terror,[67] but the administrative law strategy is becoming more common. For example, France instated the state of emergency after the terror attacks in 2015 and 2016, and the UK has similar administrative procedures in place (and for example the discussion on Belmarsh Prison).[68] Specifically, France has, until very recently, had a permanent state of emergency since 2015, and other European countries have also favoured administrative procedures in which detention times can be greatly prolonged, and with cross-over issues with migration law and the question of the criminalisation of immigration ('crimmigration').[69] After the terrorist attacks in Paris on 13 November 2015, the French government declared a formal state of emergency. The emergency regime devolved to the police and other authorities, including the Ministry of the Interior and the Prefects (who represent the state at local level), a broad array of powers, including to search houses day or night, and issue house arrest orders without prior judicial authorisation. The new French counter-terrorism bill is now absorbing the exceptional powers employed under the state of emergency into ordinary law.[70] Suspects may need to wear electronic bracelets as a monitoring measure, and the restrictions can be renewed after six months for up to one year with new or complementary information from the intelligence services.[71] Interestingly, under the criminal law framework, this kind of monitoring is usually not permitted until there is a conviction and a guilty verdict, and the monitoring option would then be a less severe form of punishment for those committing a crime for the first time, for example.[72] By using the

[66] Günter Frankenberg, 'Human Rights and the Belief in a Just World' (2013) 12 *I-CON* 35–60.

[67] See eg Cian C Murphy, *EU Counter-Terrorism: Pre-Emption and the Rule of Law* (Oxford, Hart Publishing, 2012).

[68] *A, K, M, Q & G v HM Treasury* [2007] EWHC 869 (Admin), 24 April 2008. See, for example, Myriam Feinberg, *Sovereignty in the Age of Global Terrorism: The Role of International Organisations* (Leiden, Brill-Nijhoff, 2016).

[69] Jennifer M Chacón, 'Human Trafficking, Immigration Regulation, and Subfederal Criminalization' (2017) 20 *New Criminal Law Review* 96–129, at 129; Andrew Ashworth and Lucia Zedner, *Preventive Justice* (Oxford, Oxford University Press, 2014); David Dyzenhaus, *The Constitution of Law: Legality in a Time of Emergency* (Cambridge, Cambridge University Press, 2006), Kaarlo Tuori, 'Ultima Ratio as a Constitutional Principle' (2013) 3 *Oñati Socio-legal Series* 6–20.

[70] A-S Chassany (2017) 'France: The Permanent State of Emergency', *The Financial Times*, 2 October.

[71] Enregistré à la Présidence de l'Assemblée nationale le 5 juillet 2016, available at: www.assemblee-nationale.fr/14/rap-enq/r3922-t1.asp.

[72] See, for example, the Swedish system, 'villorlig dom, fotboja, etc'.

emergency provisions, the normal criminal law framework is set aside. Interestingly, the new Counter Terrorism Directive at EU level adopted in 2017 mainly uses the criminal law framework and not the administrative one, which would mean that the countries cannot derogate from their obligations to ensure a fair trial, and, in any case, they have to comply with proportionality.[73]

Interestingly, scholars like Michel Rosenfeld distinguish between times of crisis, and times of stress, and the question of political rights. According to him, the most significant nexus between the war on terror and the political concerns the boundary between a state of crisis and the conditions of stress. As he argues, what is needed now is comprehensive pluralism to help steer the enlightenment project in the direction of equal liberty.[74] Rosenfeld does not say what this comprehensive pluralism consists of, just that it requires an understanding of the complexity at stake.

III. MIGRATION ETHICS AND THE AFSJ CHALLENGE

This section will now try to take stock of the situation in Europe by starting from the argument of ethics and immigration, and then zoom in on the European project. As Joseph Carens notes, it is through the granting of citizenship that a modern state recognises someone as a member of the political community.[75] According to Carens, what happens in the country of origin over time should become irrelevant to the question of whether refugees have a right to remain in the place where they have started a new life.[76] However, only relying on non-refoulement (protection against return to a country where a person has reason to fear persecution) places a disproportionate burden on neighbouring states. Thus, Carens argues, freedom of movement contributes to equality of opportunity. Carens thus links his argument for open borders and equality. As he points out, global justice is a matter of achieving global distributive justice and requires a massive transfer of resources from rich to poor states, not open borders. For him, the fact that freedom of movement is subject to various restrictions, does not mean that it is not an important freedom or basic human right.[77] For Carens, essentially, free movement is still an important moral goal. He stresses that, while the open border argument might be utopian and,

[73] Directive 2017/541 on combating terrorism, replacing Council Framework Decision 2002/475/JHA and amending Council Decision 2005/671/JHA.

[74] Michel Rosenfeld, *Law, Justice, Democracy and the Clash of Cultures: A Pluralist Account* (Cambridge, Cambridge University Press, 2011) chs 7–10.

[75] Joseph Carens, The Ethics of Immigration (Oxford, Oxford University Press 2013), 20.

[76] ibid, 205.

[77] Carens uses the example of traffic regulation, where the idea of taking turns of freedom is seen as an overall contribution to freedom as it is a restriction that serves to make competing freedoms compatible. So different freedoms, like the right to private property is constrained by right to freedom of movement and freedom of expression.

as such, an unrealisable aspiration, it removes all justification for complacency and inaction.[78]

Against this background, it is interesting to ask, with Itamar Mann, how exactly members of the social contract fulfil their obligations towards each other in the face of the seemingly infinite number of potential incoming refugees?[79] In the idea that human beings have rights, as initiated by the French and American revolutions, the rights of humans were to be legally secured to their membership in political communities. For Carens, the central question is what justice requires to make the world a just place. Are democratic states acting justly when they exclude? In essence, for Carens, giving states a moral licence to exclude because of self-determination is going too far. He points out that, with Rawls, liberties are always potentially subject to restrictions. For Rawls, a hypothetical risk of a threat is not enough; there has to be a reasonable expectation that damage will occur and this has to be based upon evidence and reasoning that is acceptable to all.[80] For Carens, this means that states could allow a lot more immigration than they currently do. Moreover, he ties the question of open borders to that of global justice. If the differences in living standards are not that great, then people will stay in their country of origin in a world in which the inequality between states has been reduced. The goal of the open borders argument is to challenge complacency in order to make us aware of how routine democratic practices in immigration help to maintain unjust inequality.

How does this open borders argument fit with the more common international law argument of national self-determination? As Liav Orgad explains, self-determination is a human right and essentially a right relating to self-realisation and the autonomy to determine a community's political, social and cultural status.[81] This brings us back to the discussion on membership. Walzer argued that, if states are open, our neighbours will be closed. Each society has a distinctive structure. For him, the human rights encounter should be juxtaposed with sovereignty and its normative basis in the social contract. Moreover, Mann suggests that, by potentially opening the social contract and letting new members in, this sense of responsibility implicates sovereignty, the most fundamental political structure that positive international law recognises. This is what Walzer discussed as the ethics of immigration. We might give our bread, but, in the wake of enormous migration flows, how much bread can we really give?[82]

There are many accounts of human rights and their justification and impact in constitutional law, and while I have only been able to briefly touch upon them, this chapter will now adopt a slightly more hands-on approach and turn to

[78] ibid, 235.

[79] Mann (n 21) 206.

[80] Carens, *Ethics* (2013) 279.

[81] Liav Orgad, *The Cultural Defense of Nations: A Liberal Theory of Majority Rights* (Oxford, Oxford University Press, 2015) 174.

[82] ibid and Mann (n 21). When, during the horrors of the Second World War, massive populations in Europe became stateless, for Hannah Arendt, humans with no effective citizenship had no place in the world.

two areas of particular importance: the migration crisis, and the fight against terrorism.

Let me first turn to the EU migration crisis. The word 'crisis' is used here as it was portrayed in 2015, with the huge influx of refugees and other categories of migrants. In this context, one could argue that discussing the question of justification to outsiders pre-supposes a constitutional environment at the EU meta level. As will be discussed in this chapter, one of the difficulties is the phenomenon of mixed migration and how to distinguish the different categories of migration, as, parallel to smuggled people, the migrants may be refugees seeking protection.

A. The EU Migration and Refugee Crisis and the Notion of Mixed Migration

While the migration and refugee turmoil in Europe has hardly escaped anyone, the EU's strategy for tackling these questions remain undeveloped.[83] What exactly are the implications of a right to justification with regard to the construction of the AFSJ as a justice space when we are discussing humanitarian questions such as the ongoing refugee crisis? Is it even legitimate that the EU sets out to establish an AFSJ within the EU's territory? What does it tell us about the EU's obligations towards outsiders?[84]

While these questions are indeed huge issues, both practically and philosophically, they still need to form the backbone of what we are discussing in the AFSJ. Should we accept a cosmopolitan claim of a duty of justice towards outsiders?[85] While it would seem politically utopian to claim cosmopolitan-based justice, the conception of justice could still inform the European Treaty-based interpretation of what it means to refer to solidarity. As noted above, and, as Ripstein explains, for Kant, a cosmopolitan right is not only a right to be treated without hostility, but also a right to settle anywhere one pleases. Yet, as Ripstein also notes and as mentioned above, for Kant, humans have a right to world citizenship: if they have nowhere to go, no one can be denied their innate humanity.[86]

One challenge of the migration crisis is that of mixed migration. But first we should ask what the phenomenon of mixed migration is, and what are the

[83] See, however, Cathryn Costello, *The Human Rights of Migrants and Refugees in European Law* (Oxford, Oxford University Press, 2016), for a recent account on EU migration law and human rights protection. And see Peter Niesen, "What Kant would have said in the Refugee Crisis", *Danish Yearbook of Philosophy* 50, (2017), 83–106 for a political theory account.

[84] See, in a different context, Ian Ward, 'Identifying the European Other' (2002) 14 *International Journal of Refugee Law* 219–37 at 221.

[85] See, for example, Mattias Kumm, 'The Cosmopolitan Turn in Constitutionalism: An Integrated Conception of Public Law' (2013) 20 *Indiana Journal of Global Legal Studies* 605–28, and Alexander Somek, *The Cosmopolitan Constitution* (Oxford, Oxford University Press, 2014).

[86] Ripstein (n 13).

new challenges that it poses for the European AFSJ project. Mixed flows of people may include undocumented, unauthorised, smuggled, trafficked, or other migrants seeking refuge and asylum.[87] The concept poses numerous questions as to what legal framework is applicable to address this open-textured phenomenon, as well as broader theoretical questions concerning rights and territoriality.

Clearly, the complexity of mixed migration has intensified in the recent and current refugee crises in the EU. Dublin Regulation III[88] sets out to ensure that refugees are sent back to the state in which they entered the EU,[89] but they cannot be sent back to countries where they would or could be subject to persecution (for example) and must be allowed to acquire membership somewhere.[90] In our case, this somewhere for the most needy to call a home is Europe. This claim rests on two incongruent states of affairs: on the one hand, the EU system broadly complies with the principle of non-refoulement according to which 'No Contracting State shall expel or return (refouler) a refugee in any manner whatsoever to the frontiers of territories where his life or freedom would be threatened on account of his race, religion, nationality, membership of a particular social group or political opinion'.[91] On the other hand, however, EU law does grant a general right to refuge, even though such a right is contingent on the Geneva Convention, as Article 18 Charter of Fundamental Rights makes clear. In addition, legal systems that deal with mixed migration and trafficking are challenged by the question of the causal origins that generate the geographical movement in question, alternately framed in terms of objective cause or subjective motive, when attempting to categorise subjects and allocate legal entitlements.

As seen above, contemporary constitutional law has for a long time been absorbed with the discussion of the question of outsiders and justification in the context of the Kantian idea of a cosmopolitan right that requires those who arrive in the territory of a foreign state to be received without hostility or discrimination. Thus, Buchanan stands for a certain cosmopolitan tradition in claiming that the basic idea behind the international legal regime of human rights is to regulate the behaviour of states towards all individuals within their jurisdiction. This, however, is a problem at the regional and global stage if one wants to achieve a universal rights system beyond the state, as is the case in the EU. This may even be extended to a requirement that the EU has expressed and applied in order to accord safety and protection through operations that extend beyond its territory by, for example, the European coastguard (Frontex) outside the shores of Europe. Such externalisation and extension of EU law

[87] See UNHCR, 'Mixed Migration,' available at: www.unhcr.org/pages/4a16aac66.html.

[88] Regulation (EU) No 604/2013.

[89] Regulation (EU) No 604/2013.

[90] Max Cherem, 'Refugee Rights: Against Expanding the Definition of a "Refugee" and Unilateral Protection Elsewhere' (2016) 24 *The Journal of Political Philosophy* 183–205.

[91] www.unhcr.org/en-us/excom/scip/3ae68ccd10/note-non-refoulement-submitted-high-commissioner.html.

would require a compelling discursive construction of the relationship between the EU and the trafficked/migrant/refugee/smuggled person, whereby the relationship enters into force before the person enters the EU space.

As Ayalet Shachar has noted, the EU has in essence authorised border officials responsible for border surveillance and the monitoring of foreign nationals to carry out their activities within an area of 20 kilometers from the border, creating a European variant of the constitution-free zone.[92] Why is this so? Does the EU not have its own constitution and where does it end? In the *Melki* and *Adeli* cases (C-188/10 and 189/10), the Court of Justice was asked whether the French national criminal law code that authorises border controls at the borders with other Member States is contrary to the principle of freedom of movement for persons, as set out in Article 67(2) TFEU, which provides that the EU is to ensure the absence of internal border controls for persons. The Court held that national legislation may not grant a blanket use of policing powers to the police where that legislation does not provide the necessary framework for that power to guarantee that its practical exercise cannot have an effect equivalent to border checks. Perhaps it is that the EU Court seems more interested in constructing a European framework of borders and security within those borders and also curbing national powers than depriving individuals of their rights. In the *Melki* and *Adeli* cases, the Court held that:

> ([P]ara. 75) Article 67(2) TFEU, and Articles 20 and 21 of Regulation No 562/2006, preclude national legislation which grants to the police authorities of the Member State in question the power to check, solely within an area of 20 kilometres from the land border of that State with States party to the CISA [the Convention implementing the Schengen Agreement in 1990], the identity of any person, irrespective of his behaviour and of specific circumstances giving rise to a risk of breach of public order, in order to ascertain whether the obligations laid down by law to hold, carry and produce papers and documents are fulfilled, where that legislation does not provide the necessary framework for that power to guarantee that its practical exercise cannot have an effect equivalent to border checks.

On the other hand, all of the European EU territory must comply with the values set out in the Treaty of Lisbon and the rights of the Charter of Fundamental Rights and the ECHR. The idea of trust in the EU should also mean that the same constitutional values apply in all Member States. And this is connected to what Seyla Benhabib has referred to as 'the right of others' (and, perhaps more broadly, to Hannah Arendt's the 'right to have rights').[93]

It is often said that migrants are often economically driven to seek a home elsewhere, while refugees fleeing war, political persecution or natural disasters are forced to leave their homes. Thomas Pogge, for example, has argued that, from a global justice perspective, there is no good reason to distinguish

[92] Ayelet Shachar, 'New Borders and Citizenship Constellations' (draft conference paper presented at WZB Berlin December 2015 on file with the author).

[93] Benhabib, *The Right of Others* (2004). Citizenship of the EU is also exclusive to the EU territory.

so sharply between someone being imprisoned for his or her beliefs, and someone working in a factory for 16 hours a day under slavery-like conditions.[94] As Max Cherem points out: 'While immigrants and refugee-like outsiders lucky enough to make it to well-off shores would be benefitted by (and have strong interests in) membership in the new state, they are only entitled to have their unfulfilled basic needs met.'[95] In addition, there seems to be no binding duty among other Member States to assist an overburden Member State, and even entering in such a debate has been criticised for mimicking debates about carbon trading and not being sufficiently humanity-centred.[96] The notion of solidarity in the EU should oblige the Member States to act in joint solidarity and provide assistance, but the principle seems to be merely rhetorical and depends very much on political willingness (Article 222 TFEU).

Consider the case of trafficking and smuggling. Much legislative action has taken place globally in the fight against the trafficking of persons, particularly since the entry into force of the Trafficking in Persons Protocol in 2003. The EU has had legislation in place for a long time, first under the former third pillar adopted in 2002 and since the Lisbon Treaty in the form of a Directive adopted in 2011.[97] The Directive was recently evaluated by the EU Commission and is under constant monitoring and updating.[98] The prohibition of trafficking is also listed in the EU Charter of Fundamental Rights as a priority for the EU to combat still.

Specifically, in Article 5 the EU Charter, on the prohibition on trafficking and forced labour, it is stated that:

(1) No one shall be held in slavery or servitude.
(2) No one shall be required to perform forced or compulsory labour.
(3) Trafficking in human beings is prohibited.

In addition, Article 83 TFEU makes it clear that the EU is to adopt criminal measures to fight trafficking in human beings. Specifically, Article 83 singles

[94] Thomas Pogge, 'Migration and Poverty' in Veit Bader (ed), *Citizenship and Exclusion* (Basingstoke, Macmillan, 1997) 12–27.

[95] Benhabib (n 43).

[96] Matthew J Gibney, 'Refugees and Justice between States' (2015) 14 *European Journal of Political Theory* 448–63.

[97] Directive 2011/36/EU of the European Parliament and of the Council of 5 April 2011 on preventing and combating trafficking in human beings and protecting its victims, and replacing Council Framework Decision 2002/629/JHA, OJ L 101/1.

[98] www.unodc.org/documents/data-and-analysis/glotip/Trafficking_in_Persons_2012_web.pdf. The Protocol to Prevent, Suppress and Punish Trafficking in Persons, Especially Women and Children, supplementing the United Nations Convention against Transnational Organized Crime (hereafter referred to as the 'Trafficking in Persons Protocol'), defines trafficking in persons as follows: 'the recruitment, transportation, transfer, harbouring or receipt of persons, by means of the threat or use of force or other forms of coercion, of abduction, of fraud, of deception, of the abuse of power or of a position of vulnerability or of the giving or receiving of payments or benefits to achieve the consent of a person having control over another person, for the purpose of exploitation. Exploitation shall include, at a minimum, the exploitation of the prostitution of others or other forms of sexual exploitation, forced labour or services, slavery or practices similar to slavery, servitude or the removal of organs.'

out terrorism, trafficking in human beings, sexual exploitation of women and children, illicit drug trafficking, illicit arms trafficking, money laundering, corruption, counterfeiting of means of payment, cyber crime and organised crime. These are considered the specific EU crimes with a clear cross-border dimension. In addition, Article 79 TFEU, which states that the Union is to develop a common immigration policy and focuses, inter alia, on enhancing measures to combat illegal immigration and trafficking in human beings. The EU has also published its report entitled, 'Strategy towards the Eradication of Trafficking in Human Beings 2012–2016'.[99] This report refers to the migration agenda and states that there is strong evidence that the migration crisis has been exploited by criminal networks involved in the trafficking in human beings who target the most vulnerable, in particular women and children. While trafficking is inherently wrong and exploits people, with regard to smuggling, on the other hand, even the UN recognises that human smugglers are often the only way for refugees and the destitute to get out of harm's way. Unlike trafficking, commercial human smuggling is defined as 'the procurement, in order to obtain […] a financial or other material benefit of the illegal entry of a person into a State Party of which the person is not a national or a permanent resident'.[100]

While human trafficking and migrant smuggling are two distinct crimes, frequently the two phenomena overlap.[101] The distinction is crucial, however, because of the extended protection offered to the victims of trafficking. But the prevention of and fight against migrant smuggling is, as the EU Commission rightly points out, a complex process, one which is affected by contextual factors, including a high level of economic and social disparity between the EU and several non-EU countries. The EU Commission stresses the difficult co-operation with source and transit countries, and the limited legal migration channels to the EU. In the context of increasing border control in order to prevent irregular migration, many potential migrants turn to organised criminal groups to arrange their border crossings (see the European Migration Agenda 2015).

As the EU policy document points out, smuggled migrants are generally unaware of the risks involved in these transactions and they often become victims of abuse by organised crime syndicates. In addition, the European Agenda on Migration 2015 is instructive as it expressly states that, although migrant smuggling and trafficking are two diverse criminal activities perpetrated by criminal networks, they are also interlinked, since persons who start their journeys in a voluntary manner can also be vulnerable to networks of labour or

[99] The EU Strategy towards the Eradication of Trafficking in Human Beings 2012–2016 available at https://ec.europa.eu/antitrafficking/sites/antitrafficking/files/eu_strategy_towards_the_eradication_of_trafficking_in_human_beings_2012-2016_1.pdf.

[100] Julian F Muller, 'The Ethics of Commercial Human Smuggling' (2018) 17 *European Journal of Political Theory* 1–19.

[101] See for further references and discussion, Ester Herlin-Karnell, 'Understanding Trafficking in Human Beings as Mixed Migration: The European "Area of Freedom, Security and Justice" and its Global Width' in Haverkamp, Herlin-Karnell and Lernestedt (eds), *What is wrong with human trafficking, critical perspectives* (Oxford, Hart, 2018) forthcoming.

sexual exploitation.[102] One of the core criticisms of the EU's action in this area is that policies need to provide a flexible framework to meet the challenges of increasing human mobility. It has been suggested that immigration policies need to devote more attention to the regional and local specificities of the phenomenon and the enforcement of the existing EU human rights acquis. More broadly, it also raises the question about the EU's responsibility to outsiders.

While, for example, the offence of trafficking is difficult to tackle precisely because it involves mixed migration, it is also one with symbolic elements and sets the standard for how we ought to live together in Europe. While the combat of trafficking is dealt through criminal law under the criminal law provisions, trafficking, as part of the illegal immigration framework in EU law, is dealt with through administrative procedures. From this perspective, criminalisation seems to have many benefits compared to the administrative procedure and detention without trial, which seems to signify EU migration procedures at present. Moreover, as Harel interestingly argues, non-domination ought to guide us here when deciding on criminalisation. This seems particularly relevant in the context of the trafficking offence, where the rationale behind criminalisation is to prevent the master–slave relationship between individuals.[103] Dependence renders a person vulnerable to the whims of others; it exposes a person to the potential interference of a dominant agent. As noted above, the trafficking offence is one of the oldest in EU criminal law and has a clear symbolic message which is connected to the EU values and the human rights obligations set out in the EU Charter and embedded in the ECHR. It is also one with a clear expressive dimension of EU values which is why the EU legislator has decided it needs to be legislated at EU level rather than at national level. In addition, it is part of the migration policies. Given this multi-faceted nature of the mixed migration phenomenon, it seems fair to conclude that it is a constitutional right to be treated with dignity.

The point, for our purposes, is that there is a connection between the EU and the national responses to the emergency-driven natures of both the migration crisis and that of terrorism, and the ways to tackle the risks that they pose. In EU Migration Agenda 2015, managing crisis is high on the agenda. As Mann argues, managerialism is an institutionalised attempt to elide deep normative commitments.[104] As he moreover argues, managerialism is a way of avoiding the ethical questions of open or closed borders. He argues that managerialism is a way of detaching the law from the human rights encounter and that leaving people to die on a boat amounts to violence.[105] While I agree with Mann, it is still difficult to explain why this obligation is restricted to the EU territory. Why is there no trusteeship obligation of global justice at large if it is the universality of human rights which matters?

[102] European Agenda on Migration COM(2015) 240 final.

[103] Alon Harel, Why Law Matters (Oxford, Oxford University Press 2014); Philip Pettit, 'A Republican Law of Peoples' (2010) 9 *European Journal of Political Theory* 70–94.

[104] Mann (n 21) 192–93.

[105] ibid.

While this question has no direct answer, the chapter will now turn to the fight against terrorism and look at the security regime in this area, which has largely shaped the contours of the AFSJ.

IV. ANTI-TERRORISM, SECURITY AND PREVENTION

The above-mentioned EU Security Agenda highlights the importance of solidarity and the need for joint action when fighting terrorism and other transboundary crimes. Europe has seen attacks in Paris, Brussels, Nice, London, Manchester, Berlin, Stockholm and Barcelona in recent times. The EU has been active in legislating against terrorism, particularly, since the terror attacks of 9/11, with the adoption of the European Arrest Warrant, which was one of the first instruments in the fight against terrorism and crime in general through the use of mutual recognition. Subsequently, the Madrid bombings in 2004 and the London bombings in 2005 resulted in a framework decision against terrorism, which was translated into a new Directive on the fight against terrorism in 2017.[106] The fight against radicalism is high up on the EU agenda, as stipulated in the EU Security Agenda 2015 mentioned above. As Myriam Feinberg points out, Security Agenda 2015 with its five-year action plan containing 200 individual measures is the most comprehensive security plan adopted by the EU to date.[107] The EU Security Agenda also highlights the importance of solidarity among the Member States in order to support one another when states are attacked, as is also a constitutional duty under Article 222 TFEU.

The recent terror attacks have led to a new European debate on how to tackle the threat of radicalisation and combating terrorism in the most effective way while complying with human rights as set out in the EU Charter of Fundamental rights and the ECHR. The EU is currently negotiating a Directive on the trafficking of firearms and has issued Guidelines on how to fight radicalisation.[108] It has also recently adopted a new Directive on the fight against terrorism, which was adopted in 2017.[109] In short, these accompany the Cybercrime Directive (including terrorism), the Data Transfer Directive, and the

[106] Directive 2017/541 on Combating terrorism and replacing Council Framework Decision 2002/475/JHA, COM(2015) 625 final. See, for example, among many commentators, Feinberg, *Sovereignty* (2016) ch 6, Cian C Murphy, *EU Counter-Terrorism: Pre-Emption and the Rule of Law* (Oxford, Hart Publishing, 2012), Sara Poli, 'The EU External Anti-terrorism Policy in its External AFSJ Policy' in Maria Fletcher, Ester Herlin-Karnell and Claudio Matera (eds), *The EU as an Area of Freedom, Security and Justice* (Abingdon, Routledge, 2016) 389–416, Raphael Bossung, *The Evolution of EU Counter-Terrorism: European Security Policy after 9/11* (Abingdon, Routledge, 2012).

[107] Feinberg (n 67) 89, with further references. The agenda also highlights the importance of the fight against radicalisation.

[108] The European Agenda on Security, COM(2015) 185 final.

[109] Directive 2017/ 541 on Combating terrorism and replacing Council Framework Decision 2002/475/JHA, COM(2015) 625 final.

Money Laundering and Terror Financing Directives, as well as the Terrorist Tracking Directive.[110]

Over the past decade, the internal security mission has gone hand in hand with the development of EU criminal law in particular, while we have also seen the emergence of a European criminal law space, largely built on the virtues of pre-emption and prevention. The prime example of this has been in the EU's fight against money laundering and the financing of terrorism, as well as the more general fight against organised crime.[111] But there are many other examples, too. The recent Directive on the freezing and confiscation of criminal assets is just one of the latest endeavours in the EU's internal security strategy.[112] The notion of cybercrime, and the establishment of a European Cybercrime Centre,[113] is yet another clear example of the elasticity of the security concept in this internal context. Thus, we can see how the EU's security mission is shaping the internal face of criminal justice and what this means for the EU's involvement as a criminal law legislator.

The Regulation on Europol, adopted in 2016, is also instructive. It states (in the preamble) that large-scale criminal and terrorist networks pose a significant threat to the internal security of the Union and to the safety and livelihood of its citizens. The threat assessments show that criminal groups are becoming increasingly poly-criminal and cross-border in their activities. National law enforcement authorities therefore need to co-operate more closely with their counterparts in other Member States. In this context, it is necessary to equip Europol to support Member States better in Union-wide crime prevention, analyses and investigations.[114]

In the light of the EU's promise of establishing an AFSJ, the often one-sided current focus on security appears highly problematical. Nevertheless, the EU's security mission equally follows from the ambitions set out in the Treaty since the EU promises to ensure a high level of security even where there is no clear division between internal and external security. The focus on security, and the

[110] Directive of the European Parliament and of the Council on the Prevention of the Use of the Financial System for the Purpose of Money Laundering and Terrorist Financing, Directive (EU) 2015/849, Directive 2013/40/EU, L 218/8 directive on attacks against information systems.

[111] Directive (EU) 2018/843 of the European Parliament and of the Council of 30 May 2018 amending Directive (EU) 2015/849 on the prevention of the use of the financial system for the purposes of money laundering or terrorist financing. For an overview, see for example Maria Bergström, 'The Many Uses of Anti-Money Laundering Regulation – Over Time and into the Future' (2018) *19 German Law Journal*, 1149–67 and Valsamis Mitsilegas, *Money Laundering Counter-Measures in the EU: A New Paradigm of Security Governance versus Fundamental Legal Principles* (The Hague, Kluwer Law Publishing, 2003).

[112] Directive 2014/42/EU, of the European Parliament and of the Council of 3 April 2014 on the freezing and confiscation of instrumentalities and proceeds of crime in the European Union.

[113] Communication from the Commission to the Council and the EP – Tackling Crime in our Digital Age: Establishing a European Cybercrime Centre, COM (2012) 140 final.

[114] Regulation 2016/794 on the European Union Agency for Law Enforcement Cooperation (Europol) and replacing and repealing Council Decisions 2009/371/JHA, 2009/934/JHA, 2009/935/JHA, 2009/936/JHA and 2009/968/JHA, L135/53.

desire and often obligation to import norms from the global arena in the fight against terrorism and crime, has overshadowed the need to ensure due process rights within the EU.[115] And although the EU is currently improving the situation for suspects by adopting legal safeguards, and the CJEU has from time to time handed down rulings in favour of the individual, it is currently not enough from the AFSJ, which places equal value on all components of freedom, security and justice. Security has functioned as an identity-building power which has largely shaped Europe with regard to security governance.[116]

As Kaarlo Tuori puts it, and as mentioned in chapter one, war and crime, and external and internal security are hard to keep separate in combating terrorism, which leads to the emergence of a security constitution.[117] This is similar to Bruce Ackerman's 'The Emergency Constitution', in which he claimed that we need 'new constitutional concepts' in order to avoid the downward spiral in the protection of civil liberties while we wait for politicians to respond to each new terror attack by enacting laws that become increasingly repressive with each attack.[118] As David Dyzenhaus points out, a crucial part of meeting this test is the demonstration that judges can play a meaningful role in keeping legislatures and governments within the rule of law project. Moreover, judges can play this role both when the legislature and the executive are co-operating and keeping them within the project when the legislature and executive seem to indicate that they wish to avoid control by the rule of law. Similarly, with Aron Barak then (as discussed in chapter four), judicial review is not necessarily undemocratic, but is, in fact, a democratic institution which consists of an extra check, and shows that the legislator has done its job. For Dyzenhaus, if the judges fail to carry out their duty, they also fail to clarify to the people what constitutes responsible government – government in compliance with the rule of law.[119]

A recent policy report by Amnesty International, illuminatingly shows how emergency has become normalised.[120] As noted above, after the attacks in Paris on 13 November 2015, the French government declared a formal state of emergency. The emergency regime granted a broad array of powers, including to search houses day or night and issue assigned residence orders without prior judicial authorisation. The state of emergency was extended on 26 November 2015 for three months, on 26 February 2016 for three months,

[115] The EU is following the international trend, see the Financial Action Task Force, http://www.fatf-gafi.org/. See for a discussion, E. Herlin-Karnell, 'The EU as a Promoter of Values and the European Global Project' (2012) 13 *German Law Journal* 1225.

[116] See, for example, Monica den Boer, 'Preventive Empires: Security Dynamics at Multiple Levels of Governance' (2011) 3 *Amsterdam Law Forum* 102–13.

[117] Tuori'Ultima Ratio' (2013).

[118] Bruce Ackermann, 'The Emergency Constitution' (2004) 113 *Yale Law Journal* 1029–91, discussed in David Dyzenhaus, 'The Constitution of Law' (2006).

[119] Dyzenhaus (n 69).

[120] En register à la Présidence de l'Assemblée nationale le 5 juillet 2017, available at: www.assemblee-nationale.fr/15/ta-commission/r0017-a0.asp.

and on 26 May 2016 for two months.[121] In July 2016, following the attack in Nice, the state of emergency was extended for six months. A new bill providing for the fifth extension of the state of emergency was concluded in the National Assembly in December 2016.[122] And in 2017, as noted above, instead of ending the state of emergency, Emmanuel Macron tabled a new French counter-terrorism bill which absorbs the exceptional powers used under the state of emergency into ordinary law.[123] As was argued in chapter four, there still needs to be a proportionality assessment to administrative procedures. As Wanda Mastor recently asked in the context of the French counter-terrorism strategies: 'What is the criteria for an emergency to become an "absolute" emergency? Perhaps more than any other legislation, the Intelligence Act raises the difficult question of balance between the respect for freedom and safeguarding public order.'[124]

As Myriam Feinberg argues, measures to prevent the movement of terrorists raise questions of burden-sharing and distribution of responsibility between the Member States. It therefore merits a more comprehensive approach, as well as the development of further mechanisms to increase co-operation between Member States.[125] As noted above, in the EU context, it asks interesting questions about a solidarity obligation. It should be recalled that, in the wake of the Paris attack in November 2015, France invoked the solidarity clause Article 222 TFEU. However, France also chose to invoke the mutual assistance clause in Article 42(7) TEU. The latter states that:

> If a Member State is the victim of armed aggression on its territory, the other Member States shall have towards it an obligation of aid and assistance by all the means in their power, in accordance with Article 51 of the United Nations Charter. This shall not prejudice the specific character of the security and defence policy of certain Member States.[126]

As Giovanni Faleg observed, Article 42(7) allowed France to send a strong political signal that Europe stands united against a common threat to its territory and society, especially as it implies a common European response in internal and border security domains in which NATO could not take action. As he also

[121] ibid, available at: www.assemblee-nationale.fr/14/rap-enq/r3922-t1.asp and Chassany, 'France: The Permanent State of Emergency' (2017). For a critical study of France and emergency laws practices, see Pasquale Pasquino, 'Constitutionalizing Emergency Power in a Time of Jihadist Terrorism: France 2016 as a Case of Misunderstanding and Failure' (2018) 19 *German Law Journal* 251–65.

[122] 'Dangerously Disproportionate: The ever Expanding National Security State in Europe', Amnesty International 2017 report.

[123] Chassany (n 70).

[124] Wanda Mastor, 'The French Intelligence Act: "The French Surveillance State?"' (2017) 23 *European Public Law* 707–22.

[125] Myriam Feinberg, 'Terrorism Inside Out: Legislating for Humanity to Cooperate Against Terrorism' (2017) 42 *North Carolina Journal of International Law* 505–43. See, also, Ben Saul, 'Terrorism as a Transnational Crime', Sidney Law School working paper (2014), available at: http://ssrn.com/abstract=2386462.

[126] See discussion in Giovanni Faleg, 'European Security after the Paris Attack', CEPS commentary (2015), available at: www.ceps.eu/system/files/GF%20European%20Security%20after%20Paris.pdf.

observes, the solidarity clause would have activated a wider array of EU instruments, but these require complex inter-institutional co-operation and a longer timeframe for their execution.[127]

A. The Question of Jurisdiction and Recent Security Measures

The extensive reach of the EU Court's jurisdiction, and to slightly move back in legal time, in external security matters was demonstrated in the famous *Kadi* cases. While, in *Kadi I* (Case C-402/05), the Court of Justice famously extended the jurisdiction of the EU to review, albeit indirectly, UN measures, and while this was a ground-breaking development in the context of sanctions, the adoption of the Treaty of Lisbon means that the previous jurisdictional shortcomings have been resolved thanks to a specific legal basis in the Treaty (Article 75 TFEU).[128] In *Kadi II*, the Court of Justice made it clear that the reasoning given by the UN for having listed Kadi as an alleged terrorist were not reasonable as they only contained summary claims (C-584/10 P, C-593/10 P and C-595/10 P). The Court required a more sophisticated way of reasoning. In both Kadi cases, the internal and external security dimension of the EU was blurred. The main difference between the internal and external security agenda is that the AFSJ is subject to the same constitutional framework as the internal market, both within the EU, with ordinary legislative procedure, and within the EU Court's jurisdiction, while the foreign policy area is still largely subject to intergovernmental co-operation. For example, the Court has stated that the argument that it is impossible to distinguish between the combating of internal terrorism, on the one hand, and the combating of external terrorism, on the other, does not matter for the choice of the legal basis or for the scope of Article 215(2) TFEU as the legal basis of a contested regulation. Thus, in *European Parliament v Council*,[129] the Court stressed the political considerations behind the drafting of the Treaty of Lisbon and accepted that, when choosing between legal bases, it is not just the role of the European Parliament and the increased democratic input that are the decisive factors.[130] The Court did not specify what these critical factors entailed, but it seems reasonable to conclude that the choice of sanctions, and thereby also the legal basis, mattered at the political level as much as the effectiveness of the actual enforcement or definition of a sanction. While the *European Parliament v Council* case is one which mainly concerns the dividing line between the internal and the external fight against terrorism, it is also a case which arguably highlights the choice by the legislator to fight terrorism by means of the administrative model and not the criminal

[127] ibid.

[128] For a case commentary, see eg Katja Ziegler, 'Strengthening the rule of law but fragmenting international law: the Kadi decision of the ECJ from the perspective of human rights' (2009) 9 *Human Rights Law Review* 288.

[129] Case C-130/10, *European Parliament v Council*, judgment of 19 July 2012.

[130] Case C-300/89 *Commission v Council* [1991] ECR I-2867.

law model. The new Counter-terrorism Directive as mentioned above, explicitly uses the criminal law framework, while the measures for countering terror financing such as the Anti-Money Laundering Directive and the Directive on the Freezing of Assets rely predominantly on administrative law.

Accordingly, the recently adopted Directive on the Fight against Terrorism states that: 'The objectives of fighting crime and terrorism cannot be sufficiently achieved by EU Member States acting alone, since legislation only at the national level would not have the effect of establishing minimum rules on the definitions of and penalties for terrorist offences applicable throughout the EU.'[131]

The EU reason for the new Directive is consequently that the EU framework for addressing the risks must be synchronised and must incorporate global norms into the EU acquis and corpus. Otherwise, according to the Commission, certain Member States will be party to the international agreements to fight terrorism through the UN, but there would be a possible divergence between the Member States' obligations under EU law and their obligations under international law. According to the EU legislator, the Directive strengthens the EU's legal framework for preventing terrorist attacks by criminalising acts such as receiving training for terrorism and travel for terrorist purposes, as well as organising or facilitating such travel. Hence, it is stated that: 'A comprehensive and sufficiently homogeneous legal framework can therefore be better achieved at the level of the Union. The Union may therefore adopt measures, in accordance with the principle of subsidiarity.'

Other examples of the EU's fight against terrorism include the Money-Laundering Directives, and the Directive on the Freezing of the Proceeds of Crime as mentioned above.[132] The European Commission's Action Plan for Strengthening the Fight against Terrorist Financing of February 2016 highlights the importance of updating the EU's arsenal against terrorism financing.[133] In this legislative instrument, ie the Fifth Money Laundering Directive,[134] the EU justifies its presence on the security scene by a simple reference to Article 67 TFEU and the proclamation that the Union is to provide citizens with a high level of security by both preventing and combating crime. It also states that confiscating criminal assets is increasingly recognised as an important tool in combating organised crime, which is very often transnational in nature and thus needs to be tackled upon a joint basis. According to the Commission, the EU

[131] Directive 2017/541 on combating terrorism, replacing Council Framework Decision 2002/475/JHA and amending Council Decision 2005/671/JHA.

[132] Directive (EU) 2018/843 of the European Parliament and of the Council of 30 May 2018 amending Directive (EU) 2015/849 on the prevention of the use of the financial system for the purposes of money laundering or terrorist financing, OJ L 156, 19.6.2018 43–74. Directive 2014/42/EU of the European Parliament and of the Council of 3 April 2014 on the freezing and confiscation of instrumentalities and proceeds of crime in the European Union.

[133] COM/2016/050 final, Action Plan for strengthening the fight against terrorist financing, www.europarl.europa.eu/legislative-train/theme-area-of-justice-and-fundamental-rights/file-revision-of-the-anti-money-laundering-directive-(aml).

[134] Directive (EU) 2018/843 (n 132).

is better placed than the individual Member States to regulate the freezing and confiscation of criminal assets. This Directive also has its starting-point in the EU's internal security strategy. It is based upon a dual legal basis (Article 82(2) and Article 83 TFEU) and also covers criminal activities not specifically listed in Article 83(1) if those activities are committed by the participants in a criminal organisation, as defined in Framework Decision 2008/841/JHA on the Fight against Organised Crime. This is because it has been suggested that the main achievements of the EU in combating money laundering and terrorism should be sought in the former intergovernmental sphere, while they are also to be found in related areas such as that of the confiscation of criminal proceeds, rather than in the money laundering/terrorism instruments themselves.[135]

The regime for a Terrorist Finance Tracking Programme (TFTP) is a further early example of the EU's internal security agenda in interaction with the external sphere. The TFTP agreement between the European Union and the United States came into force on 1 August 2010.[136] It concerns the transfer and processing of data for purposes of identifying, tracking and pursuing terrorists and their networks. The EU has multiple ties with the international community, not least with the USA, and the TFTP is a central bilateral EU–US agreement in the security domain which was created to address legal concerns arising out of revelations that the CIA was secretly monitoring financial messaging data effectively in the EU territory in order to track terrorism financing.[137] Moreover, in the context of data protection and security regulation, the EU–US Data Protection Umbrella Agreement is one of the key measures in the EU fight against terrorism. The Umbrella Agreement supplements data protection safeguards in existing and future data transfer agreements and national provisions authorising such transfers.[138] In the US framework, the Judicial Redress Act grants non-US

[135] Nicholas Kaye, 'Freezing and Confiscation of Criminal Proceeds' (2006) 77 *Revue Internationale de Droit Penal* 323–31, 326 and Herlin-Karnell, *The Constitutional Dimension of European Criminal Law* (n 2).

[136] EU Commission website is instructive, available at: http://europa.eu/rapid/press-release_IP-17-99_en.htm.

[137] Agreement between the European Union and the United States of America on the processing and transfer of financial messaging data from the European Union to the United States for the purposes of the Terrorist Finance Tracking Programme, 27 July 2010 OJ L 195/5 and Council Decision of 28 June 2010 on the signing on behalf of the Union of the agreement between the European Union and the United States of America on the processing and transfer of financial messaging data from the European Union to the United States for the purposes of the Terrorist Finance Tracking Programme (TFTP) 2010/411/EU 2010 OJ L 195/1. See eg Maria Fletcher and Ester Herlin-Karnell, 'Is there a TransatlanticSecurity Strategy? Area of Freedom, Security and Justice Law and its Global Dimension' in Fletcher, Herlin-Karnell and Matera (eds), *Area of Freedom, Security and Justice* (2016) 417–38. See also the proposal for a Regulation, COM(2017) 352 final, on the European Agency for the operational management of large scale IT systems in the area of freedom, security and justice. See also Mara Wesseling, A European Terrorist Finance System, policy paper 2016, Occasional Paper Royal United Services Institute, available at https://rusi.org/sites/default/files/op_wesseling_an_eu_terrorist_finance_tracking_system.1.pdf.

[138] Umbrella Agreement EU-US, available at: http://europa.eu/rapid/press-release_MEMO-16-4183_en.htm?locale=en. See also Directive (EU) 2016/680 of the European Parliament and of the

citizens certain rights, including a private right of action for alleged privacy violations that occur in the US.[139] Given the increased US–EU co-operation in the fight against crime and terrorism and the recent agreement on judicial redress for EU citizens with regard to data protection in the US, this is constitutionally important for European security co-operation.[140]

To date, EU co-operation has been limited to the right to request data from the providers of international financial messaging services, ie, those services used for effecting transnational financial transactions, including transactions between EU Member States, but do not include financial messaging data related to the Single Euro Payments Area. A further example of the EU's internal security agenda can be found in the EU's fight against cybercrime, as previously mentioned. The recent Directive tackling such threats appears closely linked to the EU's fight against organised crime.[141] The Commission had indicated early on that its intention to create a European Cybercrime Centre was a priority of the Internal Security Strategy.[142] Thus, the new Directive is based upon Article 83(1) TFEU, which covers computer crime in its broad sense.[143] For the past ten years, the EU has made important efforts to develop a framework capable of dealing with cyber security in the EU space.[144] Cyber criminality is emphasised in the Security Agenda 2015 as a particularly important challenge to the EU and the global community. The Agenda states that it requires the competent judicial authorities to rethink the way in which they co-operate within their jurisdiction and the applicable law in order to ensure swifter cross-border access to evidence and information.[145]

Yet another example can be found in the Fourth Money Laundering Directive, which, as mentioned, is already updated to a Fifth Directive.[146] The revision of the current anti-money laundering and counter-financing of terrorism Directive was proposed on 5 July 2016. The revised directive addresses five tasks:

Council of 27 April 2016 on the protection of natural persons with regard to the processing of personal data by competent authorities for the purposes of the prevention, investigation, detection or prosecution of criminal offences or the execution of criminal penalties, and on the free movement of such data, and repealing Council Framework Decision 2008/977/JHA, OJ L 119, 4.5.2016 89–131.

[139] Available at: http://europa.eu/rapid/press-release_MEMO-16-4183_en.htm.

[140] Umbrella Agreement EU-US. http://europa.eu/rapid/press-release_MEMO-16-4183_en.htm?locale=en. Alec Walen, 'Fourth Amendment Rights for Nonresident Aliens' (2016) 16 *German Law Journal* 1131–162, Ian Brown and Douwe Korff, 'Foreign Surveillance: Law and Practice in a Global Digital Environment' (2014) 3 *European Human Rights Law Review* 243–51.

[141] Proposal for a directive on attacks against information systems COM(2010) 517.

[142] The EU Internal Security Strategy in action: five steps towards a more secure Europe, COM(2010) 673 final, 22 November 2010.

[143] Directive 2013/40/EU, L 218/8 directive on attacks against information systems and repealing Council Framework Decision 2005/222/JHA.

[144] For example, Directive 2013/40/EU, on attacks against information systems.

[145] The European Agenda on Security, COM(2015) 185 final at p 19.

[146] www.europarl.europa.eu/legislative-train/theme-area-of-justice-and-fundamental-rights/file-revision-of-the-anti-money-laundering-directive-(aml), see Directive 2018/843 of the European Parliament and of the Council of 30 May 2018 on the prevention of the use of the financial system for the purposes of money laundering or terrorist financing.

(i) ensuring a high level of safeguards for financial flows from high-risk third countries; (ii) enhancing the powers of EU Financial Intelligence Units and facilitating their co-operation; (iii) ensuring centralised national bank and payment account registers or central data-retrieval systems in all Member States; (iv) tackling terrorist financing risks linked to virtual currencies; and (v) tackling risks linked to anonymous pre-paid instruments (eg, pre-paid cards).[147] The revision is part of a Commission action plan against terrorist financing, which was announced in February 2016. In Article 9 of the recently adopted Directive against Terrorism,[148] travelling for the purpose of terrorism is criminalised. Each Member State is to take the necessary measures to ensure that travelling to a country for the purpose of committing, or contributing to the commission of, a terrorist offence, is punished.[149] The Directive defines the term 'terrorist group' as meaning a structured group of more than two persons, established for a period of time and acting in concert to commit terrorist offences; 'structured group' means a group that is not randomly formed for the immediate commission of an offence and which does not need to have formally defined roles for its members. The Counter Terrorism Directive prescribes in its preamble (recital 13) that illicit trade in firearms, oil, drugs, cigarettes, counterfeit goods and cultural objects, as well as trafficking in human beings, racketeering and extortion have become lucrative ways for terrorist groups to obtain funding, and that the increasing links between organised crime and terrorist groups constitute a growing security threat to the Union and should therefore be taken into account by the authorities of the Member States involved in criminal proceedings. The Directive is cross-referenced to the Fourth Money Laundering Directive.[150] The Directive also says that attempts to travel for the purpose of terrorism, to provide training for terrorism and to recruit for terrorism should be punishable.[151]

A real test case for testing the right to justification can be found in the area of adjudication in the emergency context. The next section will offer a short glimpse of what David Scharia has dubbed 'security in real time', drawing on the Israeli system and its emergency legislation from 1948. Emergency and security contexts, such as the fight against terrorism, pose difficult questions.

V. ADJUDICATION AND SECURITY IN REAL TIME

David Scharia has recently suggested that, when a country is in crisis or under threat to its national security, a judiciary can be satisfied with a determination

[147] ibid.

[148] Directive 2017/541 on combating terrorism and replacing Council Framework Decision 2002/475/JHA and amending Council Decision 2005/671/JHA, OJ L 88, 31.3.2017 6–21.

[149] On 7 March 2017, the Council adopted the directive on combating terrorism.

[150] Directive (EU) 2015/849.

[151] On 7 March 2017, the Council adopted a directive on combating terrorism.

of the constitutionality of a law but can – and arguably should – also go further than that.[152] According to Scharia, the way that the judiciary can go further is by engaging in a dialogue in which the courts can propose solutions that may be applied within a relatively short timeframe without its judgment necessarily leading to a security vacuum in the country, if interim decisions are used. For Scharia, what is important is the techniques adopted, in this case by the Supreme Court of Israel, and used to convey its disapproval of practices.[153] In the framework of real-time scenarios and the otherwise slow working of the judiciary, interim decisions in emergency situations have proved to be crucial in anti-terrorism law and armed conflict. As Scharia puts it, the Court obliges the other branches to appear before the Court and accepts its institutional superiority, even during times of actual combat.[154]

Specifically, Scharia focuses on an important strategy when the judiciary communicates with the military and law enforcement: to wit, signalling. Signalling is how the Court expresses its position on the constitutionality of certain laws or their legality without giving a formal, binding decision.[155] Yet, these kinds of advisory message, no matter how efficient they be, cannot replace clear and binding decisions. Where human rights suffer serious infringement and the Court does not make a statement in a clear and binding way, not only are the rights infringed but the Court is harmed as well, along with the infringement. What Scharia means is that the legitimacy of the Court is harmed. As he points out, even those who completely question the use of advisory dialogue must recognise that, when other systems are not functioning, the Supreme Court may be the final barrier to protect the state from a serious infringement of human rights in times of crisis.[156] Moreover, he argues that advisory messages, particularly in the area of case law, could help courts and society in enhancing the rule of law in times of crisis and high levels of uncertainty.

Could national courts in the EU use this kind of method? While the EU has its own urgent preliminary ruling system (Article 267 TFEU states that if a question is raised in a case pending before a court or a tribunal of a Member State with regard to a person in custody, the Court shall act with the minimum of delay), the way that national courts deal with emergency in cases of EU terrorism seems a largely unexplored question and still very important considering, inter alia, the French case as mentioned earlier. One problem as discussed above is the increased use of administrative measures where real-time decisions are

[152] David Scharia, *Judicial Review of National Security* (Oxford, Oxford University Press, 2015) 91.

[153] *Public Committee Against Torture in Israel v The General Security Service et al* (5 May 1998, January) http://elyon1.court.gov.il/Files_ENG/94/000/051/A09/94051000.A09.htm; *Public Committee against Torture in Israel v The Government of Israel et al* (11 December 2005), available at: http://elyon1.court.gov.il/Files_ENG/02/690/007/A34/02007690.A34.HTM.

[154] Scharia, *Judicial Review* (2015) 233.

[155] ibid, 81.

[156] ibid, 242, also fn 6 citing Cass Sunstein, *One Case at a Time: Judicial Minimalism on the Supreme Court* (Cambridge MA, Harvard University Press, 2001) 46.

often not made by Courts but law enforcement officers. Other issues include the outsourcing of responsibility to EU agencies and the obligations to ask a court, and the individual's right to judicial review of decisions made, which are often unclear, as well as the question of who the actual legislator is.

This chapter will now briefly address the question of security and emergency regulation in the context of the growing impact of agencies in AFSJ legislation. Hence, this last section will tentatively address some of the key challenges facing the EU with regard to the function of EU agencies in this area and which are considerably less dramatic as compared to the real time security scenarios.

VI. AGENCIES AND THE ACCOUNTABILITY DEFICIT

Agencies are important players in the AFSJ, and are often said to represent a step in the direction of better regulation in EU law.[157] In the AFSJ context, EU agencies as actors include: Europol, Eurojust, the European Border and Coastguard agency (Frontex), the European Police College, the European Asylum Office, and the EU Agency for large-scale IT-Systems within the AFSJ.[158]

The exact positioning of these agencies in the legislative context and their place in the AFSJ machinery are, however, unclear. Areas such as medical authorisation, electricity regulation, and health regulation have all been reformed in recent years and offer examples of hybrid governance in terms of combining traditional EU legal instruments with network models relying on agencies and new forms of governance, such as Comitology and the Open Method of Co-ordination. This is all new, however, in the AFSJ. Although this chapter does not delve into this complex debate, the technocratic approaches clearly pose difficulties from a democratic perspective, given that many issues, including medical regulation, touch upon ethical issues that require democratic legitimation and accountability.[159] Nevertheless, the prospect of adopting a technocratic model for the AFSJ with regard to criminal law should raise concern. This complex interaction of the AFSJ policies and the financial regulation at the heart of the internal market is intensified by the fact that the European Banking Authority has been asked to carry out an assessment of the money-laundering and terrorist-financing risks facing the EU.

Moreover, while the AFSJ agencies of Europol and Eurojust do not have direct regulatory enforcement powers, they are increasingly important players

[157] See Frank Vibert, 'Better Regulation and the Role of Agencies' in Stephen Weatherill (ed), *Better Regulation* (Oxford, Hart Publishing, 2007) 387–403.

[158] See, for example, Juan Santos Vara, 'AFSJ Agencies' in Ariadna Ripoll Servent and Florian Trauner (eds), *The Routledge Handbook of Justice and Home Affairs Research* (Abingdon, Routledge, 2017), and Irene Wieczorek, 'Understanding JHA Agencies in Context' in Maria Fletcher, Ester Herlin-Karnell and Claudio Matera (eds), *The European Union as an Area of Freedom, Security and Justice* (Abingdon: Routledge, 2017) 445–57.

[159] Jürgen Neyer, *The Justification of Europe: A Political Theory of Supranational Integration* (Oxford, Oxford University Press, 2012) 25–27.

in the AFSJ regulatory machinery. However, the Member States themselves have retained law enforcement powers and have not delegated such powers to the AFSJ agencies, with the exception of Frontex in the area of migration law policies.[160] As Itamar Mann points out, since 2006, Frontex has facilitated joint operations, in which the forces of different European Member States act together to enforce borders.[161] As the European Commission points out, Frontex can provide additional technical support for Member States facing severe migratory pressure. It does this by co-ordinating the deployment of additional technical equipment (eg, aircraft and boats) and specially trained border staff.[162]

In addition, Europol is the main player in the EU anti-terrorism tracking system.[163] Europol is mandated with, inter alia, the collection, storing, processing, analysis and exchange of information, including criminal intelligence across the Member States.[164] According to Article 88 TFEU, 'Europol's mission shall be to support and strengthen action by the Member States' police authorities'. It is therefore meant to act as a complementing authority, but it is becoming a primary actor. The present chapter can do no more than point out the complex interrelationship between the need to decentralise and make the Commission more effective, and basic concerns about the rule of law and legitimacy as well as accountability in AFSJ law. Notwithstanding this, Europol has been given extended powers to supervise the EU crime-fighting agenda within the AFSJ, and this has resulted in a complex relationship between AFSJ legislation and the role played by Europol in, for example, the financial tracking programme and the measures, such as the Money Laundering Directive discussed above, which are part of the internal market acquis. The European Securities and Market Authority (ESMA) is responsible for supervising the relevant instruments adopted within the internal market, and the ESMA Regulation contains a review clause that grants the Court of Justice the power to review fines imposed by this agency.[165] It is not clear, however, to what extent Europol and Eurojust can be called to account for their actions.[166] Specifically, it appears difficult for

[160] Jörg Monar, 'Experimentalist Governance in Justice and Home Affairs' in Charles F Sabel and Jonathan Zeitlin (eds), *Experimentalist Governance in the European Union* (Oxford, Oxford University Press, 2010) 237–60.

[161] See, for example, Jorrit J Rijmpa, 'Frontex and the European System of Border Guards: Guards: The Future of European Border Management' in Maria Fletcher, Ester Herlin-Karnell and Claudio Matera (eds), *The European Union as an Area of Freedom, Security and Justice* (Abingdon: Routledge, 2017) 217–44. See https://frontex.europa.eu/media-centre/focus/frontex-analysis-countering-organised-crime-at-sea-bCCCZy.

[162] https://europa.eu/european-union/about-eu/agencies/frontex_en.

[163] Regulation (EU) 2016/794, of the European Parliament and of the Council of 11 May 2016 on the European Union Agency for Law Enforcement Cooperation.

[164] ibid, Article 4 of the Regulation.

[165] Regulation (EU) No 1095/2010 establishing a European Supervisory Authority (European Securities and Markets Authority), amending Decision No 716/2009/EC and repealing Commission Decision 2009/77/EC.

[166] On agencies, see, for example, Madalina Busuioc, Deirdre Curtin and Martijn Groenleer, 'Agency Growth between Autonomy and Accountability: The European Police Office as a "Living

an individual to challenge a decision taken by an agency and have the question addressed in the EU Court, and asserting standing or going through the preliminary procedure system may not be a straightforward path. The same holds true for the establishment of a European Public Prosecutor's Office (EPPO) with far-reaching powers to investigate financial crimes with very little transparency as to how it could be held accountable.[167] The EU Commission has very recently suggested that the jurisdiction of the EPPO is extended to cover also terrorist offences and thereby better protect citizens across Europe.[168]

There is a clear accountability deficit, therefore, with regard to the role and function of agencies as key agents in the sanction game. It asks fundamental questions about the legitimacy of any enforcement of sanctions through agencies. And yet the EU needs to have this kind of coopertion to adequatly gurantee that the EU remains a secure space where freedom and equaliy is guranteed.

However, it remains unclear to what extent agencies can be called to account for their actions. According to the *Meroni* case, only executive powers can be delegated from the EU institutions to agencies, and their use must be entirely subject to the supervision of the delegating institution. Nevertheless, in a recent case concerning Regulation No 236/2012, which lays down a common regulatory framework concerning short selling and credit default swaps, the Court of Justice made some updates.[169] It stated that the EU legislature has a wide discretion particularly where the measures to be adopted are dependent on specific professional and technical expertise and the ability of such a body to respond swiftly and appropriately.

The outsourcing of responsibility in the fight against, for example, financial crimes and the financing of terrorism has several dimensions and is problematical.[170] For example, Europol plays an increasing role as a global information hub. The agency collects, processes, retains and exchanges data in an unprecedented way. There is, as noted, however, a clear accountability deficit, which is often stressed in scholarship but needs to be scrutinised in the context of EU financial crimes and the AFSJ with regard to the role and function of agencies as key agents in EU security regulation. In addition, it is extremely

Institution"' (2011) 18 *Journal of European Public Policy* 848–67. See, also, Pierre Schammo, 'The European Union Securities and Market Authority: Lifting the Veil on the Allocation of Powers' (2011) 48 *Common Market Law Review* 1887–913.

[167] Regulation 2017/1939, of 12 October 2017 Implementing Enhanced Cooperation on the Establishment of the European Public Prosecutor's Office, 2017 O.J. (L 106) 1, 1–71 and Gerard Conway, 'The European Public Prosecutor – Holding to Account a Possible European Public Prosecutor' (2013) 24 *Criminal Law Forum* 371–401.

[168] State of the Union 2018: A reinforced European Public Prosecutor's Office to fight cross-border terrorism, European Commission press release, http://europa.eu/rapid/press-release_IP-18-5682_en.htm.

[169] Case C-270/12, *UK v Council and European Parliament*, nyr; see, for example, Emiliano Grossman and Patrick Leblond, 'European Integration: Finally the Great Leap Forward' (2011) 49 *Journal of Common Market Studies* 413–35.

[170] See Harel (n 63) ch 3, discussing what is problematical with privatisation in criminal law.

important to focus research on how the enforcement powers of these EU agencies live up to and could be reconciled with the EU constitutional structure of a high human rights protection. Are agencies legitimate as imposers of sanctions?

There is a delicate dividing line between administrative procedures and those pertaining to constitutional rights. In addition, the recent Digital Single Market Strategy for Europe and the Cybercrime Agenda confirms the hybridity of the area: the global dimension of the AFSJ as well as its internal market interrelationship.[171]

With agencies having a larger function as enforcers of EU law and with private actors also part of the supervision of anti-money laundering and counter-terrorism financing measures, is the right to justification lived up to? Perhaps, in the future, a focus on real-time judicial dialogue with a focus on interim decisions when needed in security cases and in line with the EU case law on proportionality discussed above is something that would be beneficial for Europe which admittedly would confirm a consequentialist view in this regard.

VII. WHAT KIND OF JUSTIFICATION FOR WHAT KIND OF SOLIDARITY?

When attempting to understand the legal corpus which forms the AFSJ, we also need to take the political dimension into account and the need for the EU legislator to supply a justification for its action not only to the Member States, but also to the citizens of the EU. However, even if we agree that the EU has adopted an overly preventive stance towards the creation of the AFSJ, what can be done about it, and what is the function of justice to remedy this accusation? After all, it seems as if the security crisis is not isolated from, but closely related to, the broader constitutional crisis in Europe, and one that links up with the financial crisis in recent years, in that there is an increased focus of the effectiveness in the EU system as a whole. The main issue for the EU, in this respect, is its often too one-sided focus on prevention and enforcement, while it has largely ignored the need to ensure adequate protection of the individual so as to ensure a 'just' AFSJ space. In short, the focus on international security has often overshadowed the need to ensure due process rights. The identity-building power of security is strong, and how the events of 9/11 have shaped Europe with regard to security governance at the interface between hard (ie, border controls) and

[171] Niamh Moloney, *EU Securities and Financial Markets Regulation* (Oxford, Oxford University Press, 2014), Guido Ferrarini and Niamh Moloney, 'Reshaping Order Execution in the EU and the Rule of Interest Groups: From MiFID I to MiFID II' (2012) 13 *European Business Organization Law Review* 557–97. See, also, Elliot Posner, 'The Lamfalussy Process: Polyarchic Origins of Networked Financial Rule-Making in the EU' in Charles Sabel and Jonathan Zeitlin (eds), *Experimentalist Governance in the European Union: Towards a New Architecture*, 108 (Oxford, Oxford University Press, 2012) 43–60, and Lucia Quaglia, *The EU and Global Securities Markets Regulation* (Oxford, Oxford University Press, 2014).

soft (ie, information technology) security.[172] When understanding the security concept and the impact that it has on the EU's policy agenda, the ambition here was to take the well-trodden security discourse as its starting point and look at it through a constitutionalism lens.

Some scholars have, of course, long argued against constitutionalism as the appropriate analytical take on EU governance because this has failed to deliver what it promises.[173] However, the constitutional law framework, as explained in the previous chapters, has the rule of law, commitment to human rights protection, and democracy as its key concerns, which is still an attractive framework for the AFSJ project. The rule of law really is, therefore, the backbone upon which to base AFSJ co-operation. But it needs substantiating. This is especially so in the current debate on 'backsliding' – or regression – and the current challenges to the rule of law in certain EU Member States such as Poland and Hungary.[174] For example, Article 7(1) TEU provides for the possibility for the EU Council, acting by a majority of four-fifths of its members, to determine that there is a clear risk of a serious breach by a Member State of the common values referred to in Article 2 TEU. Given this risk of divergent standards, what does solidarity really mean in the EU with its motto of united in diversity?

At international level, there seems, for example, to be no binding duty among states to assist an overburdened state.[175] The EU is increasingly legislating on migration issues at the borders of Europe, or even outside its territories, extending the reach of EU law. Should there be an obligation for the EU to take into account the needs of those outside the EU territory when legislating on new security regulation? And what does non-domination mean in this case? As this chapter has tried to explore, there is both an empirical and normative importance of a constitutional dimension.

In a recent policy document on the rule of law, the Commission points out that where Member State mechanisms to secure the rule of law cease to operate effectively, this endangers the functioning of the EU's need to protect this principle as a common value of the Union.[176] For sure, the EU needs to be firm on its commitment thereto, as it is so closely related to the protection of human rights globally, and the kind of AFSJ that will emerge in Europe 2020 and beyond (the Commission's vision).[177] This seems particularly important as,

[172] For example, Lucia Zedner, *Security* (Abingdon, Routledge, 2009).

[173] Kalypso Nicolaïdes, 'The Idea of European Demoicracy' in Julie Dickson and Pavlos Eleftheriadis, *Philosophical Foundations of European Union Law* (Oxford, Oxford University Press, 2012) 247–74.

[174] See Laurent Pech and Kim Lane Scheppele 'Illiberalism Within: Rule of Law Backsliding in the EU' (2017) 19 *Cambridge Yearbook of European Legal Studies* 3–47 and see 'Rule of Law: European Commission acts to defend judicial independence in Poland', http://europa.eu/rapid/press-release_IP-17-5367_en.htm, press release 20 December 2017.

[175] Matthew J. Gibney, 'Refugees and Justice between States' (2015) 14 *European Journal of Political Theory* 448–63.

[176] COM/2014/0158 final, A new EU Framework to strengthen the Rule of Law.

[177] COM(2014) 144 final, The EU Justice Agenda for 2020 – Strengthening Trust, Mobility and Growth within the Union.

in its Opinion 2/13,[178] the CJEU concluded that the present EU legal framework could not be acceded with the ECHR, as the planned arrangements for complying with the obligation imposed on the EU by Article 6(2) TEU to accede to the ECHR are not compatible with EU law. It begs the question of whether the Court's commitment to fundamental rights is an instrumental strategy for tying its claims to supremacy. What is important from the perspective of this chapter is that the Court, in its judgment in Opinion 2/13, especially singled out the AFSJ as a crucial area in which the EU's relationship to the European Convention of Human Rights and the notion of trust is crucial, but understudied. The Court held that the trust principle requires, particularly with regard to the AFSJ, each Member State, save in exceptional circumstances, to consider all the other Member States to be complying both with EU law and particularly with the fundamental rights recognised by the EU Charter. This highlights how critical it is to understand the parameters that make up the AFSJ and the difficulties with 'AFSJ-justice' when there is no conclusive solidarity within the EU space. It also pose some problematic questions as to the legitimacy of the EU regime and its claims to justice. We will return to this in chapter six below.

VIII. CONCLUSION

The EU promises that it will continue engaging beyond its borders and strengthen co-operation with its global partners, address root causes, and promote modalities of legal migration that foster circular growth and development in the countries of origin and destination.[179]

This expansion of legal responsibilities beyond borders poses familiar questions about legitimacy and human rights protection.[180] It is also a question that seems essential from a constitutionalism perspective and, as such, crucial for discussing the corpus of the AFSJ: What justifies the EU's expanding action and is it better suited as a collective actor as compared to the Member States themselves? As explained above, the recent migration and refugee crisis in Europe has demonstrated that the legal framework for addressing and tackling these issues is increasingly blurred; for example, the EU criminalises trafficking in human beings (but asserts the protection of the victim) but trafficking occurs in parallel to smuggling and asylum-seekers. Asylum-seekers are entitled to different legal protection (in comparison with, for example, migrants and trafficked people) under international, regional and domestic law. Frequently, however, they share the same routes of passage as the victims of trafficking.[181] The regulation of trafficking and smuggling in human beings is one that poses difficult questions

[178] Opinion 2/13 delivered 18 December 2014.
[179] ibid.
[180] Buchanan, 'Legitimacy of the International Order' (2008).
[181] See UNHCR, 'Mixed Migration,' available at: www.unhcr.org/pages/4a16aac66.html.

in the EU setting, and, as such, is increasingly connected to the general security theme discussed above. The EU has proposed to criminalise the smugglers of migrants and thereby systematically identify, capture and destroy the vessels used by smugglers. According to the EU, such action under international law will be a powerful demonstration of the EU's determination to act.[182]

As expounded on, the EU also has a very wide-ranging regime for tackling terrorism and related activity, and there is a strong connection between the internal market legislation on market law and the AFSJ legal framework on security. This chapter has tried to outline some of the main instruments and actions, such as the new Counter-terrorism Directive of 2017, which establishes common rules to fight terrorism, and other EU and Member State responses to emergency and risks.

The challenge for justice reasoning and the right to justification is what is really meant by non-domination in the EU security framework, but to what extent does it mean the same thing in the context of migration governance as in counter-terrorism policies? Only by critically engaging in the reasoning of the CJEU and by the examining the policy choices within this complex mixture of security concerns, made by the EU legislator, and by understanding how interlinked the EU policy areas are within the AFSJ and its relationship to mainstream EU law can we begin to understand this question.

[182] European Agenda on Migration, May 2015.

6

The Dimensions of Constitutional Justice: The Multi-Speed Scenario

I. INTRODUCTION

THIS PENULTIMATE CHAPTER addresses the question of how the constitutional framework outlined in this book works when applied in the context of multi-speed co-operation, in which not all the Member States of the EU are on-board the ship of integration. The chapter then moves on to look at the possibilities for the CJEU to function as a trustee court in this, and the role of national courts for upholding constitutional safeguards. This chapter is different from the previous chapter in that it is initially more doctrinal and concerned with the actual implications of the AFSJ policies of so-called flexible integration in this area and its legal consequences. The chapter concludes by returning to the turf of normative theory and discussing the possibility of fiduciary obligations for the CJEU and national courts respectively.

The phenomenon of multi-speed co-operation in Europe means that AFSJ co-operation functions in an archipelago-like landscape. Indeed, the AFSJ has always been marked by a multi-speed character. For example, Denmark has opted out of the whole AFSJ acquis, and the UK and the Republic of Ireland have been granted various opt-outs, or rather, they have a possibility to opt in to measures that are attractive to them. How, then, can this fragmented landscape be kept (and hang) together and contribute to the establishing of an AFSJ within a constituent framework of EU constitutional rights? There are two main concerns here: legitimacy; and the function of constitutional rights in this fragmented area. Expressed differently, the chapter briefly assesses the distinctive character of proportionality in this regard as a balancing mechanism, and thereby follows on from the work in chapter four. Hence, the chapter will discuss the meaning of 'justification' and 'solidarity' in this multi-speed context. It discusses them in the broader framework of differentiated integration. For example, it could be asked whether constitutionalism pre-supposes a global or European environment? In any case, the increasingly fragmented AFSJ represents a particularly tricky test of how to apply justice theory in practice. In concrete legal terms, the consequence of any opt-out is that the CJEU will not have jurisdiction to monitor Member State compliance in that field and, furthermore, (clearly) that the Member State in question is not participating in co-operation in this area. An opt-out also applies to any international agreement concluded by the European Union in relation to the specific form of co-operation. In other words, an opt-out has serious consequences for the EU as a whole.

This chapter begins by sketching some main questions about the landscape of flexibility in AFSJ matters, and addresses the question of how justice can be achieved in a flexible landscape. Thereafter, the chapter discusses the function of the CJEU as a possible trustee court as a way of ensuring the right to justification. Subsequently, the chapter sets out tentatively to explore obligations for national courts, and possible fiduciary obligations, when the regime offered by the EU is not robust enough. Indeed, a notorious problem when debating the characterisation of the EU legal structure and its source of legitimation is the fact that the EU has no single demos, but rather a people of different Member States. The well-known EU motto – 'united in diversity' – has, of course, sought to tackle this problem.

Perhaps one of the greatest challenges that the EU is facing in practical terms is the constructing of the AFSJ as a 'just' – justice – space when not all the Member States are on-board. Indeed, multi-speed Europe offers what is conceivably the best example of when too much politics leads to too much uncertainty and possible injustice for the individual. For example, the UK and the Republic of Ireland have an option to opt into AFSJ legislation, but have, as their default choice, an exemption from AFSJ grid. The UK is now about to leave the EU project through its Brexit negotiations (which started in 2016), but, depending on what instruments it chooses to remain in, and subject to EU agreement, the reality of 'multi-speed' might remain an active concept. While, in the past, the EU was constantly moving forward, with no clear direction other than the unilateral desire for more integration, the situation today seems a lot more complex. Rather than there being a single destination, the trend is likely to become one of multiple choice: in other words, a Europe at different speeds.[1] The task of identifying a European core has therefore also become multi-dimensional. In line with this European theme, Kalypso Nicolaïdis has long advocated a solution to the much debated argument on the 'absence of a demos' theory: in her view, democracy is, at best, an illusion in the EU context, and what is needed is a new version of it.[2] As she sees it, therefore, it would be better to seek recourse to the notion of 'demoicracy' as 'a Union of peoples', understood both as states and as citizens, who govern together, but not as one. She has, moreover, advocated the idea of managed mutual recognition within the EU as a form of pluralism.[3]

[1] Ester Herlin-Karnell and Poul F Kjaer, 'Dimensions of Justice and Justification in EU and Transnational Contexts' (2017) 8 *Transnational Legal Theory* 1–7, and Joseph HH Weiler, 'Journey to an Unknown Destination: A Retrospective and Prospective of the European Court of Justice in the Arena of Political Integration' (1993) 31 *Journal of Common Market Studies* 417–446, 437.

[2] Kalypso Nicolaïdis, 'European Demoicracy and its Crisis' (2013) 2 *Journal of Common Market Studies* 351–69. See, also, extensive case law on EU citizenship *Martínez Sala*, Case C-85/96, ECR 1998, I-02691.

[3] Ester Herlin-Karnell, 'Europe's Area of Freedom, Security and Justice through the Prism of Constitutionalism: Why the EU Needs a Grammar of Justice to Improve its Legitimacy' (2014) WZB discussion paper, SP IV 2014-801, Berlin.

II. JUSTICE AND FRAGMENTATION: CHERRY-PICKING AFSJ STANDARDS

The idea of flexibility in EU law means that not all Member States are part of a given legal instrument and, in cases in which they are, that there are possibilities to derogate. But how can the EU construct an area of justice within this thorny terrain of human rights protection and security-related instruments if not all the Member States are part of the game? Specifically, I have chosen to refer to the notions of flexibility and differentiation interchangeably without implying a second-class two-tier Europe or making any actual substantive distinction between a two-speed Europe and multi-speed Europe. A recent example of the possible use of the multi-speed concept of enhanced co-operation is that of the establishment of a European Public Prosecutor's Office (EPPO), which, before its adoption, sparked two yellow card procedures in the Member States because of how controversial it was. The EPPO has, with regard to the original draft, triggered reasoned opinions or so-called 'yellow cards', issued by 14 chambers of 11 different national parliaments.[4] This has attracted a lot of attention and debate in academia and legal practice.[5] The only possibility for the EPPO project to survive was the invocation of the enhanced co-operation mechanism, according to which some Member States (nine or more) could pursue flexible integration. This could be considered as a subsidiarity-friendly alternative, as it allows for differentiation between Member States in the EU and thereby for national divergence between the Member States. Moreover, Member States such as Sweden and The Netherlands announced early on that they would not participate due to what they consider to be the far-reaching competences of the EPPO including the possibility of extending the competences of the EPPO to criminality not related to the EU budget, although recently The Netherlands has changed its mind[6] and has decided to participate in the establishment of the EPPO.[7] For example,

[4] Article 12(b) TEU provides for a competence of national Parliaments to see that the principle of subsidiarity is respected in accordance with Protocol No 2.

[5] Council Regulation (EU) 2017/1939 of 12 October 2017 implementing enhanced co-operation on the establishment of the European Public Prosecutor's Office (EPPO). For more on this see the discussion in Carlos Gómez-Jara Díez and Ester Herlin-Karnell, 'Prosecuting EU Financial Crimes: The European Prosecutor's Office in Comparison to the US Federal Regime' (2018) 19 *German Law Journal* 1191–220, and see eg Willem Geelhoed, Leendert H Erkelens and Arjen WH Meij (eds), *Shifting Perspectives on the European Public Prosecutor's Office* (Berlin-Heidelberg, Springer Verlag, 2018) and Jacob Öberg, *Limits to EU Powers: A Case Study of EU Regulatory Criminal Law* (Oxford, Hart Publishing, 2017), ch 7.

[6] Sofie Wolf, 'The Netherlands will Join the European Public Prosecutor's Office', available at: www.maastrichtuniversity.nl/blog/2018/05/netherlands-will-join-european-public-prosecutors-office-eppo.

[7] As to Sweden's position for not joining the EPPO, see Council 2017, EPPO General Approach, point no 11. On the Dutch position see NRC Handelsblad of 24 November 2016: 'Nederland doet toch niet mee aan Europees OM', available at: www.nrc.nl/nieuws/2016/11/23/nederland-doet-toch-niet-mee-aan-europees-openbaar-ministerie-a1533218; see, also, Willem Geelhoed, Leendert H Erkelens and Arjen WH Meij (eds), *Shifting Perspectives on the European Public Prosecutor's Office* (Berlin-Heidelberg, Springer Verlag, 2018).

the EU Commission has recently suggested that EPPO will be responsible for terrorism investigations as well.[8] Indeed, Article 86(4) provides for the possibility of a future European Council to adopt a decision amending the competences of such a prosecutor to include serious crime with a cross-border dimension in a broader sense and we will return to this below. From the perspective of the establishment of an EPPO through the notion of flexible integration, it also raises concerns about a system that seems to offer a half-baked solution. After all, it may be asked what the function of an EPPO is if it is not joined by the whole of the EU? When discussing the concept of 'flexibility' in terms of differentiation, the starting point is often the enhanced co-operation mechanisms as the most clear-cut example of flexible integration.

Moreover, while the EU Treaties and jurisprudence have always granted exceptions to the mantra of EU conformity, such divergence in the minimum level of human rights protection appears particularly undesirable in the AFSJ. But flexibility as a concept is found throughout the Treaty and could be said to represent a form of codified pluralism,[9] given that the EU acquis is full of examples of mini opt-outs. This area offers a new challenge, with the EU and the CJEU currently shaping the AFSJ sphere by seeking to apply mainstream EU constitutional principles that have existed in the traditional playing field of the EU constitutional setting for some time. The idea of flexibility seems to provide an attractive European model which can avoid the accusation of a one-size-fits-all approach to the highly complicated project of an EU composed of such divergent Member States. However, as much as the notion of flexibility seems to be an attractive concept, it is nonetheless also a rather vague one.

Despite mainstream EU principles – such as direct effect, supremacy and effectiveness, which could be described as unifying constitutional (embryonic) principles – being applied in the AFSJ, there are also certain challenges ahead in respect of how these principles should be applied in the flexibility landscape of opt-outs and opt-ins. As mentioned, the UK and the Republic of Ireland, for example, have negotiated a complete smorgasbord approach to the AFSJ

[8] 'State of the Union 2018: A reinforced European Public Prosecutor's Office to fight cross-border terrorism', European Commission press release, http://europa.eu/rapid/press-release_IP-18-5682_en.htm.

[9] See Bruno De Witte, 'Old-fashioned Flexibility: International Agreements between Member States of the European Union' in Gráinne de Búrca and Joanne Scott (eds), *Constitutional Change in the EU: From Uniformity to Flexibility?* (Oxford, Hart Publishing, 2000) 31–58. Andrea Ott, 'EU Constitutional Boundaries to Differentiation: How to Reconcile Differentiation with Integration?' in Andrea Ott and Ellen Vos (eds), *Fifty Years of European Integration: Foundations and Perspectives* (The Hague, TMC Asser Press, 2009) 113–38; Ester Herlin-Karnell and Theodore Konstadinides, 'The Rise and Many Expressions of Consistency in EU Law: Legal and Strategic Implications for European Integration' (2013) 15 *Cambridge Yearbook of European Legal Studies* 139–67. On the notion of flexibility, see, for example, Deirdre Curtin, 'The Constitutional Structure of the Union: A Europe of Bits and Pieces' (1993) 30 *Common Market Law Review* 17–69; Alexander C-G Stubb, 'A Categorization of Differentiated Integration' (1996) 34 *Journal of Common Market Studies* 283–95.

project. Under the Treaty of Lisbon, Protocol Number 21, these Member States have the opportunity to opt out of criminal law co-operation provisions. They can later opt in under the conditions set out in the said Protocol. This confirms the highly complex nature of the AFSJ landscape. Arguably, the opt-out area offers a fascinating, yet complicated, test case of exactly which constitutional principles apply and how they work in the AFSJ. This, in turn, begs the question as to how the EU can achieve justice at different speeds in this area, and also the question of whether justice necessarily means centralisation?

In addition, closely related to the notion of differentiation and also within the specific area of EU criminal law is the example of Schengen, which demonstrates that the Court can effectively police the Member States' level of participation in a given policy area by gate-keeping their preferences, which amounts to non-unitary integration.[10] The Schengen *acquis*,[11] where some Member States have sought to go further than other, less integrative Member States by establishing the highest possible standard of co-operation, is one of the first examples of a flexible style of integration method in AFSJ-related matters. Such co-operation has already been taking place, especially by means of information exchange, in particular in combating terrorism, cross-border crime and illegal migration.[12]

The UK (despite its Brexit drama) was never part of the Schengen *acquis*, but it may make a request to the Council for authorisation to participate in part or all of the Schengen provisions, and, in addition, to contribute to the adoption of measures based upon the Schengen *acquis* (Articles 4 and 5 of the Schengen Protocol).[13] Such was the case in *UK v Council*,[14] where the UK sought the annulment of Regulation 2007/2004 adopted in 2004 with a view to establishing the external border-control agency Frontex.[15] The UK was not included in the adoption of the challenged Regulation that was built on the provisions of

[10] See, also, Maria O'Neill, 'EU Cross-border Policing Provisions: The View from One of the Schengen Opt Out States' (2010) 18 *European Journal of Crime, Criminal Law and Criminal Justice* 73–89.

[11] 1985, The Schengen Agreement, [2000] OJ L239. More specifically, the Schengen *acquis* comprises, inter alia, the Convention implementing the Schengen Agreement of 14 June 1985 between the Governments of the States of the Benelux Economic Union, the Federal Republic of Germany and the French Republic on the gradual abolition of checks at their common borders signed at Schengen (Luxembourg) on 19 June 1990.

[12] See, for example, Steve Peers, *EU Justice and Home Affairs*, vols 1 and 2 (Oxford, Oxford University Press, 2015).

[13] See, for example, Estella Baker, 'Criminal Justice and the "New, Deep and Special Partnership" between the EU and the UK: A Critical Test for the Area of Freedom, Security and Justice?' (2018) 26 *European Journal of Crime, Criminal Law and Criminal Justice* 1–19. The Council has to decide on such a request by unanimity unless the legislative proposal in question is built on the pre-existing Schengen *acquis*, to which the UK has secured an opt-out. See also Mar Jimeno-Bulnes, 'Brexit and the Future of European Criminal Law – a Spanish Perspective' (2017) 28 *Criminal Law Forum* 325–47.

[14] Case C-77/05 *UK v Council* ECR I-11459; Case C-137/05 *UK v Council* [2007] ECR I-11593.

[15] Council Regulation (EC) No 2007/2004 of 26 October 2004 establishing a European Agency for the Management of Operational Cooperation at the External Borders of the Member States of the European Union [2004] OJ L349/1.

the pre-existing Schengen *acquis*. In yet another case, the UK again sought the annulment of a regulation on the standards for security features and biometrics in passports and travel documents issued by Member States. As in the previous case, the UK was excluded from participating in the adoption of the Regulation.[16] In both cases, the Court upheld the Council's discretion to refuse to allow the UK to take part in the adoption of these regulations.[17] These judgments can be characterised as consistency-driven.[18]

Against this background, it may be asked what it actually means to refer to flexibility in AFSJ law. In answering this question, arguably, we first need to know what flexibility means in EU law proper. While the notion of flexibility is far from a new concept and has traditionally been defined as the possibility of one or more Member States choosing to remain outside the scope of certain activities pursued within the Union's legal framework, or conversely choosing to move forward by leading a select group of avant garde Member States that want to go further in integration processes than the others, the very notion of flexible integration poses some pertinent questions in the current financial (and constitutional) crisis of the EU. Indeed, while Deirdre Curtin was right in her early assessment and prediction of a Europe consisting of 'bits and pieces',[19] in connection with the creation of the intergovernmental pillars and its exclusion from the Community method, what seems to be emerging in contemporary EU law is a Court-led era of differentiation.[20] When discussing the concept of flexibility in terms of differentiation, the starting point is often the enhanced co-operation mechanisms as the most clear-cut example of flexible integration.[21] The concept accepts that there is room for action outside the EU model, and that not all Member States have to be 'in the same boat', while still respecting each other through the fundamental loyalty principle of the Article 4(3) Treaty of the European Union.

Despite its novel nature in an EU context, or perhaps precisely because of it, criminal law offers a good example of the limits, and the varied meaning, to the concept of flexibility as a tool for European integration. The consequence of any opt-out (that is, of not participating in a measure) is that the CJEU will

[16] Council Regulation (EC) No 2252/2004 of 13 December 2004 on standards for security features and biometrics in passports and travel documents issued by Member States [2004] OJ L385/1.

[17] ibid.

[18] Herlin-Karnell and Konstadinides, 'Many Expressions of Consistency' (2013).

[19] Curtin, 'The Constitutional Structure' (1993). This section borrows from Ester Herlin-Karnell, 'Between Flexibility and Fragmentation: The Example of Criminal Law' in B de Witte, A Ott, E Vos (eds), *Between Flexibility and Disintegration: The State of EU law today* (Cheltenham, Edward Elgar, 2017).

[20] Gráinne de Búrca, 'Legal Principles as an Instrument of Differentiation?' in Bruno De Witte, Dominik Hanf and Ellen Vos (eds), *The Many Faces of Differentiation in EU Law* (Antwerp, Intersentia, 2003) 131–44.

[21] For example, Stephen Weatherill, 'If I'd Wanted you to Understand I would have Explained it Better: What is the Purpose of the Provisions on Closer Co-operation Introduced by the Treaty of Amsterdam?' in David O'Keeffe and Patrick Twomey (eds), *Legal Issues of the Amsterdam Treaty* (Oxford, Hart Publishing, 1999) 21–38.

generally not have jurisdiction to monitor it. An opt-out also applies to any international agreement concluded by the Union in relation to the co-operation in question. In other words, an opt-out has serious consequences for the EU endeavour to ensure consistency across its policies.

Needless to say, any opt-out decision is bound to be a political decision and will be the cause of further complexity in the legal discussion of the AFSJ. As indicated above, the UK and Ireland (soon with relevance only to Ireland) have negotiated a complete *smörgåsbord* – or pick and choose – approach to the AFSJ project. Yet, in the area of, for example, the fight against money laundering, countering terrorism financing and financial crime, it appears less likely that the UK and Ireland would wish to remain outside EU co-operation. This is because that it is not only the EU which initiated these initiatives that is, the international obligations set as the guidelines by the Financial Action Task Force upon which the EU Directives are based the compliance threat would remain from the international fora and that the UK has been one of the leading proponents of further co-operation against money laundering and against terror financing across the EU.[22] Indeed, it raises some delicate questions about the delimitation of EU internal and external powers with regard to the EU's strategy to counter terrorism effectively.

Denmark offers a unique test case for the practicality of the AFSJ project. Protocol No 22, as attached to the Lisbon Treaty, allows Denmark a special position by granting it the right to remain outside the project.[23] This Protocol means that Denmark participates in Schengen-related measures and Pre-Lisbon third pillar instruments upon the basis of international law, which continue to be binding and applicable to Denmark as before. Denmark may, however, notify the other Member States that it wishes to join the EU criminal law/AFSJ venture. Likewise, amendments of pre-Lisbon instruments do not apply to Denmark and the old version will still apply to Denmark.[24] According to Article 8 of Protocol No 22, at any time, Denmark may, in accordance with its constitutional requirements, inform the other Member States that it no longer wishes to avail itself of all or part of this Protocol. The relationship between Denmark and all the other Member States in the EU (except the UK and Irish opt-outs) is based upon intergovernmental co-operation, and Council of Europe Treaties, such as, most prominently, the European Convention of Human Rights standards (and the Convention rights are, of course, binding on the EU).[25]

[22] Herlin-Karnell, "Between Flexibility and Fragmentation" (2017).

[23] See eg Ester Herlin-Karnell, 'Denmark and the European Area of Freedom, Security and Justice: A Scandinavian Arrangement' (2013) 5 *Amsterdam Law Forum* 95–105.

[24] Notoriously, ever since the Maastricht Treaty, Denmark has had some serious objections to the EU project. As a brief historic account, it is worth recalling that, in accordance with the Danish Protocol attached to the previous Amsterdam Treaty, Denmark was exempted from almost all measures adopted within the framework of former Title IV of the old EC Treaty. In addition, Denmark had special rules in place regarding the Schengen acquis. These rules are now transferred to and bundled together in one document under the regime provided by Lisbon, namely, Protocol No 22.

[25] Herlin-Karnell, 'Between Flexibility and Fragmentation' (2017).

Arguably, the Danish approach of rejecting the whole AFSJ threatens the consistency of the practicability of the operation of mutual recognition of criminal law, as the judicial system is largely based upon mutual recognition in this area. Nevertheless, others have argued that the approach adopted by Denmark strengthens sovereignty without undermining uniformity in the AFSJ. Specifically, Rebecca Adler-Nissen, for example, argues that differentiated integration is not a threat to the notion of 'an ever closer Union', but instead offers an innovation that is quite consistent with the rationale of integration.[26] It could be argued that this is a confirmation of the CJEU's approach, as demonstrated in *Spain and Italy v Council*,[27] albeit in the context of enhanced co-operation and not in the specific context of criminal law. But there is one important difference: exporting the 'bits and pieces' approach to the AFSJ also runs the risk of undermining fundamental rights protection and thereby lowering the standard of human rights protection where it is most needed in the EU.

This chapter will now discuss the question of judicial review and constitutional justice in AFSJ matters.

III. CONSTITUTIONAL JUSTICE, TRUST AND THE CJEU

A central player in EU security regulation is, of course, the CJEU, which has been a prominent game-changer in the AFSJ, especially in the area of mutual recognition.[28] Specifically, the idea of mutual recognition in the EU context is that states should mutually trust one another in Europe, and recognise, inter alia, a judgment, product, qualification or an arrest warrant from another EU state.

As noted, the area of mutual recognition has been one of the most important playing fields for the CJEU.[29] Indeed, much of the EU's co-operation in the AFSJ has been built on the principle of mutual recognition as underpinning co-operation in justice and home affairs matters. Indeed, the concept of mutual recognition constitutes the main rule-of-thumb in the structure, as provided by the Treaty of Lisbon in AFSJ matters where trust plays an increasingly important role. It is often suggested that the main problem with mutual recognition in

[26] Rebecca Adler-Nissen, 'Opting Out of an Ever Closer Union: The Integration Doxa and the Management of Sovereignty' (2011) 34 *West European Politics* 1092–113.

[27] Allan Rosas and Lorna Armati, *EU Constitutional Law* (Oxford, Hart Publishing, 2010) 108–10. Joined Cases C-274/11 and C-295/11, *Spain and Italy v Council*, judgment of 16 April 2013.

[28] Koen Lenaerts and José Gutiérrez-Fons, 'The European Court of Justice and Fundamental Rights in the Field of Criminal Law' in Valsamis Mitsilegas, Maria Bergström and Theodore Konstadinides (eds), *Research Handbook on EU Criminal Law* (Cheltenham, Edward Elgar Publishing, 2016), 7–28.

[29] Lenaerts and Gutiérrez-Fons (ibid). Henri de Waele, 'Entrenching the Area of Freedom, Security and Justice: Questions of Institutional Governance and Judicial Control' in Maria Fletcher, Ester Herlin-Karnell and Claudio Matera, *The European Union as an Area of Freedom, Security and Justice* (Abingdon, Routledge, 2016) 485–508.

the AFSJ is the absence of sufficient trust in this area, and that this is problematical, as Article 67 TFEU pre-supposes that mutual recognition plays the key role in this area. Hence, the notion of trust in this area as a quasi-constitutional standard for justifying EU action and has been the subject of must discussion in the legal doctrine.

In particular, the CJEU has used the notion of trust in the area in order to overcome the lack of uniformity in national systems. For example, and as mentioned in chapter four, in the *NS* case, the Court held that the *raison d'être* of the EU and its creation of an AFSJ and, in particular, the Common European Asylum System, based upon mutual trust and a presumption of compliance, by other Member States, must be in compliance with fundamental rights.[30] Furthermore, a common problem, and, as such, one which is frequently highlighted by academic commentary, which arises when discussing the notion of EU criminal law co-operation is that there is no definition of 'mutual trust' in the field of criminal law.[31] This lack of conceptualisation has been considered to be a significant lacuna in EU criminal law co-operation. In this regard, there is currently insufficient mutual trust between the Member States and no adequate European regime for the protection of human rights within the former third pillar to justify such an analogy with the internal market and mutual recognition.[32]

Indeed, several fairly recent cases on the limits to mutual recognition in the AFSJ demonstrate that the concept of mutual trust is not an absolute requirement, but one that can be set aside if necessary for the adequate protection of human rights (Case C-123/08). In the *NS* (Case C-411/10) case in EU asylum law, the CJEU asserted that, if there were substantial grounds for believing that there are systematic flaws in the asylum procedure in the Member State responsible, then the transfer of asylum-seekers to that territory would be incompatible with the Charter of Fundamental Rights.

As explained in chapter four, in the recent *Aranyosi* and *Căldăraru*[33] case concerning the execution of an EAW and the risk of inhuman and degrading treatment, the Court emphasised Article 4 of the Charter of Fundamental Rights, that prohibition is absolute in that it is closely linked to respect for human dignity. The Court held that the executing judicial authority must

[30] *NS*, C-411/10. See, also, Case C-578/16 *PPU, CK*.

[31] Hans Lindahl (ed), *A Right to Inclusion and Exclusion? Normative Fault Lines of the EU's Area of Freedom, Security and Justice* (Oxford, Hart Publishing, 2009); Neil Walker, 'The Problem of Trust in an Enlarged Area of Freedom, Security and Justice: A Conceptual Analysis' in Malcolm Anderson and Joanna Apap (eds), *Police and Justice Cooperation and the New European Borders* (The Hague, Kluwer Law International, 2002) 19–34. Thus, the mutual recognition of judicial decisions across the Member States pre-supposes a level of trust between the domestic legal orders that appears particularly difficult to achieve in an area as sensitive as criminal law. In general, criminal law deals with the deprivation of liberty, which contrasts with the imperative of EU free movement.

[32] Peers, *EU Justice* (2015).

[33] Case C-404/15 and C-659/15 *PPU*.

postpone its decision on the surrender of the individual concerned until it obtains the supplementary information that allows it to exclude the existence of such a risk.

Moreover, as indicated above, in the *NS* case, in the context of the EU asylum system, the CJEU asserted that, if there are substantial grounds for believing that there were systematic flaws in the asylum procedure it would be incompatible with the Charter of Fundamental Rights to enforce the legislative obligation. For the CJEU, there is no doubt that, where there is a serious risk that the applicant's rights, as guaranteed by the Charter of Fundamental Rights, may be breached, Member States should enjoy a wide margin of discretion. This permits the Member State in which the application was lodged to examine it even when the criteria set out by Chapter III of the Dublin III Regulation[34] do not apply, in particular, when the state that should be responsible is to be deemed dangerous. The question is the extent to which this margin of appreciation should operate in the light of potential political or ideological conflicts.[35] The Court has yet to answer this question.

The CJEU has to ensure consistency between the rights under the EU Charter of Fundamental Rights and the European Convention on Human Rights (ECHR).[36] This means that it often looks at the case law of the Strasbourg Court for guidance.

For example, prior to the above-mentioned *NS* case, in 2011, the European Court of Human Rights (ECtHR), in the case *MSS v Belgium and Greece*, held that the conditions of detention and the living conditions of asylum-seekers in Greece were to be regarded as a violation of Article 3 of the ECHR.[37] Likewise, in the area of EU criminal law, the Court copies the ECHR with regard to the minimum standard adopted, which was both the case in *Melloni* (Case C-399/11) (the ECHR does not give wider protection but leaves it often to the 'margin of appreciation' test whether to allow trial in absentia), and in *Aranyosi* and *Căldăraruas* mentioned above. In spite of this, the CJEU continues to have a rather complicated relationship with Strasbourg and the ECHR in particular. In its recent Opinion 2/13 on the EU's accession to the ECHR, the CJEU rejected the possibility of EU accession to the ECHR partly on the

[34] Dublin Regulation No 604/2013.

[35] Massimo Fichera and Ester Herlin-Karnell, 'The Margin of Appreciation Test and Balancing in the Area of Freedom Security and Justice: A Proportionate Answer for a Europe of Rights?' (2013) 19 *European Public Law* 759–87.

[36] See, especially, Charter of Fundamental Rights of the European Union [2000] OJ C364/01, Article 52(3): 'In so far as this Charter contains rights which correspond to rights guaranteed by the Convention for the Protection of Human Rights and Fundamental Freedoms, the meaning and scope of those rights shall be the same as those laid down by the said Convention. This provision shall not prevent Union law providing more extensive protection.'

[37] Article 3 ECHR: 'No one shall be subjected to torture or to inhuman or degrading treatment or punishment'.

grounds that as 'EU law imposes an obligation of mutual trust between those Member States, accession is liable to … undermine the autonomy of EU law'.[38]

The Court has adopted a yo-yo-like approach with regard to its relationship with national courts and with regard to any conception of EU justice. Sometimes, the Court has maintained its Solange doctrine and, at other times, simply focused on the enforcement of EU law at all costs. The case law, if you like, is contextualised, albeit sometimes a bit unclearly, as to why some cases are different from others. Apart from the importance of consistency as a value in shaping legal drafting, and, as such, a prominent theme in the case law of the CJEU, consistency theoretically plays an important part in judicial decision-making. In the aforementioned Opinion 2/13 the Court held that:

> In so far as the ECHR would require a EU Member State to check that another Member State has observed fundamental rights, even though EU law imposes an obligation of mutual trust between those Member States, accession [to the ECHR] is liable to upset the underlying balance of the EU and undermine the autonomy of EU law.

Regarding the relationship between the CJEU and the ECtHR, the ECtHR's case law has been rather more solicitous of asylum-seekers' fundamental rights, as in *MSS v Belgium and Greece* mentioned above. According to Daniel Halberstam, by asking for an express exemption for Convention violations by EU Member States caused by EU law's mutual confidence obligations, the CJEU is trying to mimic the existence of a federal state in international law.[39] Thus, one of the challenges for the CJEU is to convince the highest national courts that, despite the non-accession of the EU to the ECHR, the EU system of rights is, at a minimum, as good as that offered by the ECHR. In a recent article, Anneli Albi has argued that what is really needed in AFSJ matters (and, more generally, in EU constitutional law) is a turn to 'substantive co-operative constitutionalism'.[40] With this, she means that the Court needs to adopt a conceptual approach through which scholars, courts and national and transnational institutions would be able to explore how to develop European and global governance in a way that would seek to uphold and enhance the achieved standards of the classic, substantive, more 'guarantistic' and democratically responsive version of constitutionalism. Clearly, this is work in progress. It is also an area in which the CJEU is likely to continue to be a game-changer in the future, and with either more co-operation on the table, or by promoting a closed-door approach. What, then, does all this tell us about the Court at the apex of AFSJ-integration?

[38] Daniel Halberstam, '"It's the Autonomy, Stupid!" A Modest Defence of Opinion 2/13 on EU Accession to the ECHR, and the Way Forward' (2015) 16 *German Law Journal* 105–46.

[39] ibid, 105.

[40] Anneli Albi, 'Erosion of Constitutional Rights in EU Law: A Call for "Substantive Co-operative Constitutionalism"' (2015) 9 *Vienna Journal on International Law* 291–343.

What is interesting from the perspective of this book is that the Court, and as was briefly discussed above, in its judgment in Opinion 2/13, especially singled out the AFSJ as a crucial area in which the EU's relationship to the ECHR and the notion of 'trust' is severely understudied. The Court held that the trust principle requires, particularly with regard to the AFSJ, each Member State, save in exceptional circumstances, to consider all the other Member States to be complying both with EU law and, in particular, with the fundamental rights recognised by EU law. Again, this highlights how critical it is to understand the parameters that make up the AFSJ.

Specifically, a debate has arisen as to what the term 'exceptional circumstances' really means. As mentioned above, the notion of trust in this area has, in many ways, worked as claimed panacea for a lack of uniformity. This question has become the crucial testing ground for the credibility of the EAW. In the recent *Artur Celmer* case,[41] before the Irish High Court of Justice, concerning the question of whether surrendering someone to Poland would undermine the rule of law and EU values, and the because of the risk of degrading treatment, the High Court stated that:

> The judgment of the CJEU in *Aranyosi* and *Caldararu* [*sic*] [*Căldăraru*], proposes a two-step approach in determining whether fundamental rights have been breached. An initial finding of general or systemic deficiencies in the protections in the issuing state must be made, and the executing judicial authority must then seek all necessary supplementary information from the issuing state as to the protections for the individual concerned. These tests have been predicated on mutual trust and mutual recognition. A problem with adopting that approach in the present case is that the deficiencies identified are to the edifices of a democracy governed by the rule of law. In those circumstances, it is difficult to see how individual guarantees can be given by the issuing judicial authority as to fair trial when it is the system of justice itself that is no longer operating under the rule of law.

The CJEU delivered its judgment on 25 July 2018 and thereby partly confirmed the worry expressed by the Irish court but pointed out that it is chiefly for the European Council to monitor the Member States compliance with the rule of law.[42] The CJEU held that in 72–73§§ of its judgment that:

> It is only if the European Council were to adopt a decision determining, as provided for in Article 7(2) TEU, that there is a serious and persistent breach in the issuing Member State of the principles set out in Article 2 TEU, such as those inherent in the rule of law, and the Council were then to suspend Framework Decision 2002/584 [the EAW] in respect of that Member State that the executing judicial authority would be required to refuse automatically to execute any European arrest warrant issued by it, without having to carry out any specific assessment of whether the individual concerned runs a real risk that the essence of his fundamental right to a fair trial will be affected […] as long as such a decision has not been adopted by the European Council, the executing judicial authority may refrain, on the basis of Article 1(3) of

[41] *The Minister for Justice and Equality v Celmer* [2018] IEHC 119 (2018).
[42] Case C-216/18, *PPU, LM*, 25 July 2018.

> Framework Decision 2002/584, to give effect to a European arrest warrant issued by a Member State which is the subject of a reasoned proposal as referred to in Article 7(1) TEU only in exceptional circumstances where that authority finds, after carrying out a specific and precise assessment of the particular case, that there are substantial grounds for believing that the person in respect of whom that European arrest warrant has been issued will, following his surrender to the issuing judicial authority, run a real risk of breach of his fundamental right to an independent tribunal and, therefore, of the essence of his fundamental right to a fair trial.

Similarly in the *Petruhhin* case,[43] delivered in 2016, the CJEU in the context of extradition agreements with third states (non-EU states), stipulated that: 'where a Member State receives a request from a third State seeking the extradition of a national of another Member State, that first Member State must verify that the extradition will not prejudice the rights referred to in Article 19 of the Charter.'

Article 19 of the Charter, in turn, requires that 'No one may be removed, expelled or extradited to a State where there is a serious risk that he or she would be subjected to the death penalty, torture or other inhuman or degrading treatment or punishment'. As has recently been suggested, the criteria with regard to the EAW might soon be very similar to that of Article 19 of the Charter, and the Member States will have to assure that prison conditions are acceptable from a human dignity perspective.[44]

IV. THE COURT OF JUSTICE AS A TRUSTEE COURT IN THE AFSJ?

The CJEU considers itself to be not only at the top of the judicial integration chain, but also to be a court with fiduciary obligations to protect EU law rights in all the Member States in the autonomous European legal order, which is largely based upon trust between the Member States.[45] Thus, for example, according to Alec Stone-Sweet and Thomas Brunel, the CJEU is not a simple agent of the Member States; instead, it is the latter that are the trustees of its regimes, ie, of EU law at large. In reaching this conclusion, the authors mention three criteria: first, that the Court is recognised as the authoritative interpreter of the law of the regime, which is the case of the CJEU; secondly, that the Court's jurisdiction, with regard to state compliance, is compulsory; and, thirdly, that it is virtually impossible, in practice, for contracting states to reverse the Court's important rulings on treaty law. Accordingly, a trustee court is a kind of super agent empowered to enforce the law against the Member States themselves.[46]

[43] Case C-182/15, *Petruhhin*, 6 September 2016.

[44] See André Klip, 'Europeans First!: Petruhhin, an Unexpected Revolution in Extradition Law' (2017) 25 *European Journal of Crime, Criminal Law and Criminal Justice* 195–204.

[45] COM(2014) 144 final, 'The EU Justice Agenda for 2020 – Strengthening Trust, Mobility and Growth within the Union'.

[46] Alec Stone Sweet and TL Brunell, 'Trustee Courts and the Judicialization of International Regimes: The Politics of Majoritarian Activism in the ECHR, the EU, and the WTO' (2013) Faculty

By legislating a right-based constitution, it has been argued, and in line with Kantian theory, that the people have placed the ultimate value and their freedom in trust, and that it places officials under the obligation to secure a public right.[47] The constitution confers judicial review powers on the Court for the purpose of enforcing rights as positive requirements of legality.[48]

Does this description fit the CJEU with regard to the AFSJ? A tentative expression of trusteeship might be found in the AFSJ, where the Court has to balance freedom, security and justice. An example of the CJEU acting as a successful guardian of the AFSJ can, perhaps, be found in the case of *Digital Rights*,[49] discussed in chapter four, which is instructive also as a touchstone of justice-inspired reasoning in the CJEU. It should once again be briefly recalled that the Court annulled the 2006 Data Retention Directive, which was aimed at fighting crime and terrorism, and which allowed data to be stored for up to two years. It concluded that the measure breached proportionality on the grounds that the Directive had a too-sweeping generality and therefore violated, inter alia, the basic right of data protection as set out in Article 8 of the Charter of Fundamental Rights. The Court pointed out that the access by the competent national authorities to the data retained was not made dependent on a prior review carried out by a Court or by an independent administrative body whose decision sought to limit access to the data to what was strictly necessary for the purpose of attaining the objective pursued. Nor did it lay down a specific obligation on Member States designed to establish such limits. According to the Court, there was not a sufficiently good enough justification provided by the EU legislator.

As elaborated in chapter four, constitutional rights in the AFSJ appear to be largely contingent on the proportionality (or reasonableness) test in national courts in order to realise the justice component of Freedom, Security and Justice, as courts are often asked to strike the right balance between security and freedom.[50] Similarly, Stone-Sweet and Ryan have recently argued that a trustee court ought to embrace the proportionality principle if it is to fulfil its mission.[51]

Scholarship Series, Paper 4625, available at: http://digitalcommons.law.yale.edu/fss_papers/4625, and Evan J Criddle and Evan Fox-Decent, *Fiduciaries of Humanity: How International Law Constitutes Authority* (Oxford, Oxford University Press, 2016). See, also, the recent work by Alec Stone Sweet and Clare Ryan, *A Cosmopolitan Legal Order: Constitutional Justice and the European Convention on Human Rights* (Oxford, Oxford University Press, 2018), ch 2, 'A Kantian System of Cnsituional Justice' 31–72, written with Eric Palmer.

[47] Stone Sweet and Ryan (ibid).

[48] ibid.

[49] Case C-293/12, *Cruz Villalón*, 8 April 2014.

[50] On the difference between reasonableness and proportionality, see Paul Craig, 'The Nature of Reasonableness Review' (2013) 66 *Current Legal Problems* 131–67, and Matthias Klatt, 'Positive Rights: Who Decides? Judicial Review in Balance' (2015) 13 *I-CON*, 354–82.

[51] Stone Sweet and Ryan, *Cosmopolitan Legal Order* (2018). See, also, Ester Herlin-Karnell, 'The European Court of Justice as a Game changer: fiduciary obligations in the area of freedom, security and justice' in Ariadna Ripoll Servent and Florian Trauner (eds), *Routledge Handbook of Justice and Home Affairs Research* (Abingdon, Routledge, 2017) 396–408.

For these scholars, fiduciary obligations will optimise the polity's capacity to progress its goals of achieving a rightful constitutional condition, and it will use (inter alia) the proportionality assessment as an operating system for dialogue which shapes the evolution of policy and the content of the rights-based constitution.[52]

However, the more technical aspects of the proportionality doctrine – particularly, the requirement of a rational connection between the means and end of a restriction on rights – helps to show that constitutional rights are not simply moral rights which have been institutionalised, but are, instead, controls on the predicates of state power.[53] In turn, this makes rights-based constitutional adjudication quite consistent with a political concept of rights, and accommodates the fact of disagreement about rights.[54]

Arguably, the Court considers itself to be not only at the top of judicial integration chain, but also as a court with fiduciary obligations to protect EU law rights in all Member States via its extensive case law on trust in the autonomous European legal order.

Therefore, according to Alec Stone-Sweet and Thomas Brunell, the CJEU is not a simple agent of the Member States, but it is, instead, the latter that are the trustees of its regimes, ie, of EU law at large.[55] Subsequently, and as mentioned in chapter four, in *Schrems*, the Court ruled, in effect, that US law allows US intelligence services to access the personal data of EU citizens without sufficient privacy safeguards as a matter of EU law.[56] The EU law in question was the so-called Commission Adequacy Decision 2000/520, adopted pursuant to Article 25 of the Data Protection Directive 95/46. Under Directive 95/46, the transfer of personal data outside the European Economic Area to a third country is only permissible when the third country de facto ensures an 'adequate level of protection'. The Commission may find that a third country meets this standard

[52] Stone Sweet and Ryan (n 46) 68–69.

[53] See chapter four above, and again Aharon Barak, *Proportionality: Constitutional Rights and their Limitations* (Cambridge, Cambridge University Press, 2012); Robert Alexy, *A Theory of Constitutional Rights* (Oxford, Oxford University Press, 2002); Vicki C Jackson, 'Constitutional Law in an Age of Proportionality' (2015) 124 *Yale Law Journal* 3094–96; Mattias Kumm, 'The Idea of Socratic Contestation and the Right to Justification: The Point of Rights-based Proportionality Review' (2010) 4 *Law & Ethics of Human Rights* 142–75; Matthias Klatt and Moritz Meister, *The Constitutional Structure of Proportionality* (Oxford, Oxford University Press, 2012), Kai Möller, *The Global Model of Constitutional Rights* (Oxford, Oxford University Press, 2012); and the contributions in Grant Huscroft, Bradley W Miller and Grégoire Webber (eds), *Proportionality and the Rule of Law* (Cambridge, Cambridge University Press, 2014), Grégoire CN Webber, *The Negotiable Constitution: On the Limitations of Rights* (Cambridge, Cambridge University Press, 2009), Moshe Cohen-Eliya and Iddo Porat, *Proportionality and Constitutional Culture* (Cambridge, Cambridge University Press, 2013).

[54] Eoin Daly, 'Freedom as Non-domination in the Jurisprudence of Constitutional Rights' (2015) 28 *Canadian Journal of Law and Jurisprudence* 289–316.

[55] Stone Sweet and Brunell (n 46), Criddle and Fox-Decent, *Fiduciaries of Humanity* (2016).

[56] C-362/14 *Schrems v Data Protection Commissioner*.

through its domestic law or international commitments, and by taking account of all the circumstances surrounding the data transfer. The Court declared the Adequacy Decision to be invalid. It did so, 'without there being any need to examine the content of the safe harbour principles', upon the basis that the Commission had not stated in the Adequacy Decision that the United States did, in fact, ensure an adequate level of protection through its domestic law or its international commitments.[57] This approach was confirmed in the recent *Telia 2 Sverige* case concerning the retention of the traffic and location of data in relation to subscribers and registered users, which was in breach of the Charter.[58] The Swedish Post and Telecom Authority required Telia 2 to retain traffic and location data in relation to its subscribers and registered users. The measure was found to be disproportionate and in breach of data protection (paras 95–96 of the judgment).

As seen in chapter four, the idea of balancing mechanisms of state action has for a long time been a touchstone for the EU and, as such, has been elevated to a golden rule in EU law-making, in terms of the proportionality principle. At a minimum, it has always been a key message of the CJEU's case law, and its insistence on proportionality has functioned as a way of either preventing Member States from derogating from EU law obligations or, by contrast, of granting them some leeway when asked to enforce supranational EU principles in the national arena. Thus, the potential for the Court to act as a trustee court could, arguable, be found in an ambitious reading of the proportionality principle, and one such avenue, if read in the light of the fundamental rights, could be seen as being safeguarded by the Charter of Fundamental Rights.

It is therefore a challenge for the EU Court of Justice to convince the highest national courts that, despite its non-accession, the EU system of rights is, at the very minimum, as good as that offered by the ECHR. Indeed, there is wide-ranging literature in EU constitutional law, in pluralism and in the cosmopolitan legal movement.[59] Much of this debate has been constructed around the possibility of Member States derogating from EU law and the possibility of national constitutional courts acting as a rebutter of EU law when national constitutional values are endangered (which would be contrary to supremacy in classic EU law doctrine).

[57] Maria Fletcher and Ester Herlin-Karnell, 'Is there a Transatlantic Security Strategy? Area of Freedom, Security and Justice Law and its Global Dimension' in Fletcher, Herlin-Karnell and Matera (eds), *Area of Freedom, Security and Justice* (2016).

[58] Joined Cases C-203/15 and C-698/15.

[59] See, for example, Sionaidh Douglas-Scott, 'Justice And Pluralism in the EU' (2012) 65 *Current Legal Problems* 83–118; and Klemen Jaklic, *Constitutional Pluralism in the EU* (Oxford, Oxford University Press, 2015).

V. NATIONAL COURTS AND FIDUCIARY OBLIGATIONS: WHEN THE EU STANDARD IS NOT ROBUST ENOUGH

If the constitutional concern is to ensure that equality and freedom are safeguarded, then it seems unwise to insist on a strict judicial hierarchy in those cases in which the national constitutional framework in security and criminal law-related contexts provides for a higher level of judicial safeguards.

But what sort of argument would work in a court in the AFSJ context with its emphasis on security? As Alon Harel argues, courts provide individuals with an opportunity to raise their grievances and challenge what the individuals perceive (justifiably or unjustifiably) as a violation of their rights.[60] In this way, courts engage in reasoned deliberation and provide an explanation for the alleged violation. This is the right to justification that was discussed in chapter three. Institutions that operate in this way thereby inevitably become institutions that operate in a judicial manner.[61]

As Cristina Lafont points out: 'What the political process cannot possibly guarantee, the legal process typically does: the individual right to a fair hearing in which explicit, reasoned justifications for and against a contested statute become publicly available for political deliberation.'[62]

In national context, it begs the question of whether courts have a duty of trusteeship, or a fiduciary obligation of constitutional rights for individuals, when the current EU law regime does not offer a sufficiently high human rights standard according to their constitutional culture.[63] As explained in chapter four, constitutional rights are often said to function as a filtering mechanism through which we can determine what sorts of treatment of persons by the state are consistent with their status as free and equal bearers.[64] Since limitations on rights must be 'rationally connected to the objective and not be arbitrary, unfair or based on irrational considerations', this can be interpreted as a mechanism for ensuring that coercive state interference remains non-arbitrary in the republican sense, in that it tracks 'commonly avowable' public interests.[65] As stated above, it is true that, the proportionality test will often effectively require judges to make substantive, appraisals as to the relative merits of competing claims of

[60] Alon Harel, *Why Law Matters* (Oxford, Oxford University Press, 2014) ch 2. And draft paper Robust Constitutionalism (on file with the author).

[61] Daly, 'Freedom as Non-domination' (2015).

[62] Cristina Lafont, 'Philosophical Foundations of Judicial Review' in David Dyzenhaus and Malcolm Thorburn (eds), *Philosophical Foundations of Constitutional Law* (Oxford, Oxford University Press, 2016) 265–81.

[63] On trustees, see Eyal Benvenisti, 'Sovereigns as Trustees of Humanity: On the Accountability of States to Foreign Stakeholders' (2013) 107 *American Journal of International Law* 295–333, and Criddle and Fox-Decent (n 46).

[64] Malcolm Thorburn, 'Proportionality' in David Dyzenhaus and Malcolm Thorburn (eds), *Philosophical Foundations of Constitutional Law* (Oxford, Oxford University Press, 2016) 305–21.

[65] Philip Pettit, *On the People's Terms: A Republican Theory and Model of Democracy* (Cambridge, Cambridge University Press, 2012), chs 4 and 5.

public and private rights. According to Eoin Daly, this implicates judges in a more far-reaching normative endeavour which extends beyond an assessment of arbitrariness in its republican sense.[66]

But, if, returning to the discussion in chapter three, a fiduciary obligation for national courts to ensure a high level of human rights protection and thereby the robustness of the EU system seems crucial. This means that courts are the institutions that effectively test the robustness of the EU regime and what justification is offered to the victim and due process standards for the suspected.

The constitutional structure of the AFSJ is largely dependent on reasonableness and proportionality in order to ensure that arbitrary domination does not exist. Reciprocity and trust is, in turn, guaranteed by a pluralistic structure of the AFSJ where enforcement depends on the robustness of the system. National courts are sometimes better placed than the CJEU to secure the highest level of human rights and this should be recognised under EU law. In the relation between the CJEU and the national courts, the free and equal paradigm should, perhaps, fall within the national margin of appreciation (not just ECHR, but also EU law proportionality).[67]

Consider the case of the United Kingdom and its Brexit negotiations for leaving the EU project. Are there any constitutional consequences of the UK leaving the EU, and could these consequences have an impact on criminal law co-operation in civil law jurisdiction? The UK, with its unwritten constitution, is interesting in the context of the constitutional law impact on criminal law. Given that the UK is a member of the ECHR and given that the EU values and rights are almost identical to the ECHR, what is the effect of this? If, for example, criminal law procedural co-operation is seen as a constitutional project and thereby obliged to guarantee freedom and equality for all, then I would like to ask the question of to what extent national courts have a duty or a fiduciary obligation of constitutional rights for individuals. In the specific case of Brexit, if human rights protection would be weakened by the UK's exit, but the UK still chooses to participate in some EU repressive measures, such as the fight against terrorism, and the EAW, etc, then, it could be argued that, if the UK does not offer a sufficiently high human rights standard according to established EU law culture, national UK courts would still have an obligation to apply EU fundamental rights in criminal law procedures. Likewise, national courts in mainland Europe would not have an obligation to blindly execute a judgment or arrest warrant on behalf of the UK if not all EU safeguards were guaranteed. Here, the implications of a constitutional structure for understanding criminal law procedure and the importance of constitutionalism in this process are crucial. The effect of global regulation, for example (think of the fight against

[66] Daly (n 54).

[67] On margin of appreciation, for example, Yuval Shany, 'Toward a General Margin of Appreciation Doctrine in International Law?' (2005) 16 *European Journal of International Law* 907–40.

cyber-crime, money laundering or terrorism) in this context, would mean the duty for national constitutional courts to apply the highest standard in national criminal law procedures, even when those rules come from the outside, if they wish to ensure a more robust protection of human rights.

VI. CONCLUSION

The aim of this chapter has been to look at the effects of a balancing right to justice in the complex area of opt-outs and enhanced co-operation mechanisms. The chapter has argued that the balancing mechanism largely resembles a proportionality test, and that the classic loyalty mantra in EU law (where Member States have to ensure the full effectiveness of EU law) has slowly emerged into a fairness- and dignity-oriented test, as demonstrated in a number of recent cases in the context of the EAW, asylum law and data protection cases. Subsequently, the chapter set out to explore tentatively the idea of the CJEU acting as a trustee court, and argued that the Court has fiduciary obligations to maintain the values set out in the Charter and the Treaty of Lisbon Treaty. Thereafter, I set out to look cautiously at the question of the obligation of national courts to adopt the highest standard of human rights obligations and show that such a pluralistic approach is in line with the model of flexible integration and a method for achieving a just constitutional structure in this area.

7

Conclusion

I. CONCLUSION

In Michael Walzer's spheres of justice and in John Rawls' theory, justice is still an essentially state-bound concept. For Rawls, the very point of developing a conception of justice is to discover more precisely our understanding of what is reasonable and unreasonable in matters of justice.[1] Moreover, for Rawls, respect for human decency is a condition of justice, but not all decent societies are just.[2] A decent society, as Avishai Margalit reminds us, is one that treats people with respect and dignity.[3] And, a just society also allows individuals equality and freedom and a right to justification for arbitrary decisions that concern the people within its jurisdiction.[4] While the EU is not a state, the idea of justice in the EU legal setting has become a new lens for viewing the European enterprise and, as such, is largely inspired by the greater debate in political theory on how to imagine a just society. This book has tried to explore the meaning and function of justice-oriented reasoning in the EU legal discourse by deconstructing it from a perspective of non-domination and legitimacy, and by asking what justice can add to the debate on EU constitutionalism in the specific AFSJ territory. As explained throughout this volume, the AFSJ bundles together the most sensitive nation-state questions, such as criminal law, security, migration, border control and civil law co-operation. It is a very divergent policy area and one in which the EU is currently working out what mainstream principle in EU law can successfully be transplanted to govern this new area of the law. With the rather unchartered territory of EU security regulation, a fundamental question is what form of justification in legal terms could the Member States and the citizens of the EU rightly demand as the EU project expands? In this volume, I have explored the question of how to understand the conditions of constitutional

[1] Michael Walzer, *Spheres of Justice: A Defence of Pluralism and Equality* (Chicester, Wiley-Blackwell, 1983); John Rawls, *A Theory of Justice* (Cambridge MA, Harvard University Press, 1971).

[2] Samuel Freeman, 'Introduction, John Rawls – An Overview' in Freeman (ed), *The Cambridge Companion to Rawls* (Cambridge, Cambridge University Press, 2003) 1–61 at 45.

[3] Avishai Margalit, *The Decent Society* (Cambridge MA, Harvard University Press, 1998).

[4] Rainer Forst, *Justification and Critique: Towards a Critical Theory of Politics* (Cambridge, Polity Press, 2014).

legitimacy by arguing for a meaning of justice as non-domination which forms part of the EU's constitutional structure and helps to ensure a sufficiently high human rights standard that would foster European culture and a sense of fairness. I argued that this is particularly needed for the construction of the AFSJ to a successful 'justice' space. The starting point of the book has been the normative argument that the EU currently suffers from a justice deficit and that something needs to be done. And so, the underlying question of the project has been this: What are the core constitutional challenges facing the EU in the area of security regulation and how can justice function as a device for improving the lives of both Europeans and all those subject to the EU's regulation?

As discussed in the preceding chapters, for Rainer Forst, the basis of the demand for justice is the claim to be respected as an agent of justification; that is, in one's dignity as a human being who can ask for and give justification. For him, the concepts of justice and justification are interwoven. Specifically, as this book has tried to show, conceptions of justice offer a compelling perspective for understanding the wider governance structure of the EU. Rather than merely anchoring the individual's array of legal rights and the access to justice that it expresses, justice would then constitute a broader normative, as well as institutional, principle for arranging the values underlying the EU's AFSJ. Such a conception of the AFSJ would not only value security, but equally strive to ensure freedom and justice – and thereby the overall fairness of the system.

In particular, it is through an engagement with the concepts of non-domination, justice and justification that I have tried to show the uniqueness of the constitutional structure of the AFSJ and why it constitutes a particularly useful testing field of justifications. This is because the AFSJ is one of the most urgent and dynamic EU policy domains at present, and where the idea of justice as non-domination will add to a grammar of justice and thereby help to improve the EU's credibility. The first part of the book has tried to demonstrate that a turn to justice as a theoretical concept could help the EU framing of the questions that it ought to be asking and, as such, are needed for the development of the AFSJ. This could usefully be referred to as a constitutionalised vision of justice for the AFSJ. At its core, the question relates to the connection between a theoretical understanding of justice and the practical implications of it in AFSJ matters.

A. Summary of the Arguments

As explained above, the AFSJ is an area that is currently marked by too little justice-oriented reasoning in the EU's institutions, and where security-related measures have tilted the balance in the AFSJ. As indicated, the notion of access to justice has always played a vital role in the ongoing construction of Europe, but this book has explored whether there is a need for an elaborated understanding of justice as a theoretical concept. It has tried to show that the debate on

EU constitutionalism is, in essence, a debate on legitimacy and on ensuring justice. In the EU context, justice must be politically grounded, assuming that we start from a common justice platform, where fundamental rights are fully respected in practice. Seen in Forstian terms, the concept is about the basic right to justification. Applying a Rawlsian account to the theory of justice would, moreover, imply using reasonableness as an adequate standard for measuring legitimacy at EU level and for linking it to the broader debate on justice. Clearly, or at least arguably, the principle of proportionality can be viewed as pointing in the same direction as reasonableness, which was explored in chapter four.

Accordingly, it could be argued that the EU legal system encompasses a broader notion of justice than the basic constitutional principle upon which other EU principles are based. For all these reasons, therefore, there has to be a connection between the aspiration for justice and that of the overall legal architecture, or the governance ambition of securing legitimacy in the European system.

In chapter one, a picture was sketched of what an AFSJ looks like and why the current focus on security could be seen as problematical, as it poses challenges as to what kind of security the EU specifically sets out to establish, and how it can be reconciled with the notions of freedom and justice. Thereafter, in chapter two, an explanation was provided of the role of security within the AFSJ, which was linked to the long-standing debate in political theory on the connection between freedom and power. Specifically, the chapter started from the position that there is currently an over-reliance on security in the current law-making in the EU, and that it is useful to turn to the republican benchmark of freedom as non-domination when assessing the EU's security agenda.[5] The chapter then connected this question to the wider issue of legitimacy and set out to argue that an understanding of freedom as non-domination and, by extension, justice as non-domination, offers a useful lens for viewing and understanding the EU's AFSJ endeavour.

Subsequently, in chapter three, this line of reasoning was developed further by focusing on the connection between justice seen as non-domination and the right to justification in EU security law. The right to justification, as developed in the rich political theory literature, was then tested in both the EU context, and, more broadly, in the constitutional legal framework for EU security regulation. It is suggested that the question of justice and justification is ultimately one of sufficiently good reasons, in which the establishment of the AFSJ is a question of constitutionalism, as such.[6] The idea of chapter four, and largely inspired by Mattias Kumm's work on the right to Socratic contestation,[7] was then to make the case that, in order to give the notion of justification concrete legal meaning,

[5] Philip Pettit, 'A Republican Law of Peoples' (2010) 9 *European Journal of Political Theory* 70–94.

[6] Alon Harel, *Why Law Matters* (Oxford, Oxford University Press, 2014).

[7] Mattias Kumm, 'The Idea of Socratic Contestation and the Right to Justification: The Point of Rights-based Proportionality Review' (2010) 4 *Law & Ethics of Human Rights* 142–75.

we need to look at the principle of proportionality. Again, as was suggested in chapter 4 Rawlsian account to the question of proportionality would, for example, imply using reasonableness as an adequate standard for measuring legitimacy at EU level and for linking it to the wider discourse on justice.[8] According to Rawls' liberal principle of legitimacy, the use of political power is fully proper only when 'it is exercised in accordance with a constitution the essentials of which all citizens as free and equal may reasonably be expected to endorse in light of the principles and ideals acceptable to their common human reason'.[9] Regardless of whether one agrees with all the elements in Rawls' argument and the question of public reason, this chapter explored the practical legal implications of a right to justification – in terms of public reason – in a legal context. As the chapter set out to track, the principle of proportionality can be viewed as pointing in the same direction as reasonableness. Specifically, the framework of proportionality was then applied to the AFSJ. In doing so, it investigated proportionally as a bridging principle in the intersection of the internal and external security dogma in the AFSJ. The chapter examined the varied meanings of proportionality as well as the possibilities of a margin of appreciation test (dangers and merits) and, although the chapter is primarily theory-oriented, it aimed to marry theory and practice by testing the power of justification in context by looking at the recent case law (for example, the Digital Rights case). Next, in chapter five, a case study was provided and in parts of the chapter a considerably more hands-on approach was adopted. In this chapter, two areas (admittedly moving targets, but of particular importance) were dissected: the EU's response to the refugee/migration crisis; and the ongoing EU fight against terrorism and crime. Both examples seriously challenge the EU's legitimacy claim. Thus, the chapter also discussed the extent to which the Charter of Fundamental Rights successfully provides for a right to justification in EU decision-making, particularly with regard to how the proportionality principle is applied. Finally, in chapter six, the difficult question as to how the constitutional framework outlined in this book works when applied in the context of the multi-speed context, in which not all Member States are on board the ship of integration, was addressed. This means that AFSJ co-operation operates in an archipelago-like landscape. The chapter tentatively asked whether constitutionalism pre-supposed a global or European environment. It examined the meaning of 'justification' and solidarity in this multi-speed context. Moreover, the chapter discussed the broader framework of differentiated integration by looking at it within the broader framework of differentiated integration in order to place the AFSJ in context and also addressed some of the current and important doctrinal questions in this area.

Finally, we may still have to justify what exactly is the message of the book.

[8] John Rawls (ed), *Justice as Fairness: A Restatement, Erin Kelly*, (Cambridge MA, Harvard University Press, 2001).

[9] John Rawls, *Political Liberalism* (Ithaca NY, Columbia University Press, 1993).

II. THE JUSTIFICATION OF THE BOOK

Critics may still ask how useful a justice-oriented approach in AFSJ law is. And they may still wonder why justice is different in the EU, as compared to the different Member State spheres. As I have attempted to show in this work, given the EU's authority to decide on traditionally nation-state questions and its extensive reading of EU security as opposed to national security, the EU, in its attempt to establish an AFSJ, also has to have an ambition of establishing a just *justice* space. I adopted the Forst-inspired view that justice and justification are interlinked. The right to justification, as developed in political theory, can – as this book has argued – be mapped on to the EU's constitutional legal framework as providing a good framework. Justice as non-domination is also intrinsic to the constitutional structure of the AFSJ. The critic may well ask what is the added value of this view? In reply, I have argued that viewing justice as non-domination informs and shapes the constitutional structure of the AFSJ in the direction of a culture of fairness.

A reading of justice that is linked to the question of justification – as a key idea of the overall structure and fairness of the AFSJ–EU system – could help construct a fair AFSJ which fully takes into account how sensitive this area is. A turn to justification via the legal tool of proportionality could facilitate and benefit the debate on the future of the AFSJ in the sense that it offers a better chance for justice to inform the outcome, helping to ensure a balance in the AFSJ as a force of good governance. One core idea of the book then is that the need for justice seen as non-domination in the EU does not pre-suppose a merely consequentialist approach, although it is important that serious attention to justice as a critical legal concept could add democratic credibility to the AFSJ if it is read as a basic right to justification, which safeguards due process rights. Its usefulness thus lies in its potential to place the focus on the individual by requiring a sufficiently coherent (entailing generality and reciprocity) system. A turn to justification via the legal tool of proportionality could also help benefit the debate on the future of the AFSJ in the sense that it offers a better chance for justice to inform the outcome, thereby helping to ensure a balance in the AFSJ as a force of good governance in this area. Such an understanding, however, requires a largely political reading of justice that takes it beyond mere moralism or what it means to be a good European, and forces the EU to work out a sufficiently thought-through policy agenda with a constitutional structure of the project, with the Member States to follow, and with the concerns of the individuals in the EU being central to this agenda. This is also central for the question of the burden of justification. As was chartered in this book, the impact of a constitutional meaning of justice that could be grounded in the EU Charter and EU treaty values, and the extent to which it could function as a visualising tool for remedying some of the problems facing the EU in the current wave of populism and isolationism in some Member States, remains a considerable challenge and dilemma for the construction of the AFSJ (and of course the EU in general).[10] What is more, the place of the burden of justification for attaining freedom seems often to lie on citizens and not on the EU or its Member States when they are determining AFSJ policies such as security regulation. This apparent revised burden of justification in an area that often involves coercion is highly problematic in a security-related context and confirms a current tendency of the security concept being used in a way that amounts to domination and has been traced in this work.

But, above all, this book has argued that justice seen as non-domination has important implications for how we think about the AFSJ, and has attempted to start the process with regard to why and how such awareness matters.

[10] TRS Allan, *Constitutional Justice: A Liberal Theory Of The Rule Of Law* (Oxford, Oxford University Press, 2003). See also Aharon Barak, 'On Constitutional Implications and Constitutional Structure' in David Dyzenhaus and Malcolm Thorburn (eds), *Philosophical Foundations Of Constitutional Law* (Oxford, Oxford University Press, 2016) ch 3.

Bibliography

Ackermann, Bruce, 'The Emergency Constitution' (2004) 113 *The Yale Law Journal* 1029–91.

Adler-Nissen, Rebecca, 'Opting Out of an Ever Closer Union: The Integration Doxa and the Management of Sovereignty' (2011) 34 *West European Politics* 1092–13.

Albi, Anneli, 'Erosion of Constitutional Rights in EU Law: A Call for "Substantive Co-operative Constitutionalism"' (2015) 9 *Vienna Journal on International Constitutional Law* 291–343.

Alexy, Robert, *A Theory of Constitutional Rights* (Oxford, Oxford University Press, 2002).

—— 'The Absolute and the Relative Dimensions of Constitutional Rights' (2017) 37 *Oxford Journal of Legal Studies* 31–47.

Allan, TRS, *Constitutional Justice: A Liberal Theory of the Rule of Law* (Oxford, Oxford University Press, 2003).

Amstutz, Marc, 'Eroding Boundaries: On Financial Crisis and an Evolutionary Concept of Regulatory Reform' in Poul F Kjaer, Gunther Teubner and Alberto Febbrajo (eds), *The Financial Crisis in Constitutional Perspective: The Dark Side of Functional Differentiation* (Oxford, Hart Publishing, 2011) 223–68.

Anderson, David, and Cian C Murphy, 'The Charter of Fundamental Rights' in Andrea Biondi, Piet Eeckhout and Stefanie Ripley (eds), *EU Law After Lisbon* (Oxford, Oxford University Press, 2012) 155–79.

Arendt, Hannah, *On Violence* (Orlando FL, Harcourt Brace & Company, 1970).

Ari-Takahshi, Yutaka, 'Proportionality' in *The Oxford Handbook of International Human Rights Law*, Dinah Shelton (ed) (Oxford, Oxford University Press, 2015) 446–68.

Arnull, Anthony, and Daniel Wincott (eds), *Accountability and Legitimacy in the European Union* (Oxford, Oxford University Press, 2002).

Ashworth, Andrew, and Lucia Zedner, *Preventive Justice* (Oxford, Oxford University Press, 2014).

Bachvarova, Mira, 'Non-domination's Role in the Theorizing of Global Justice' (2013) 9 *Journal of Global Ethics* 173–85.

Bajaj Sameer and Rossi Enzo, 'Noumenal Power, Reasons and Justification: A Critique of Forst' chapter in E Herlin-Karnell and M Klatt (eds), *Constitutionalism Justified* (Oxford, Oxford University Press 2019), forthcoming.

Baker, Estella, 'Criminal Justice and the "New, Deep and Special Partnership" between the EU and the UK: A Critical Test for the Area of Freedom, Security and Justice?' (2018) 26 *European Journal of Crime, Criminal Law and Criminal Justice* 1–19.

Barak, Aharon, 'The Role of a Supreme Court in a Democracy and the Fight Against Terrorism' (2005) 35 *Hong Kong Law Journal* 287–308.

—— Proportionality: Constitutional Rights and their Limitations (Cambridge, Cambridge University Press, 2012).

—— *Human Dignity: The Constitutional Value and the Constitutional Right* (Cambridge, Cambridge University Press, 2015).

—— 'On Constitutional Implications and Constitutional Structure' in David Dyzenhaus and Malcolm Thorburn (eds), *Philosophical Foundations of Constitutional Law* (Oxford, Oxford University Press, 2015) 53–74.

Beatty, David M, *The Ultimate Rule of Law* (Oxford, Oxford University Press, 2005).

Beck, Ulrich, and Edgar Grande, *Cosmopolitan Europe* (Cambridge, Cambridge University Press, 2007).

Beetz, Jan Pieter and Rossi, Enzo, 'EU Legitimacy in a Realist Key', WZB Centre for Global Constitutionalism Discussion Paper 2015, SP IV 2015-802 (2015).

Beitz, Charles R, *The Idea of Human Rights* (Oxford, Oxford University Press, 2009).

Bellamy, Richard, *Political Constitutionalism: A Republican Defence of the Constitutionality of Democracy* (Cambridge, Cambridge University Press, 2007).

Benhabib, Seyla, *The Rights of Others: Aliens, Residents, and Citizens* (Cambridge, Cambridge University Press, 2004).

—— 'Democratic Sovereignty and Transnational Law. On Legal Utopianism and Democratic Skepticism' (2014) available at: http://papers.ssrn.com/sol3/papers.cfm?abstract_id=2455436.

Benvenisti, Eyal, 'Sovereigns as Trustees of Humanity: On the Accountability of States to Foreign Stakeholders.' (2013) 107 *American Journal of International Law* 295–333.

Berlin, Isaiah, 'Two Concepts of Liberty' in Berlin, *Four Essays of Liberty* (Oxford, Oxford University Press, 1958).

Bergström, Maria, 'The Many Uses of Anti-Money Laundering Regulation – Over Time and into the Future' (2018) 19 *German Law Journal* 1149–67.

Blake, Michael and Smith, Patrick Taylor, 'International Distributive Justice' *The Stanford Encyclopedia of Philosophy* (Spring 2015 edn), Edward N Zalta (ed), https://plato.stanford.edu/archives/spr2015/entries/international-justice.

Bohman, James, 'Nondomination and Transnational Democracy' in Cécile Laborde and John Maynor (eds), *Republicanism and Political Theory* (Oxford, Blackwell, 2008) 190–218.

—— 'A Response to my Critics: Democracy across Borders' (2010) 3 *Ethics & Global Politics* 71–84.

Bongiovanni, Giorgio, Antonino Rotolo and Corrado Roversi, 'The Claim to Correctness and Inferentialism: Alexy's Theory of practical Reason Reconsidered' in George Pavlakos (ed), *Law, Rights and Discourse: The Legal Philosophy of Robert Alexy* (Oxford, Hart Publishing, 2007) 275–300.

Bongiovanni, Giorgio, Giovanni Sartor and Chiara Valentini (eds), *Reasonableness and Law* (Dordrecht, Springer, 2009).

Bossung, Raphael, *The Evolution of EU Counter-Terrorism: European Security Policy after 9/11* (Abingdon, Routledge, 2012).

Brems, Eva, and Janneke Gerards (eds), *Shaping Rights in the ECHR: The Role of the European Court of Human Rights in Determining the Scope of Human Rights* (Cambridge, Cambridge University Press, 2014).

Buchanan, Allen, 'Human Rights and the Legitimacy of the International Order' (2008) 14 *Legal Theory* 39–70.

—— *The Heart of Human Rights* (Oxford, Oxford University Press, 2013).

—— 'Why International Legal Human Rights?' in Rowan Cruft, S Matthew Liao and Massimo Renzo (eds), *The Philosophical Foundation of Human Rights* (Oxford, Oxford University Press, 2015) 244–62.

Busuioc, Madalina, Curtin, Deirdre and Groenleer, Martijn, 'Agency Growth between Autonomy and Accountability: The European Police Office as a "Living Institution"' (2011) 18 *Journal of European Public Policy* 848–67.

Caney, Simon, *Justice beyond Borders: A Global Political Theory* (Oxford, Oxford University Press, 2005).

Carens, Joseph H, The Ethics of Immigration (Oxford, Oxford University Press, 2013).

Chacón, Jennifer, 'Immigration Detention: No Turning Back?' (2014) 113 *South Atlantic Quarterly* 621–28.

Cherem, Max, 'Refugee Rights: Against Expanding the Definition of a 'Refugee' and Unilateral Protection Elsewhere' (2016) 24 *The Journal of Political Philosophy* 183–205.

Cohen, Gerald A, *Rescuing Justice and Equality* (Cambridge MA, Harvard University Press, 2008).

Cohen, Jean L, *Globalization and Sovereignty: Rethinking Legality, Legitimacy, and Constitutionalism* (Cambridge, Cambridge University Press, 2012).

Cohen-Eliya, Moshe and Porat, Iddo, *Proportionality and Constitutional Culture* (Cambridge, Cambridge University Press, 2013).

Colón-Ríos, Joel I, 'The Legitimacy of the Juridical: Constituent Power' (2010) 48 *Osgoode Hall Law Journal* 199–245.

—— *Weak Constitutionalism: Democratic Legitimacy and the Question of Constituent Power* (Abingdon, Routledge, 2012).

Conway, Gerard, 'Holding to Account a Possible European Public Prosecutor: Supranational Governance and Accountability across Diverse Legal Traditions' (2013) 24 *Criminal Law Forum* 371–401.

Cooke, Maeve, 'Law's Claim to Correctness' in George Pavlakos (ed), *Law, Rights and Discourse: The Legal Philosophy of Robert Alexy* (Oxford, Hart Publishing, 2007) 225–48.

Costello, Cathryn, (2016) The Human Rights of Migrants and Refugees in European Law (Oxford, Oxford University Press, 2016).

Corradetti, Claudio, 'Constructivism in Cosmopolitan Law: Kant's Right to Visit', (2017) 6 *Global Constitutionalism* 412–41.

Craig, Paul, 'Proportionality, Rationality and Review' (2010) *New Zealand Law Review* 265.

—— 'Integration, Democracy and Legitimacy' in Paul Craig and Gráinne de Búrca (eds), *The Evolution of EU Law* (Oxford, Oxford University Press, 2011) 13–40.

—— *EU Administrative Law* (Oxford, Oxford University Press, 2012).

—— 'Subsidiarity: A Political and Legal Analysis' (2012) 50 *Journal of Common Market Studies* 72–87.

—— 'The Nature of Reasonableness Review' (2013) 66 *Current Legal Problems* 131 –67.

—— 'Proportionality and Judicial Review: A UK Historical Perspective' in Stefan Vogenauer and Stephen Weatherill (eds), *General Principles of Law, European and Comparative Perspectives* (Oxford, Hart Publishing, 2017) 145–66.

Craig, Paul and de Búrca, Gráinne (eds), The Evolution of EU Law, 2nd edn (Oxford, Oxford University Press, 2011).

Criddle, Evan J and Fox-Decent, Evan, *Fiduciaries of Humanity: How International Law Constitutes Authority* (Oxford, Oxford University Press, 2016).

Cromartie, Alan, 'Legitimacy' in Richard Bellamy and Andrew Mason (eds), *Political Concepts* (Manchester: Manchester University Press, 2003) 93–104.

Crum, Ben, 'Public reason and Multi-layered Justice' (2017) 8 *Transnational Legal Theory* 42–58.

Curtin, Deirdre, 'The Constitutional Structure of the Union: A Europe of Bits and Pieces', (1993) 30 *Common Market Law Review* 17–69.

—— 'Overseeing Secrets in the EU: A Democratic Perspective' (2014) 52 *Journal of Common Market Studies* 684–700.

Daly, Eoin, 'Freedom as Non-domination in the Jurisprudence of Constitutional Rights' (2015) 28 *Canadian Journal of Law and Jurisprudence* 289–316.

—— *Rousseau's Constitutionalism: Austerity and Republican Freedom* (Oxford, Hart Publishing, 2017).

Dawood, Yasmin, 'The Antidomination Model and the Judicial Oversight of Democracy' (2008) 96 *The Georgetown Law Journal* 1411–85.

De Búrca, Gráinne, 'The Principle of Subsidiarity and the Court of Justice as an Institutional Actor' (1998) 36 *Journal of Common Market Studies* 217–35.

—— 'Legal Principles as an Instrument of Differentiation? The Principles of Proportionality and Subsidiarity' in Bruno De Witte, Dominik Hanf and Ellen Vos (eds), *The Many Faces of Differentiation in EU Law* (Antwerp, Intersentia, 2001) 131–44.

De Goede, Marieke, 'The SWIFT Affair and the Global Politics of European Security' (2012) 50 *Journal of Common Market Studies* 214–30.

De Waele, Henri, 'Entrenching the Area of Freedom, Security and Justice: Questions of Institutional Governance and Judicial Control' in Maria Fletcher, Ester Herlin-Karnell and Claudio Matera (eds), *The European Union as an Area of Freedom, Security and Justice* (Abingdon, Routledge, 2016) 485–508.

De Witte, Bruno, 'Old-fashioned Flexibility: International Agreements between Member States of the European Union' in Gráinne de Búrca and Joanne Scott (eds), *Constitutional Change in the EU: From Uniformity to Flexibility?* (Oxford, Hart Publishing, 2000) 31–58.
De Witte, Floris, *Justice in the EU: The Emergence of Transnational Solidarity* (Oxford, Oxford University Press, 2015).
Den Boer, Monica, 'Preventive Empires: Security Dynamics at Multiple Levels of Governance (2011) 3 *Amsterdam Law Forum* 102–13.
Douglas-Scott, Sionaidh, 'Justice and Pluralism in the EU' (2012) 65 *Current Legal Problems* 83–118.
—— 'The Problem of Justice in the European Union' in Julie Dickson and Pavlos Eleftheriadis (eds), *Philosophical Foundations of EU Law* (Oxford, Oxford University Press, 2012) 412–48.
—— *Law after Modernity* (Oxford, Hart Publishing, 2013).
—— 'Human Rights as a Basis for Justice in the European Union', (2017) 8 *Transnational Legal Theory* 59–78.
Durieux, Jean-François 'The Duty to Rescue Refugees' (2016) 28 *International Journal of Refugee Law* 637–55.
Dworkin, Ronald M, 'Hard Cases' *Harvard Law Review* (1975), pp 1057–1109.
—— *Law's Empire* (Oxford, Hart Publishing, 1998).
—— *Justice for Hedgehogs* (Cambridge MA, Harvard University Press, 2011).
—— 'A New Philosophy for International Law' (2013) 41 *Philosophy & Public Affairs* 2–30.
Dyzenhaus, David, *The Constitution of Law: Legality in a Time of Emergency* (Cambridge, Cambridge University Press, 2006).
—— 'Consent, Legitimacy and the Foundation of Political and Legal Authority' in Jeremy Webber and Colin Murray McLeod (eds), *Between Consenting Peoples: Political Community and the Meaning of Consent* (Vancouver, UBC, 2010) 163–87.
—— 'Process and Substance as Aspects of the Public Law Form' (2015) 74 *The Cambridge Law Journal* 284–306.
Eleftheriadis, Pavlos, 'The Moral Distinctiveness of the European Union' (2011) 9 *International Journal of Constitutional Law* 695–713.
Endicott, Timothy AO, 'Proportionality and Incommensurability', Oxford Legal Studies Research Paper No 40/2012 (2012).
Estlund, David M, *Democratic Authority: A Philosophical Framework* (Princeton NJ, Princeton University Press, 2008).
Faleg, Giovanni, 'European Security after the Paris Attack', CEPS commentary (2015), available at www.ceps.eu/system/files/GF%20European%20Security%20after%20Paris.pdf.
Farmer, Lindsay, *The Making of Modern Criminal Law: Criminalization and Civil Order* (Oxford, Oxford University Press, 2016).
Feinberg, Myriam, *Sovereignty in the Age of Global Terrorism: The Role of Organisations* (Leiden, Brill, 2016).
—— 'Terrorism Inside Out: Legislating for Humanity to Cooperate Against Terrorism' (2017) 42 *North Carolina Journal of International Law* 505–43.
Ferrarini, Guido and Moloney, Niamh, 'Reshaping Order Execution in the EU and the Rule of Interest Groups: From MiFID I to MiFID II' (2012) 13 *European Business Organization Review* 557–97.
Fichera, Massimo and Herlin-Karnell, Ester, 'The Margin of Appreciation Test and Balancing in the Area of Freedom Security and Justice: A Proportionate Answer for a Europe of Rights?' (2013) 19 *European Public Law* 759–87.
Fichera, Massimo and Kramer, Jens (eds), *Law and Security in Europe: Reconsidering the Security Constitution* (Cambridge, Intersentia, 2013).
Fichera M, 'Sketches of a Theory of Europe as an Area of Freedom, Security and Justice', in: M. Fletcher, E. Herlin-Karnell and C. Matera (eds), *The EU as an Area of Freedom, Security and Justice*, (Abingdon: Routledge, 2016), Chapter 3, pp. 34–56.
Fletcher, Maria, Herlin-Karnell, Ester and Matera, Claudio (eds) *The EU as an Area of Freedom, Security and Justice* (Abingdon, Routledge, 2016).

Flikschuh, Katrin, 'A Regime of Equal Private Freedom? Individual Rights and Public Law in Ripstein's Force and Freedom' in Sari Kisilevsky and Martin J Stone (eds), *Freedom and Force: Essays on Kant's Legal Philosophy* (Oxford, Hart Publishing, 2017) 55–74.

Føllesdal, Andreas, 'Appreciating the Margin of Appreciation' in Adam Etinson (ed), *Human Rights: Moral or Political?* (Oxford, Oxford University Press, 2018) 269–312.

Føllesdal, Andreas and Hix, Simon, 'Why there is a Democratic Deficit in the EU: A Response to Majone and Moravcsik' (2006) 44 *Journal of Common Market Studies* 533–62.

Forst, Rainer, *The Right to Justification: Elements of a Constructivist Theory of Justice* (Chichester-New York, Columba University Press, 2012).

—— 'Transnational Justice and Democracy: Overcoming Three Dogmas of Political Theory' in Eva Erman and Sofia Näsström (eds), *Political Equaliy in Transnational Democracy* (Basingstoke, Palgrave Macmillan, 2013) 41–59.

—— *Justification and Critique: Towards a Critical Theory of Politics* (Cambridge-Malden MA, Polity Press, 2014).

—— 'Legitimacy, Democracy and Justice', paper presented at VU Centre for European Legal Studies/ Access Europe, Amsterdam, 6–7 November 2014, 'Towards a Grammar of Justice in EU Law'.

—— 'Justice, Democracy and the Right to Justification: Reflections on Jürgen Neyer's Normative Theory of the European Union' in Dimitry Kochenov, Gráinne de Búrca and Andrew Williams (eds), *Europe's Justice Deficit?* (Oxford, Hart Publishing, 2015) 227–34.

—— 'Noumenal Power' (2015) 23 *The Journal of Political Philosophy* 111–27.

—— *Normativity and Power: Analyzing Social Orders of Justification* (Oxford, Oxford University Press, 2017).

Foucault, Michel, *The Archeology of Knowledge: And the Discourse on Language* (New York, Vintage Books, 1972).

Fox-Decent, Evan, 'Constitutional Legitimacy Unbound' in: David Dyzenhaus and Malcolm Thorburn (eds), *Philosophical Foundations of Constitutional Law* (Oxford University Press, 2016) 119–40.

Frankenberg, Günter, 'Human Rights and the Belief in a Just World' (2013) 12 *I-CON* 35–60.

Freeman, Samuel, 'Congruence and the Good of Justice' in Freeman (ed), *The Cambridge Companion to Rawls* (Cambridge, Cambridge University Press, 2003) 277–315.

Fuller, Lon L, *The Morality of Law* (New Haven CT, Yale University Press, 1964).

Ganesh, Aravind, 'Rightful Relations with Distant Strangers: A Kantian Critique of the Law of the European Union in the Wider World' (2018) unpublished PhD thesis draft, VU University Amsterdam.

Gardbaum, Stephen, 'Human Rights as International Constitutional Rights' (2008) 19 *European Journal of International Law* 749–68.

Gaus, Gerald, *The Tyranny of the Ideal: Justice in a Diverse Society* (Princeton NJ: Princeton University Press, 2016).

Geelhoed, Willem, Erkelens, Leendert H and Meij, Arjen WH (eds), *Shifting Perspectives on the European Public Prosecutor's Office* (Berlin-Heidelberg, Springer Verlag, 2018).

Gibney, Matthew J, 'Refugees and Justice between States' (2015) 14 *European Journal of Political Theory* 448–63.

Gómez-Jara Díez, Carlos and Herlin-Karnell, Ester, 'Prosecuting EU Financial Crimes: The European Prosecutor's Office in Comparison to the US Federal Regime' (2018) 19 *German Law Journal* 1191–220.

Grimm, Dieter, 'Proportionality in Canadian and German Constitutional Jurisprudence' (2007) 57 *University of Toronto Law Journal* 383–97.

Grossman, Emiliano and Leblond, Patrick, 'European Integration: Finally the Great Leap Forward?' (2011) 49 *Journal of Common Market Studies* 413–35.

Habermas, Jürgen, *Between Facts and Norms: Contributions and Discourse Theory Law and Democracy* (Cambridge-Malden MA, Polity Press, 1996).

—— *The Crisis of the European Union: A Response* (Cambridge, Polity Press, 2013).

Halberstam, Daniel, '"It's the Autonomy, Stupid!" A Modest Defence of Opinion 2/13 on EU Accession to the ECHR, and the Way Forward' (2015)16 *German Law Journal* 105–46.

Harel, Alon, *Why Law Matters* (Oxford, Oxford University Press, 2014).

—— 'Robust Constitutionalism' in Ester Herlin-Karnell and Matthias Klatt (eds), *Constitutionalism Justified* (Oxford, Oxford University Press, forthcoming).

Hart, HLA (2012) *The Concept of Law*, 3rd edn (Oxford, Clarendon Press 2012).

Hayek, Friedrich August von (1944) *The Road to Serfdom* (London: Routledge, 2001 reprint).

Herlin-Karnell, Ester, 'The Development of EU Precautionary Criminalization' (2011) 2 *European Criminal Law Review* 149–69.

—— *The Constitutional Dimension of European Criminal Law* (Oxford, Hart Publishing, 2012).

—— 'The EU as a Promoter of Values and the European Global Project' (2012) 13 *German Law Journal* 1225.

—— 'Denmark and the European Area of Freedom, Security and Justice: A Scandinavian Arrangement' (2013) 5 *Amsterdam Law Forum* 95–105.

—— 'Europe's Area of Freedom, Security and Justice Through the Prism of Constitutionalism: Why the EU Needs a Grammar of Justice to Improve its Legitimacy', WZB, discussion paper, SP IV 2014-801 (Berlin, 2014).

—— 'Two Conceptions of Justice in EU Constitutionalism. The Shaping of Security Law in Europe' (Amsterdam, VU University of Amsterdam, 2014).

—— 'The Domination of Security and the Promise of Justice: On Justification and Proportionality in Europe's "Area of Freedom, Security and Justice"' (2017) 8 *Transnational Legal Theory* 79–102.

—— 'The European Court of Justice as a Game Changer: Fiduciary Obligations in the Area of Freedom, Security and Justice' in Ariadna Ripoll Servent and Florian Trauner (eds), *Routledge Handbook of Justice and Home Affairs Research* (Abingdon, Routledge, 2017) 396–408.

—— 'Between Flexibility and Fragmentation: The Example of Criminal Law' in Bruno de Witte, Andrea Ott, Ellen Vos (eds), *Between Flexibility and Disintegration: The State of EU law today* (Cheltenham, Edward Elgar, 2017).

—— "On constitutional law parameters and EU Security regulation" *Boston University International Law Journal*, forthcoming, 2018.

—— 'The Concepts of Non-Domination and Justification in EU security-related context' in Ester Herlin-Karnell and Matthias Klatt (eds), *Constitutionalism Justified* (Oxford, Oxford University Press, 2019), forthcoming.

—— 'Understanding Trafficking in Human Beings as Mixed Migration: The European "Area of Freedom, Security and Justice" and its Global Width' in Haverkamp, Herlin-Karnell and Lernestedt (eds), *What is Wrong with Human Trafficking? Critical Perspectives on the Law* (Oxford, Hart, 2019).

Herlin-Karnell, Ester and Kjaer, Poul F, 'Dimensions of Justice and Justification in EU and Transnational Contexts' (2017) 8 *Transnational Legal Theory* 1–7.

Herlin-Karnell, Ester and Konstadinides, Theodore 'The Rise and Many Expressions of Consistency in EU Law: Legal and Strategic Implications for European Integration' (2013) 15 *Cambridge Yearbook of European Legal Studies* 139–67.

Hinsch, Wilfried, 'Justice, Legitimacy, and Constitutional Rights' (2010) 13 *Critical Review of International Social and Political Philosophy* 39–54.

Huscroft, Grant, Miller, Bradley W and Webber, Grégoire (eds), *Proportionality and the Rule of Law: Rights, Justification, Reasoning* (New York, Cambridge University Press, 2014).

Jackson, Vicki C, 'Constitutional Law in an Age of Proportionality' (2015) 124 *The Yale Law Journal* 3094–196.

Jacobs, Francis G, 'The Lisbon Treaty and the Court of Justice' in Andrea Biondi, Piet Eeckhout and Stefanie Ripley (eds), *EU Law after Lisbon* (Oxford, Oxford University Press, 2012) 197–212.

Jaklic, Klemen, *Constitutional Pluralism in the EU* (Oxford, Oxford University Press, 2015).

Janssens, Christine, *The Principle of Mutual Recognition in EU Law* (Oxford, Oxford University Press, 2013).

Jenkins, David, Jacobsen, Amanda and Henriksen, Anders, *The Long Decade: How 9/11 Changed the Law* (Oxford, Oxford University Press, 2014).

Jimeno-Bulnes, Mar, 'Brexit and the Future of European Criminal Law – a Spanish Perspective' (2017) 28 *Criminal Law Forum* 325–47.

Kaunert, Christian, Léonard, Sarah and Pawlak, Patryk (eds), *European Homeland Security: A European Strategy in the Making?* (Abingdon, Routledge, 2012).

Kaye, Nicholas, 'Freezing and Confiscation of Criminal Proceeds' (2006) 77 *Revue Internationale de Droit Penal* 323–31.

Kjaer, Poul F, 'Between Integration and Compatibility' in Paulius Jurčys, Poul F Kjaer and Ren Yatsunami (eds), *Regulatory Hybridization in the Transnational Sphere* (Leiden, Nijhoff, 2013).

—— *Constitutionalism in the Global Realm: A Sociological Approach* (Abingdon, Routledge, 2014).

—— 'The Function of Justification in Transnational Governance', WZB Berlin Social Science Center Discussion Papers, SP IV 2015-808 (2015).

—— 'Why Justification? The Structure of Public Power in Transnational Contexts' (2017) 8 *Transnational Legal Theory* 8–21.

Kjaer, Poul F, Teubner, Gunther and Febbrajo, Alberto (eds), *The Financial Crisis in Constitutional Perspective: The Dark Side of Functional Differentiation* (Oxford, Hart Publishing, 2011).

Klatt, Matthias, 'Positive Rights: Who Decides? Judicial Review in Balance' (2015) 13 *I-CON* 354–82.

Klatt, Matthias and Meister, Moritz, *The Constitutional Structure of Proportionality* (Oxford, Oxford University Press, 2012).

Klip, André 'Europeans First!: Petruhhin, an Unexpected Revolution in Extradition Law', European Journal of Crime (2017) 25 *Criminal Law and Criminal Justice* 195–204.

Kochenov, Dimitry, de Búrca, Gráinne and Williams, Andrew (eds) *Europe's Justice Deficit?* (Oxford, Hart Publishing, 2015).

Kolodny, Niko 'Being Under the Power of Others' (2017), available at http://sophos.berkeley.edu/kolodny/BeingUnderThePowerOfOthers2.pdf.

Koskenniemi, Martti 'Constitutionalism as Mindset: Reflections on Kantian Themes about International Law and Globalization' (2007) 8 *Theoretical Inquiries in Law* 9–36.

Kukathas, Chandran, 'Are Refugees Special?' in Sarah Fine and Lea Ypi (eds), *Migration in Political Theory: The Ethics of Movement and Membership* (Oxford, Oxford University Press, 2016) 249–68.

Kumm, Mattias, 'Democracy is not Enough: Proportionality and the Point of Judicial Review' (2009), NYU School of Law, Public Law Research Paper No 09-10 available at http://ssrn.com/abstract=1356793.

—— 'How does European Union Law Fit into the World of Public Law? Costa, Kadi, and Three Conceptions of Public Law' in Jürgen Neyer and Antje Wiener (eds), Political Theory of the European Union (Oxford-New York, Oxford University Press, 2010) 111–38.

—— 'The Idea of Socratic Contestation and the Right to Justification: The Point of Rights-based Proportionality Review' (2010) 4 *Law & Ethics of Human Rights* 141–75.

—— 'Alexy's Theory of Constitutional Rights and the Problem of Judicial Review' in Matthias Klatt (ed), *Institutionalized Reason: The Jurisprudence of Robert Alexy* (Oxford, Oxford University Press, 2012) 201–17.

—— 'Constitutionalism and the Moral Point of Constitutional Pluralism' in Julie Dickson and Pavlos Eleftheriadis (eds), *Philosophical Foundations of EU Law* (Oxford, Oxford University Press, 2012) 216–46.

—— 'Constitutionalism and the Cosmopolitan State: An Integrated Conception of Public Law' (2013) 20 *Indiana Journal of Global Legal Studies* 605–28.

—— 'Constituent Power, Cosmopolitan Constitutionalism, and Post-positivist Law' (2016) 14 *I-CON* 697–711.

—— 'Sovereignty and the Right to be Left Alone: Subsidiarity, Justice-sensitive Externalities and the Proper Domain of the Consent Requirement in International Law' (2016) 79 *Law and Contemporary Problems* 239–58.

—— 'The Turn to Justification: On the Structure and Domain of Human Rights Practice' in Adam Etinson (ed), *Human Rights: Moral or Political?* (Oxford, Oxford University Press, 2018) 238–61.

Laborde, Cécile, and Ronzoni, Miriam 'What is a Free State? Republican Internationalism and Globalisation' (2015) 64 *Political Studies* 279–96.

Lafont, Cristina, 'Philosophical Foundations of Judicial Review' in David Dyzenhaus and Malcolm Thorburn (eds), *Philosophical Foundations of Constitutional Law* (Oxford, Oxford University Press, 2016) 265–81.

Larmore, Charles, 'What is Political Philosophy?' (2013) 10 *Journal of Moral Philosophy* 276–306.

Lazarus, Liora, 'The Right to Security' in Rowan Cruft, Matthew Liao and Massimo Renzo (eds), *The Philosophical Foundations of Human Rights* (Oxford, Oxford University Press 2015) 423–41.

Lenearts, Koen (2015) 'The Principle of Mutual Recognition in the Area of Freedom, Security and Justice', talk delivered at the Fourth Annual Sir Jeremy Lever lecture, All Souls College, University of Oxford, 30 January 2015 (on file with the author).

Lenaerts, Koen, and Gutiérrez-Fons, José, 'The European Court of Justice and Fundamental Rights in the Field of Criminal Law' in Valsamis Mitsilegas, Maria Bergström and Theodore Konstadinides (eds), *Research Handbook on EU Criminal Law* (Cheltenham, Edward Elgar Publishing, 2016) 7–28.

Lindahl, Hans (ed), *A Right to Inclusion and Exclusion? Normative Fault Lines of the EU's Area of Freedom, Security and Justice* (Oxford, Hart Publishing, 2009).

Lindseth, Peter L, *Power and Legitimacy: Reconciling Europe and the Nation-State* (Oxford, Oxford University Press, 2010).

Locke, John, *An Essay Concerning Human Understanding: Second Treatise of Civil Government* (Ware, Wordsworth Editions, 2014).

Loughlin, Martin, 'The Concept of Constituent Power' (2014) 13 *European Journal of Political Theory* 218–37.

Maffettone, Sebastiano, 'Global Legitimation and Reasonableness' in Giorgio Bongiovanni, Giovanni Sartor and Chiara Valentini (eds), Reasonableness and Law (Dordrecht-Heidelberg-London-New York, Springer, 2009) 147–62.

Mann, Itamar, *Humanity at Sea: Maritime Migration and the Foundations of International Law* (Cambridge, Cambridge University Press, 2016).

Margalit, Avishai, *The Decent Society* (Cambridge MA, Harvard University Press, 1988).

Mastor, Wanda, 'The French Intelligence Act: "The French Surveillance State?"' (2017) 23 *European Public Law* 707–22.

Matera, Claudio, 'The Influence of International Organisations on the EU's Area of Freedom, Security and Justice: A First Inquiry' in Ramses A Wessel and Steven Blockmans (eds), *Between Autonomy and Dependence: The EU Legal Order under the Influence of International Organisations* (The Hague, Assser Press, 2013) 269–96.

Mathews, Jud, and Stone Sweet, Alec, 'All Things in Proportion? American Rights Review and the Problem of Balancing' (2010) 60 *Emory Law Journal* 797–876.

McCrudden, Christopher (ed), *Understanding Human Dignity* (Oxford, Oxford University Press, 2013).

Michelman, Frank, 'Rawls on Constitutionalism and Constitutional Law' in Samuel Freeman (ed), *The Cambridge Companion to Rawls* (Cambridge, Cambridge University Press, 2003) 394–425.

Mill, John Stuart, *On Liberty* (London, Parker, 1859).

Miller, David, *Strangers in our Midst: The Political Philosophy of Immigration* (Cambridge MA, Harvard University Press, 2016).

Mitsilegas, Valsamis, *Money Laundering Counter-Measures in the EU: A New Paradigm of Security Governance versus Fundamental Legal Principles* (The Hague, Kluwer Law Publishing, 2003).

Möller, Kai, *The Global Model of Constitutional Rights* (Oxford, Oxford University Press, 2012).

—— 'Dworkin's Theory of Rights in the Age of Proportionality' (2018) 12 *Law & Ethics of Human Rights*, forthcoming.
Moloney, Niamh, *EU Securities and Financial Markets Regulation* (Oxford, Oxford University Press, 2014).
Monar, Jörg, 'Experimentalist Governance in Justice and Home Affairs' in Charles F Sabel and Jonathan Zeitlin (eds), *Experimentalist Governance in the European Union: Towards a New Architecture* (Oxford, Oxford University Press, 2010) 237–60.
Moon, J Donald, 'Cohen vs. Rawls on Justice and Equality' (2015) 18 *Critical Review of International Social and Political Philosophy* 40–56.
Muller, Julian F, 'The Ethics of Commercial Human Smuggling' (2018) 17 *European Journal of Political Theory* 1–19.
Murphy, Cian C, *EU Counter-Terrorism: Pre-Emption and the Rule of Law* (Oxford, Hart Publishing, 2012).
Nagel, Thomas, 'The Problem of Global Justice' (2005) 33 *Philosophy and Public Affairs* 113–47.
Neal, Andrew W, 'Foucault in Guantánamo: Towards an Archaeology of the Exception' (2006) 37 *Security Dialogue* 31–46.
Neyer, Jürgen, *The Justification of Europe: A Political Theory of Supranational Integration* (Oxford, Oxford University Press, 2012).
Neyer, Jürgen and Wiener, Antje (eds), *Political Theory of the European Union* (Oxford-New York, Oxford University Press, 2010).
Nicolaïdes, Kalypso, 'The Idea of European Demoicracy' in Julie Dickson and Pavlos Eleftheriadis (eds), *Philosophical Foundations of European Union Law* (Oxford, Oxford University Press, 2012) 247–74.
Niesen, Peter, 'What Kant would have said in the Refugee Crisis', *Danish Yearbook of Philosophy* 50, 2017, 83–106.
—— 'European Demoicracy and its Crisis' (2013) 51 *Journal of Common Market Studies* 351–69.
Nili, Shmuel, 'Between Domestic and Global Justice' (2015) 12 *Journal of Moral Philosophy* 55–81.
—— 'The Moving Global Everest: A New Challenge to Global Ideal Theory as a Necessary Compass' (2016) 17 *European Journal of Political Theory* 87–108.
Nussbaum, Martha C, *Frontiers of Justice: Disability, Nationality, Species Membership* (Cambridge MA, Harvard University Press, 2007).
Öberg, Jacob, *Limits to EU Powers: A Case Study of EU Regulatory Criminal Law* (Oxford, Hart Publishing 2017).
O'Neill, Maria, 'EU Cross-border Policing Provisions: The View from One of the Schengen Opt-out States' (2010) 18 *European Journal of Crime, Criminal Law and Criminal Justice* 73–89.
Olsthoorn, Johan 'Why Justice and Injustice have no Place outside the Hobbesian State' (2014) 14 *European Journal of Political Theory* 19–36.
Orgad, Liav, *The Cultural Defense of Nations:. A Liberal Theory of Majority Rights* (Oxford, Oxford University Press, 2015).
Ott, Andrea, 'EU Constitutional Boundaries to Differentiation: How to Reconcile Differentiation with Integration?' in Andrea Ott and Ellen Vos (eds), *Fifty Years of European Integration: Foundations and Perspectives* (The Hague, TMC Asser Press, 2009) 113–38.
Pasquino, Pasquale, 'Constitutionalizing Emergency Power in a Time of Jihadist Terrorism: France 2016 as a Case of Misunderstanding and Failure' (2018) 19 *German Law Journal* 251–65.
Pech, Laurent and Lane Scheppele, Kim, 'Illiberalism Within: Rule of Law Backsliding in the EU' (2017) 19 *Cambridge Yearbook of European Legal Studies* 3–47.
Peers, Steve (2015) *EU Justice and Home Affairs*, vols 1 and 2 (Oxford, Oxford University Press, 2015).
Pettit, Philip, *Republicanism: A Theory of Freedom and Government* (Oxford, Oxford University Press, 1997).
—— 'A Republican Law of Peoples' (2010) 9 *European Journal of Political Theory* 70–94.
—— *On the People's Terms: A Republican Theory and Model of Democracy* (Cambridge, Cambridge University Press, 2012).

—— *Just Freedom: A Moral Compass for a Complex World* (New York, Norton, 2014).
—— 'Justice: Social and Political' in David Sobel, Peter Vallentyne and Steven Wall (eds), *Oxford Studies in Political Philosophy*, vol 1 (Oxford, Oxford University Press, 2015) 9–35.
Plaw, Avery, 'Does Justice Stand Alone?' (2015) 18 *Critical Review of International and Social Philosophy* 57–73.
Pogge, Thomas (1997) 'Migration and Poverty' in Veit Bader (ed), *Citizenship and Exclusion* (Basingstoke, Macmillan, 1997) 12–27.
Poli, Sara, 'The EU External Anti-terrorism Policy in its External AFSJ Policy' in Maria Fletcher, Ester Herlin-Karnell and Claudio Matera (eds), *The EU as an Area of Freedom, Security and Justice* (Abingdon, Routledge, 2016) 389–416.
Posner, Elliot, 'The Lamfalussy Process: Polyarchic Origins of Networked Financial Rule-Making in the EU' in Charles F Sabel and Jonathan Zeitlin (eds), *Experimentalist Governance in the European Union: Towards a New Architecture* (Oxford, Oxford University Press, 2010) 43–60.
Quaglia, Lucia, *The EU and Global Financial Regulation* (Oxford, Oxford University Press, 2014).
Quong, Jonathan, 'On the Idea of Public Reason' in Jon Mandle and David A Reidy (eds), *A Companion to Rawls* (Chichester, Wiley, 2014) 265–80.
Rawls, John, *A Theory of Justice* (Cambridge MA, Harvard University Press, 1971).
—— *Political Liberalism* (Ithaca NY, Columbia University Press, 1993).
—— *Justice as Fairness: A Restatement* (Cambridge MA, Harvard University Press, 2001).
—— 'The Idea of Public Reason Revisited' in John Rawls, *Collected Papers*, Samuel Freeman (ed) (Cambridge MA, Harvard University Press, 2011) 573–615.
Raz, Joseph, *The Morality of Freedom* (Oxford, Oxford University Press, 1986).
Rijmpa, Jorrit J, 'Frontex and the European System of Border Guards: The Future of European Border Management' in Maria Fletcher, Ester Herlin-Karnell and Claudio Matera, *The European Union as an Area of Freedom, Security and Justice* (Abingdon, Routledge, 2016) 217–45.
Ripstein, Arthur, 'Foundationalism in Political Theory' (1987) 16 *Philosophy & Public Affairs* 115–37.
—— 'Authority and Coercion' (2004) 32 *Philosophy & Public Affairs* 2–35.
—— 'Justice and Responsibility' (2004) 17 *Canadian Journal of Law and Jurisprudence* 361–86.
—— *Ronald Dworkin* (Cambridge, Cambridge University Press, 2007).
—— *Force and Freedom: Kant's Legal and Political Philosophy* (Cambridge MA, Harvard University Press, 2009).
—— Private Wrongs (Cambridge MA, Harvard University Press, 2016).
—— 'Property and Sovereignty: How to Tell the Difference' (2017) 18 *Theoretical Inquiries in Law* 243–68.
—— 'Reclaiming Proportionality' (2017) 34 *Journal of Applied Philosophy* 1–18.
—— 'The Innate Right of Humanity and the Right to Justification' in Ester Herlin-Karnell and Matthias Klatt (eds), *Constitutionalism Justified* (Oxford, Oxford University Press, forthcoming).
Risse, Mathias, 'Taking up Space on Earth: Theorizing Territorial Rights, the Justification of States and Immigration from a Global Standpoint' (2015) 4 *Global Constitutionalism* 81–113.
Rosas, Allan and Armati, Lorna, *EU Constitutional Law: An Introduction* (Oxford, Hart Publishing, 2010).
Rosenfeld, Michel 'Constitutional versus Administrative Ordering in an era of Globalization and Privatization, Reflections on Sources of Legitimation in the Post Westphalian Polity' (2011) 32 *Cardozo Law Review* 2339–68.
Rossi, Enzo, 'Justice, Legitimacy and (Normative) Authority for Political Realists' (2012) 15 *Critical Review of International Social and Political Philosophy* 149–64.
Rostbøll, Christian F, 'Non-domination and Democratic Legitimacy' (2015) 18 *Critical Review of International Social and Political Philosophy* 424–39.
—— 'Kant, Freedom as Independence, and Democracy' (2016) 78 *The Journal of Politics* 792–805.
Roth, Brad, *Sovereign Equality and Moral Disagreement: Premises of a Pluralist International Legal Order* (Oxford, Oxford University Press, 2011).

Rousseau, Jean-Jacques, *The Social Contract* (Harmondsworth, Penguin, 1968) ch 11.
Saadé, Eliane, *The Concept of Justice and Equality: On the Dispute between John Rawls and Gerald Cohen* (Berlin-Boston MA, Walter de Gruyter, 2015).
Sadurski, Wojciech, 'Reason of State and Public Reason' (2014) 27 *Ratio Juris* 21–46.
Sangiovanni, Andrea, 'Justice and the Priority of Politics to Morality' (2008) 16 *The Journal of Political Philosophy* 137–64.
—— 'The Irrelevance of Coercion, Imposition, and Framing to Distributive Justice' (2012) 40 *Philosophy & Public Affairs* 79–110.
—— 'Solidarity in the European Union' (2013) 33 *Oxford Journal of Legal Studies* 213.
—— 'On the Relation Between Justice and Legitimacy: A Framework for the EU', paper presented at the workshop 'Towards a Grammar of Justice in EU Law', 6–7 November 2014, at the VU Centre for European Legal Studies and Access Europe Workshop.
—— 'Human Rights, Interests, and Variation' in Ester Herlin-Karnell and Matthias Klatt (eds), Constitutionalism Justified (Oxford, Oxford University Press, 2018), forthcoming.
Santos Vara, Juan, 'The EU's Agencies: Ever more Important for the Governance of the Area of Freedom, Security and Justice' in Ariadna Ripoll Servent and Florian Trauner (eds), The Routledge Handbook of Justice and Home Affairs Research (Abingdon, Routledge, 2017) 445–57.
Saul, Ben, 'Terrorism as a Transnational Crime', Sidney Law School working paper (2014).
Schammo, P, 'The European Union Securities and Market Authority: Lifting the Veil on the Allocation of Powers' (2011) 48 *Common Market Law Review* 1887–913.
Schapiro, Martin, 'The Giving Reasons Requirement' (1992) *The University of Chicago Legal Forum* 179–220.
Scharia, David, *Judicial Review of National Security* (Oxford, Oxford University Press, 2015).
Schlink, Bernard, 'Proportionality in Constitutional Law: Why Everywhere but here?' (2012) 22 *Duke Journal of Comparative and International Law* 291–302.
Schmitt, Carl, *The Concept of the Political*, G Schwab (trans) (Chicago IL, University of Chicago Press, 2007).
—— *Political Theology: Four Chapters on the Concept of Sovereignty* (Cambridge MA, The MIT Press, 1985 trans).
Schotel, Bas, *On the Right of Exclusion: Law, Ethics and Immigration Policy* (Abingdon, Routledge, 2012).
Schuppert, Fabian, 'Non-domination, Non-alienation and Social Equality: Towards a Republican Understanding of Equality' (2015) 18 *Critical Review of International Social and Political Philosophy* 440–55.
Schutze, Robert, *From Dual to Cooperative Federalism: The Changing Structure of European Law* (Oxford, Oxford University Press, 2003).
Sen, Amartya, The Idea of Justice (Cambridge MA, Harvard University Press, 2009).
Senden, Linda, *Soft Law in European Community Law* (Oxford, Hart Publishing, 2004).
Shachar, Ayelet, 'New Borders and Citizenship Constellations' (draft conference paper presented at WZB Berlin, December 2015, on file with the author).
Shany, Yuval, 'Toward a General Margin of Appreciation Doctrine in International Law?' (2005) 16 *European Journal of International Law* 907–40.
Shapiro, Ian, 'On Non-Domination' (2012) 62 *University of Toronto Law Journal* 293–336.
Shapiro, Martin, 'The Giving Reasons Requirement' (1992) 8 *The University of Chicago Legal Forum* 179–220.
Shapiro, Scott J, 'The "Hart-Dworkin" Debate: A Short Guide for the Perplexed' in Arthur Ripstein (ed), *Ronald Dworkin* (Cambridge, Cambridge University Press, 2007) 22–55.
Simester, AP and von Hirsch, Andreas, *Crimes, Harms and Wrongs: On the Principles of Criminalisation* (Oxford, Hart Publishing, 2011).
Simmons, A John, 'Justification and Legitimacy' (1999) 109 *Ethics* 739–71.
—— 'Human Rights World Citizenship: The Universality of Human Rights in Kant and Locke' in Simmons, *Justification and Legitimacy: Essays on Rights and Obligations* (Cambridge, Cambridge University Press, 2001) 179–96.

—— *Justification and Legitimacy: Essays on Rights and Obligations* (Cambridge, Cambridge University Press, 2001).
Sleat, Matt, 'Legitimacy in Realist Thought: Between Moralism and Realpolitik' (2014) 42 *Political Theory* 314–37.
Somek, Alexander, 'What is Political Union' (2013) 14 *German Law Journal* 561–80.
—— *The Cosmopolitan Constitution* (Oxford, Oxford University Press, 2014).
Stanford Encyclopedia, available at: https://plato.stanford.edu/entries/authority.
Statman, Daniel 'Two Concepts of Dignity' (2001) 24 *Tel Aviv University Law Review* 541–603.
Stiltz, Anna, 'Nations, States and Territory' (2011) 121 *Ethics* 572–601.
Stone Sweet, Alec, and Brunell, TL, 'Trustee Courts and the Judicialization of International Regimes: The Politics of Majoritarian Activism in the ECHR, the EU, and the WTO', Faculty Scholarship Series. Paper 4625 (2013), available at http://digitalcommons.law.yale.edu/fss_papers/4625.
Stone Sweet, Alec and Ryan, Clare, *A Cosmopolitan Legal Order* (Oxford, Oxford University Press, 2018) ch 2 (with Eric Palmer).
Stubb, Alexander C-G, 'A Categorization of Differentiated Integration' (1996) 34 *Journal of Common Market Studies* 283–95.
Sunstein C, *One Case at a Time: Judicial Minimalism on the Supreme Court* (Cambridge MA, Harvard University Press, 2001).
Tan, Kok-Chor, *Justice without Borders: Cosmopolitanism, Nationalism and Patriotism* (Cambridge, Cambridge University Press, 2004).
—— 'Why Global Justice Matters' (2014) 10 *Journal of Global Ethics* 128–34.
—— 'Humanitarian Intervention as a Duty' (2015) 7 *Global Responsibility to Protect* 121–41.
—— *What is this thing called Global Justice?* (Abingdon, Routledge, 2017).
Taylor, Charles, *The Ethics of Authenticity* (Cambridge MA, Harvard University Press, 1992).
Teitel, Ruti, *Humanity's Law* (Oxford, Oxford University Press, 2011).
Teubner, Gunther, *Constitutional Fragments: Societal Constitutionalism and Globalization* (Oxford, Oxford University Press, 2012).
Thompson, Michael J, 'Reconstructing Republican Freedom. A Critique of the Neo-republication Concept of Freedom as Non-domination' (2013) 39 *Philosophy and Social Criticism* 277–98.
Thorburn, Malcolm, 'Proportionality' in David Dyzenhaus and Malcolm Thorburn (eds), *Philosophical Foundations of Constitutional Law* (Oxford, Oxford University Press, 2016) 305–21.
Tomkins, Adam, *Our Republican Constitution* (Oxford, Hart Publishing, 2005).
Tridimas, Takis, *General Principles of EU Law* (Oxford, Oxford University Press, 2012).
Tuckness, Alex, 'Locke's Political Philosophy' in *The Stanford Encyclopedia of Philosophy* available at https://plato.stanford.edu/archives/spr2016/entries/locke-political.
Tuori, Kaarlo 'Ultima Ratio as a Constitutional Principle' (2013) 3 *Oñati Socio-legal Series* 6–20.
—— 'A European Security Constitution?' in David Jenkins, Amanda Jacobsen and Anders Henriksen (eds), *The Long Decade: How 9/11 Changed the Law* (Oxford, Oxford University Press, 2014).
Tushnet, Mark, Advanced Introduction to Comparative Constitutional Law (Cheltenham, Edward Elgar Publishing, 2014).
Tyler, Tom R, *Why People Obey the Law* (Princeton NJ, Princeton University Press, 2006).
Valentini, Laura, *Justice in a Globalized World: A Normative Framework* (Oxford, Oxford University Press, 2011).
Vibert, Frank, 'Better Regulation and the Role of Agencies' in Stephen Weatherill (ed), *Better Regulation* (Oxford, Hart Publishing, 2007) 387–403.
von Bogdandy, Armin and Bast, Jürgen, *European Constitutional Law* (Munich-Oxford, Hart Publishing-Ch Beck-Nomos, 2009).
Waldron, Jeremy, *Law and Disagreement* (Oxford, Oxford University Press, 1999).
—— 'Safety and Security' (2006) 85 *Nebraska Law Review* 454–507.
—— 'Exclusion: Property Analogies in the Immigration Debate' (2017) 18 *Theoretical Inquiries in Law* 469–89.

Walker, Neil, 'The Problem of Trust in an Enlarged Area of Freedom, Security and Justice: A Conceptual Analysis' in Malcolm Anderson and Joanna Apap (eds), *Police and Justice Cooperation and the New European Borders* (The Hague, Kluwer Law International, 2002) 19–34.

—— 'Justice in and of the European Union' in Dimitry Kochenov, Gráinne de Búrca and Andrew Williams (eds), *Europe's Justice Deficit?* (Oxford, Hart Publishing, 2015) 247–78.

Walzer, Michael, *Spheres of Justice: A Defense of Pluralism and Equality* (Chicester, Wiley-Blackwell, 1983).

Ward, Ian, 'Identifying the European Other' (2001) 14 *International Journal of Refugee Law* 219–37.

Weatherill, Stephen, 'If I'd Wanted you to Understand I would have Explained it Better: What is the Purpose of the Provisions on Closer Co-operation Introduced by the Treaty of Amsterdam?' in David O'Keeffe and Patrick Twomey (eds), *Legal Issues of the Amsterdam Treaty* (Oxford, Hart Publishing, 1999) 21–38.

—— *Law and Values in the European Union* (Oxford, Oxford University Press, 2016).

Webber, Grégoire CN, *The Negotiable Constitution: On the Limitation of Rights* (Cambridge, Cambridge University Press, 2009).

Weber, Max, *Economy and Society*, vol 1 (Berkeley-Los Angeles CA, University of California Press, 2013).

Weiler, Joseph HH, 'The Transformation of Europe' (1991) 100 *The Yale Law Journal* 2403–83.

—— 'Journey to an Unknown Destination: A Retrospective and Prospective of the European Court of Justice in the Arena of Political Integration' (1993) 31 *Journal of Common Market Studies* 417–46.

Weinrib, Jacob, *Dimensions of Dignity: The Theory and Practice of Modern Constitutional Law* (Cambridge, Cambridge University Press, 2016).

Wesseling M, "A European Terrorist Finance System", policy paper 2016, Occasional Paper Royal United Services Institute, available at https://rusi.org/sites/default/files/op_wesseling_an_eu_terrorist_finance_tracking_system.1.pdf.

Wieczorek, Irene, 'Understanding JHA Agencies in Context: Where does Eurojust lie in the Constitutional Architecture of the Area of Freedom, Security and Justice?' in Maria Fletcher, Williams, Andrew, *The Ethos of Europe: Values, Law and Justice in the EU* (Cambridge, Cambridge University Press, 2010).

Williams, Bernard, 'Realism and Moralism in Political Theory' in Williams (ed), *In the Beginning was the Deed: Realism and Moralism in Political Argument* (Princeton NJ: Princeton University Press, 2005) 1–17.

Wolf, Sofie, 'The Netherlands will Join the European Public Prosecutor's Office' (2018) available at www.maastrichtuniversity.nl/blog/2018/05/netherlands-will-join-european-public-prosecutors-office-eppo.

Wolthuis, Bertjan 'Principles of Economic Union: An Extension of John Rawls's Theory of Justice' (2017) 23 *European Law Journal* 454–66.

Yovel, Yirmiyahu, *Spinoza and Other Heretics: The Marrano of Reason*, vol 1 (Princeton NJ, Princeton University Press, 1989).

Ypi, Lea, *Global Justice and Avant-Garde Political Agency* (Oxford, Oxford University Press, 2011).

Zedner, Lucia, *Security* (Abingdon, Routledge, 2009).

Ziegler, Katja, 'Strengthening the rule of law but fragmenting international law: the Kadi decision of the ECJ from the perspective of human rights' (2009) 9 *Human Rights Law Review* 288.

Zumbansen, Peer, 'Defining the Space of Transnational Law: Legal Theory, Global Governance and Legal Pluralism' in Günther Handl, Joachim Zekoll and Peer Zumbansen (eds), *Beyond Territoriality: Transnational Legal Authority in an Age of Globalization* (Leiden, Martinus Nijhoff, 2012) 53–86.

Zylberman, Ariel, 'Why Human Rights? Because of You' (2016) 24 *The Journal of Political Philosophy* 321–43.

Other Sources

Enregistré à la Présidence de l'Assemblée nationale le 5 juillet 2017, available at www.assemblee-nationale.fr/15/ya-commission/r0017-a0.asp.
European Commission, 'State of the Union 2018: A reinforced European Public Prosecutor's Office to fight cross-border terrorism, press release (2018), available at http://europa.eu/rapid/press-release_IP-18-5682_en.htm.
European Commission, 'Fact Sheet: Questions and Answers on the EU–US Data Protection "Umbrella Agreement"', available at http://europa.eu/rapid/press-release_MEMO-16-4183_en.htm?locale=en.
European Commission, https://ec.europa.eu/home-affairs/sites/homeaffairs/files/what-we-do/policies/european-agenda-security/20180612_agenda-on-security-factsheet-sis_en.pdf.
European Commission, http://www.europarl.europa.eu/legislative-train/theme-area-of-justice-and-fundamental-rights/file-revision-of-the-anti-money-laundering-directive-(aml).
European Security Union, http://europa.eu/rapid/press-release_IP-17-5202_en.htm.
Financial Action Task Force, http://www.fatf-gafi.org/.
UNHCR, 'Mixed Migration', available at: www.unhcr.org/pages/4a16aac66.html.
United Nations Office on Drugs and Crime: Global Report on Trafficking in Persons, available at www.unodc.org/documents/data-and-analysis/glotip/Trafficking_in_Persons_2012_web.pdf.

Index